Executive's Guide to Fair Value

Executive's Guide to Fair Value

*Profiting from the
New Valuation Rules*

ALFRED M. KING

John Wiley & Sons, Inc.

Library of Congress Cataloging-in-Publication Data:

King, Alfred M.
  Executive's guide to fair value : profiting from the new valuation rules / Alfred M. King.
     p. cm.
  ISBN 978-0-470-17329-9 (cloth)
  1. Fair value—United States. 2. Valuation—United States. I. Title.
  HF5681.V3K55 2008
  658.15—dc22
                                            2007033353

Printed in the United States of America.

10 9 8 7 6 5 4 3 2

For:

Mary Jane
Who is learning about Fair Value the hard way.

Tom
Who has learned about Fair Value on the job.

Contents

Preface

"I am bound by my own definition of criticism: a disinterested endeavor to learn and propagate the best that is known and thought in the world."
Matthew Arnold, *Essays in Criticism*

Who can be against "Fair Value"? After all, isn't UnfairValue the opposite of Fair Value? Nobody has ever been heard to say that he is in favor of unfair value, so logic suggests that everyone must be in favor of fair value. Unfortunately this syllogism falls apart because the term Fair Value, as it is used in accounting and financial reporting, is actually a term of art, and not what common sense might suppose.

The Financial Accounting Standards Board (FASB) is the body designated in this country to determine Generally Accepted Accounting Principles (GAAP). GAAP is like the Rules of the Road, traffic laws that must be obeyed. Further, these accounting rules are enforced by public accounting firms, backed up by the Securities and Exchange Commission; these two groups in turn are backed up by the Public Company Accounting Oversight Board.

In short, the FASB's approach to financial reporting—now enshrined in GAAP—affects every company and every executive of that company. Investment bankers, attorneys, and consultants must be aware of the latest twists and turns in GAAP, in order to provide accurate advice to financial executives.

In September 2006 a major change in the direction of GAAP was announced by the FASB in its newly issued Statement of Financial Accounting Standard 157 (SFAS 157). Titled "Fair Value

Measurements," the full import of this document is only now becoming clear.

As will become apparent in this book, the author, with almost 40 years in the Appraisal industry, criticizes the FASB and Fair Value accounting. This criticism, while perhaps intellectually stimulating, should not supersede the more important goal of the book.

The book explains, in nontechnical terms, what Fair Value (FV) is, how it must be applied, and the consequences of certain choices still permitted by GAAP. Financial executives, who often leave day-to-day application of GAAP to "the accountants," must understand the implications of FV, particularly as it impacts reported earnings and Earnings per Share (EPS).

FV accounting, set forth in SFAS 157, directly influences reported earnings both before and after any Merger and Acquisition (M&A) activity. Assets on today's balance sheet must be tested for FV, following the guidelines enunciated in SFAS 157. In short, whether you like it or hate it, almost every aspect of financial reporting will feel the impact of FV accounting.

Financial advisors must also understand the new Rules of the Road. Attorneys involved with corporate finance and investment bankers advising their clients on prospective transactions have to be at least as familiar with GAAP as is the company's audit partner.

Finally, we explain how appraisers and valuation specialists arrive at their professional conclusions. In turn, this should assist those responsible for engaging appraisers in choosing the most qualified professional, and then managing the engagement to assure a mutually satisfactory indication of value.

We provide a sample appraisal report in the Appendix. Most readers probably have not held a real appraisal in their hands, and very few of those will have read it in its entirety. One of the key points made in the book is that appraisal reports should be read and understood, because the appraiser's logic and approach can and should be challenged. This is only possible, however, if the user has actually read the report. Because it may be some period of time before any reader actually requires a specific valuation, we provide a real, but disguised report sent to one of our clients to aid in following the material in the book.

The views expressed in this book are my own, and do not represent an official position of Marshall & Stevens, Inc. or any other organization with which I am affiliated. I trust that the logic of my positions will convince every reader that what I say is correct, but in valuation as in many other fields there is always room for differences of opinion.

Undoubtedly some readers will have questions regarding this material. The author will be pleased to respond to inquiries addressed at: aking@marshall-stevens.com. Please put in the subject line the heading: Book Inquiry. This will distinguish your communication from the many spam communications each of us receives daily.

Alfred M. King
Spotsylvania, Virginia
October, 2007

Acknowledgments

With thanks to my colleagues at Marshall & Stevens, Inc.

Executive's Guide to Fair Value

CHAPTER 1

What Is Fair Value?

Most readers of this book have an intuitive understanding of the term *Fair Value*. For example, if your house were to be condemned by the local Department of Transportation to build a road through your backyard, you would want the state to pay you the Fair Value of your property.

You also have probably heard and used the term *Fair Market Value*. In common parlance, Fair Value (FV) and Fair Market Value (FMV) are used interchangeably; they represent what is considered reasonable by an outside observer if a buyer and seller are going to consummate a transaction. The notion of fairness permeates discussions about value, and the assumption is made that both parties have essentially equal knowledge about the property in question, and neither party is contemplating a forced sale or purchase.

The Fair Value of your home or your car is, in practice, a far more complex concept than may appear at first glance. Take your home: Is the current FV based on what it would cost to rebuild if it burned down (insurable value or replacement cost)? Or is it what you want your local property tax assessor to base next year's property taxes on? Or, finally, is it what you could receive if you called a broker and put the house on the market?

Minimum thought will rapidly lead to the conclusion that those are actually three *different* values. Which is correct? The truth is that all three answers are correct, but each is valid *only for the purpose for which it was developed*. You would not want to pay real estate taxes on the cost to rebuild your home, and you might not want to sell your home solely on the basis of its assessed value for taxes.

Transactions are based on current values. Transactions are never based on what you, the owner, might have paid for the asset several years ago. The real estate assessor does not care about your original cost, and neither does the prospective buyer of your house if you have to move. The insurance company might be interested in what the house cost to build if it were new, but your purchase price from the original owner tells the insurance company nothing about what a new house would cost if your existing structure burned down.

When decisions about property are concerned, the *only* relevant information is its current value today. Every decision *you* make is based on *your* evaluation about today's value to you. Somebody else's cost is irrelevant.

By the same token, if no transaction involving your property is contemplated, it is highly unlikely that you need to refine your understanding of the true FMV.

Generally Accepted Accounting Principles (GAAP) is the language of business. In today's environment, the GAAP rules are promulgated by the Financial Accounting Standards Board (FASB) under the auspices of the Securities and Exchange Commission (SEC). GAAP rules are enforced on their clients (companies) by auditing firms; in turn, the work of the auditors is reviewed by the SEC and Public Company Accounting Oversight Board (PCAOB).

GAAP is pervasive in the business world. Virtually every set of financial statements sent to people outside a firm (recipients such as bankers, suppliers, and investors) *must* be prepared following GAAP rules. Unless prepared in accordance with GAAP, auditors cannot and will not sign off on financial statements, because their certification states that the financials were in fact prepared in accordance with GAAP.

How does this discussion of GAAP tie into earlier comments about Fair Value? In fact, it ties in directly because GAAP is undergoing a transformation at the hands of the FASB. Right or wrong, the FASB is starting to require GAAP to be prepared using Fair Value concepts.

In the remainder of this book, you will learn what these new rules are, what impact they will have on both preparers and users of financial statements, and what you as an executive can do about this radical change in financial reporting.

FASB IS PUSHING FAIR VALUE

The author has debated over the past ten years with many Board members and staff of the FASB about the use of Fair Values in financial reporting. To avoid any thought that there is a conflict of interest, I am unalterably opposed to many of the actual and prospective uses of Fair Values, as defined by the FASB. Will such requirements help my business? Undoubtedly, the answer is yes. All appraisers will gain from the use of FV information—just as auditors gained following mandatory audit requirements in the Securities Acts of 1933 and 1934.

But the fact that something will help my wallet and put food on my table does not make it right. This book is not the venue for me to carry on my crusade against Fair Value reporting. I do this in many other forums.

The FASB is publicly committed to the increasing use of Fair Value in financial reporting. Actions sometimes speak louder than words, and we discuss many of the new FV rules recently promulgated by the FASB. But the situation is actually far direr. The FASB in the United States and the International Accounting Standards Board (IASB) in Europe are publicly committed to extending FV concepts in financial reporting.

In fact the only reason the two Boards have not yet mandated full FV reporting is that they would face a massive revolt by their constituents, that is, preparers, auditors, and users.

If preparers, auditors, and users are *not* clamoring for full FV financial reports, then why are the two Boards inexorably marching down that path? There are two separate, and essentially unrelated, answers. One relates to the Enron experience and the other is based on pure "accounting theory."

FINANCIAL INSTRUMENTS AND THE LEGACY OF ENRON

There were many causes of the Enron debacle, and they included auditor mistakes, fraud by management, banks enabling improper financing, and improper valuation of financial instruments. In a nutshell, Enron management, as just one example, assumed that they could develop a product using the Internet to download information and movies to users. They created a financial instrument that assumed future revenues would be generated from this as yet non-existent service. The financial instrument was then valued, by Enron—with concurrence from their audit firm—on the basis of the "present value" of the future cash flows expected to be received. The calculations, and the valuation, were all internal to Enron.

Using their own calculations, Enron effectively created *income*, which they then picked up on their income statement, with the offset as an *asset* on the Balance Sheet representing the current FV of the derivative. Of course, when Enron began to deteriorate or implode, this *asset* turned out to have no value because their Internet download never got off the ground.

Following the Enron collapse, some observers of accounting came to the conclusion that one of the factors enabling Enron to "cook the books" was its ability to value its own financial instrument. The solution, to the rule setters at the FASB, appeared simple.

Instead of allowing a company to value its own instruments on the basis of its own calculations, under the new approach the instrument would have to be valued by what outside buyers would pay for it. In other words, the market itself would be the basis of valuation. Going to the specific Enron *asset*, it is highly doubtful that an independent third party, a dealer in financial instruments, would pay very much for a highly speculative stream of *income* that extended out some 20 or more years. Thus, instead of permitting Enron to use its own assumptions, the value for financial reporting would be based on *real-world* transactions. In short, were the new rule to have been in effect then, the Enron derivatives games could not have been played.

To counter the abuse by Enron, the FASB, with encouragement from the SEC, instituted new tightened rules. The stated purpose of the new rules—and it is hard to argue against the objective—was to make sure that all Fair Values that appeared on a company's Balance Sheet would be derived from the market itself, not self-interested internal assumptions. Further, for the types of financial instruments that Enron created, there were market makers who either already dealt with that type of product or would quickly set themselves up to make a market. The market for financial instruments has been growing at a rapid rate over the past ten years, and the number of new instruments is truly endless. By making one rule for all financial instruments the FASB once and for all appeared to put a stop to this particular area of "creative accounting."

THEORETICAL MERITS OF FAIR VALUE ACCOUNTING

Accounting theoreticians have been proposing one form or another of accounting based on value for almost 40 years. The first big push came in the late 1970s when inflation rates in excess of 10% and even 15% appeared in the daily headlines. Compounding 15% inflation for several years will destroy the usefulness of accounting reports based solely on the "original cost" of assets acquired ten or more years ago. Depreciation expense based on original cost will not be sufficient to replace old assets when they must be replaced.

Certainly, the experience of countries with persistent inflations, such as Brazil, suggests that some form of adjustment must be made in order to make current financial statements relevant. Inflation is no more or less than a reduction in the value of the unit of currency. Without some form of adjustment, therefore, a dollar spent ten years ago appears to be the same as a dollar spent this year. Yet, in a period of inflation, today's dollar may be worth only 30¢ relative to $1 ten years ago. (This is without considering the time value of money, which also makes comparisons between today and previous periods difficult.) Inflation destroys accounting comparability.

So, one argument in favor of value accounting deals with trying to overcome the impact of inflation, the depreciation in the value of the unit of currency. But there is a second, and equally compelling, argument. Even in the total absence of inflation, some prices go up, and others go down. This may be the result of productivity, material shortages, new products, and many other causes, including technology.

But if current values differ from those present when the asset was acquired—either up or down—then current financial statements do not reflect the *real* value of the assets, with real value defined as what it would cost today to acquire the asset *or* what the asset could be sold for to a third party.

Under that approach, wanting financial statements to show current values, today's traditional financial reporting model, based as it is on actual historical prices paid, does not reflect economic reality. Proponents of having financial statements prepared on the basis of current values argue that such information is useful to readers of the statements, and that outdated historical costs are irrelevant for making decisions today. In short, the focus is on the *users* of financial statements and what it is assumed they want or need.

Taking this argument one stage farther, these accounting theoreticians believe that primacy among financial statements should be placed on the Balance Sheet, with the Income Statement merely reflecting the changes between the opening and closing Balance Sheets.

Most readers of this book, however, were brought up on the belief that the Income Statement should represent what management has done with the shareholders' assets. The profit-and-loss (P&L) statement should be viewed as a report card on management performance. This school of thought asserts that a theoretical current value of an asset that is not going to be sold or disposed of is of little use in evaluating management performance. Because it is difficult to make the Balance Sheet and Income Statement "articulate" if current values are introduced, most executives are willing to let the Balance Sheet be a residual, as long as the Income Statement reflects current performance.

Unfortunately, however, the Board members and staff of the FASB do not share the management perspective. Their view is that the Balance Sheet is important, that it should be correct, and that correct Balance Sheet amounts should be based on current values. This is their reality. It is easy to find fault with the Board's assumptions and approaches, but very difficult to get them to change their minds.

So, while the true merits of current value accounting can continue to be debated, it appears that this particular train has already pulled out of the station, leaving behind advocates of historical cost as well as the primacy of the Income Statement.

FAIR VALUE IS THE NEW PARADIGM

The FASB, with total support from the SEC, has determined that Fair Value is better information, and that the Balance Sheet has to be correct. Based on the Enron debacle, the Board believes that Fair

Value for financial instruments is the proper approach. In turn, these are to be valued by looking at what some outside market participant would actually pay to buy the instrument(s).

There are two key concepts here that must be clearly articulated. First, the Board believes that current or Fair Value is to be determined by what they call an *exit price*, and most observers would define this as what something could be sold for. Second, the relevant market for estimating selling prices has to be determined by looking to the perhaps somewhat theoretical concept of *market participants*.

Further, the Board's emphasis on the importance of the Balance Sheet, and the relegation of the Income Statement to third-class status, has profound implications. In practice, if the Board goes all the way in implementing its approach, changes in the Fair Value of assets will be considered income (or loss) of the period. Thus, simply holding a financial instrument that goes up or down $1 million in a year because of changes in interest rates will have the *same* P&L impact as does selling $20 million of goods and services with a 5% after-tax margin. Management, as well as many investors, feels that product or service revenues and costs are pretty important. Except for dealers in securities, changes in interest rates are irrelevant in looking at the performance of most manufacturing or service businesses.

The purpose of this chapter is only to discuss what is, and what management can do about it. While it may be satisfying to argue that the FASB is wrong, it really does not help run a business more effectively and efficiently. So from here on, this book accepts the Board's decisions, but does reserve the right to point out the possible pitfalls for management in following the new FV requirements. Given the FASB's requirements, we show you how to minimize the adverse consequences.

How Reliable Are Fair Values?

It was stated earlier that the FASB was concerned about Enron and several other horror cases in accounting, such as WorldCom and HealthSouth. In response, they feel that adoption of FV financial reporting will preclude management from developing and reporting their own values and consequently inflating reported income. Implicit in this approach is the assumption that Enron, or anyone else for that matter, can develop the true Fair Value of an asset. A direct corollary, then, is that there is one, and only one, Fair Value for any asset.

After all, if Enron has an Internet derivative, one can determine the Fair Value by going to dealers in this asset. Among dealers, at any point in time, there may be very slight differences in their individual bid and asked prices. But, in the larger scheme of things, financial markets are very efficient. Even small price differentials are quickly erased by arbitrageurs. Consequently, determining the Fair Value of a financial instrument only requires making one or two phone calls, if the price is not actually quoted in today's *Wall Street Journal*. For practical purposes, any minor discrepancies among dealers can simply be disregarded.

Implicit in this approach to developing FV information is the assumption that markets are efficient, that price differentials disappear quickly. For financial instruments such an assumption is probably correct.

However, for financial executives in manufacturing, distribution, and service businesses, as contrasted with financial institutions, the markets that they have to look to for price quotes are *not* efficient. There is very little arbitrage available when it comes to determining the Fair Value of a 40-story office building. Such assets are only rarely traded. When they do trade, they are essentially one-off transactions because no two office buildings are alike. Just because the building next door sold two years ago for $175 per square foot does not mean that your building today would sell for $175, $200, or $150. There is no way to determine the Fair Value today of an office building short of either putting it on the market and selling it, or obtaining an appraisal from a valuation specialist.

From just this one simple example it is easy to see how trying to determine the Fair Value for financial reporting opens up several difficult areas, and many of these are themselves controversial. Suppose the building owner had just obtained an appraisal report that had been given to a bank to support using the real estate as collateral for a loan. Is the amount on that appraisal report, developed for financing, valid for financial reporting? Using the new FASB criteria, could the building be *sold* for that amount? Maybe not, because the financing appraisal might well have assumed just continuing with existing tenants and existing use. A buyer might want to redevelop part of the building for retail stores, which would change the value.

Observation: The new FV rules actually provide very substantial room for potential manipulation of reported financial results. Earnings can be, and we predict will be, managed through application of the current FV requirements.

Further, the FASB insists that the value be developed based on what market participants would pay. Who are the market participants for major office buildings? There are a number of real estate investment trusts (REITs) that specialize in office properties, and many institutional investors occasionally invest in real estate. But at any one point in time, trying to identify these theoretical buyers is far from a trivial exercise.

The bottom line is that the FASB wrote the FV rules with financial instruments in mind. Trying to apply these somewhat specialized rules to the great variety of tangible and intangible assets is causing, and will continue to cause, great troubles for businessmen, their auditors, their investors, and those of us in the valuation profession that have to try and develop this information on a supportable and auditable basis. No one wants a replay of Enron, but the new rules are going to cause a new series of problems, as will be discussed throughout the book.

Relevance of Fair Value

The FASB has two separate touchstones for financial reporting. The first is *relevance* and the second is *reliability*. Massive debates have hinged on which of these two is more important. Some argue, "What good is relevant information if it is not reliable?" The opposition counters by asking what good is reliable information if it is not relevant.

Reliability, while not identical with auditability, is usually taken to mean that if several independent observers had the same fact pattern, they would come out with very similar answers. Thus, if most accountants would treat the same fact pattern the same way, the financial information could be considered reliable. An example would be the recorded cost for a 1,000-ton press; most accountants would sum up the invoice price, inbound freight, installation, and

> **Observation:** The same asset can have several different Fair Values, depending on the purpose for which the value is being developed. Put a different way, there is no such thing as "the" Fair Value of any asset. Multiple values are not only possible but often exist simultaneously. Any time the term *Fair Value* is used, the purpose and definition must be clearly stated, or major mistakes can be made.

setup. Cost accountants could argue whether some small amount of debugging should be capitalized, and practice might differ on this one factor; in any event, almost all accountants would agree within 1% or less as to the cost of the press. An auditor could satisfy herself by going to the paid invoices in the accounts payable department and comparing the amounts to the original capital expenditure request and to the respective purchase orders. In short, the cost of the press would be highly reliable by almost any standard.

When it comes to relevance, however, many critics of today's accounting, including many at the IASB and the FASB, as well as leading academics, argue that while the cost of the press is certainly reliable, it may not be relevant for today's decisions. Particularly if the press was acquired several years ago, and a new press would cost 20% to 30% more today, they believe that a more relevant piece of information for readers of the financial statements would be today's Fair Value of the press.

Of course, those same critics disagree among themselves as to whether the most relevant information is (1) what the item would sell for today in its used condition, (2) what a new press would cost to acquire, or (3) whether the cost new should or should not be adjusted for condition and location of the old press. These are in practice three quite widely dispersed amounts. So those who argue for relevance still have a burden of proving why *their* definition of relevance is better than some other definition.

The relevant Fair Value may not be totally reliable, because valuation is not an exact science. And a reliable determination of original cost may be highly reliable but not necessarily as relevant as Fair Value.

How Exact Can the Determination of Fair Value Be?

There are two questions every valuation specialist is asked prior to his engagement by a client:

1. "How often have you appraised assets in my industry?"
2. "How accurate will your answers be?"

The first question can be answered in one of two ways. If he has had prior experience valuing companies in that industry he very quickly brings out a list of prior engagements and points with pride to his undoubted experience. If, however, he has not happened to have appraised that *exact* industry, then he answers—with total conviction because it is true—that "it really makes very little difference what industry an experienced appraiser is working in because the valuation principles are always the same." In Chapter 11 we discuss briefly, from the perspective of a company, how to engage a valuation specialist and how the company should manage the work effort.

The second most frequent question deals with the accuracy and/or supportability of a specific valuation assignment. For many years, appraisers have used as a rule of thumb that if two separate appraisers are given the same assignment, for the same purpose, they will most likely come out within 10% of each other. Put a different way, we really develop a range of values, and within that range probably no one amount is better than another.

Most readers of this book will probably never have examined an actual valuation report in detail. Go to the Appendix to see an actual complete report sent to a client, disguised to protect confidentiality. Note that while this represents a real client situation, both the name of the company and the financial information have been disguised.

Reading the report you see that our firm, Marshall & Stevens, came to a very specific value as of the valuation date. The truth, however, is that there is probably a false sense of precision in most valuation reports. As mentioned earlier, we probably can only get within approximately 10% of the real value. But the report itself states a specific value, often down to the dollar.

The reason for *not* providing clients with a range is that many valuation reports are used for financial reporting, and accountants cannot book a range of values; they must prepare a journal voucher with a single point number in order to balance the debits and credits. Consequently, valuation specialists show point estimates in the report. The true underlying Fair Value, however, is actually a range. In the absence of any other information, most appraisers would choose the midpoint of the range. They can, and sometimes do, choose a value at either the upper or lower range of values.

For example, if a client is borrowing money from a bank on a mortgage, the lender may want a loan-to-value amount of 80%. If the borrower is seeking a loan of $800,000, that means the client desires that the real estate appraisal comes out at or above $1 million. If the range of values we develop is between $925,000 and $1,050,000, we probably would not report the value as $987,500, which is the arithmetic midpoint. Rather, we would say in the text that there is always a range, but our best single point estimate is $1 million. The fact is that no appraisal is ever going to be accurate to within 2%, so rounding up from $987,500 to $1 million seems appropriate. The bank will not be hurt, and the borrower can get his loan without having to ask the bank's loan committee to make an exception to their 80% loan-to-value guideline.

Many clients really "push" the valuation specialist to arrive at some predetermined answer. For tax-related valuations, clients usually want the lowest supportable amounts, while for borrowing and sales of assets, clients usually want the highest supportable values.

Because of the absence of a "bright line" in most valuations, and the ability to arrive at a supportable answer within a somewhat narrow range, clients do in practice urge the appraiser to go as far as he can go to come up with an acceptable answer that meets the client's business needs. Not every appraiser is able to stand up to such client pressure. This is commonly recognized by many parts of the business community in referring to the MAI professional designation for real estate appraisers (Member of the Appraisal Institute) as "Made as Instructed." Appraisers hear this all the time, but only in very rare situations has the author seen actual reports that were unduly influenced by client demands. However, it does happen, and the writer has been an expert witness in several cases where the other side's valuation report just did not correlate with the real economics of the situation.

DEAL EXPENSES

This chapter has dealt with several subjects concerning the FASB's push to using value information in financial reports. In September 2006, the Board issued its Statement of Financial Accounting Standards (SFAS) 157, dealing with the definition of Fair Value, and providing guidelines for the determination of Fair Value. Contrary to the opinion of some commentators, SFAS 157 did not call for the further use of FV in financial reports. What it did say was that if you were required to develop the FV of an asset or a liability, the Standard told you how to do it. Consequently, SFAS 157 has become the new "bible" for appraisers.

As mentioned earlier, two of the basic principles were:

1. Values were to be derived on the assumption that the asset were to be sold (i.e., how much cash could be realized).
2. The estimate of that sales value was to be determined based on assumptions as to what market participants would pay for the asset.

These definitions are somewhat different from what appraisers have used in the past, where the term *Fair Market Value* was pretty clearly defined by the courts, the Internal Revenue Service (IRS), and general business practice. The new definition of FV has some significant ramifications, and one that will affect many readers directly is the legal and accounting expenditures for a business combination. (The FASB prefers the term *business combination*, whereas common parlance often uses the term *merger and acquisition* [M&A] transaction.) This will be discussed in detail in Chapter 4.

Under previous practice, when a buyer consummated a merger, there were usually major out-of-pocket expenditures for investment banking, accounting, legal, printing, proxy, and (very small) appraisal costs. These costs were considered part of the deal, and were capitalized as part of the transaction, along with cash paid to the sellers and stock issued to the sellers. Inasmuch as these costs can easily amount to millions of dollars, and were incurred only to get the deal done, capitalization seemed to make good sense. In fact, without those expenditures, the deal would not have been consummated.

The FASB's new definition of Fair Value, however, precludes capitalization of deal-related expenses. Now they must be expensed as incurred. This outcome may not have been widely recognized because SFAS 157 becomes effective in 2009. But, regardless of when it becomes effective, the outcome is the same. Deal-related expenses are not considered part of FV.

Now you can argue with the FASB that capitalization of deal-related costs is virtually identical to the capitalization of inbound freight and installation for a piece of capital equipment. At least so far, the Board is not mandating expensing of inbound freight and installation—although some rumblings even here have been heard.

The logic for capitalization of freight and installation costs is that from the perspective of the buyer, the user of the asset, without such expenditures one only has a very expensive paperweight. The costs are absolutely necessary for the machine to work and produce its assigned output. So for the past 50 or more years, capitalization of freight and installation was not even considered as a matter of judgment. First-year accounting students learned the rules and that was it.

Now the FASB says, "Wait a minute. The M&A-related deal costs (investment banking, legal, audit, etc.) are *not* part of the assets acquired! If you value the assets acquired in accordance with the new definition (exit price and market participants), another buyer would not pay you for your deal expenses. They do not add intrinsically to the acquired assets from the M&A transaction. The fact that they were necessary for you to get the deal done is irrelevant to the new buyer." Hence, the Board says you cannot capitalize deal-related costs and must expense them as incurred.

The Board's new rules on deal-related expenses are totally logical *internally* and follow directly from the FASB's own new definition of Fair Value. The decision, however, just does not make sense to the buyer who *had* to incur the costs to conclude the deal process. "No expenses, no deal" is how most business executives view this issue. No matter what you think or believe, deal-related expenses are going to be expensed as incurred.

It is outside the scope of this book to argue with the FASB's rules on Fair Value. It will become abundantly clear that we feel there are major issues. But the nature of due process—and the FASB does indeed follow due process—is that once a decision is reached, you should follow it. Perhaps you can try to modify the application of the new rules, or if the new rules ultimately turn out not to be operational you can get the FASB to change their mind. Until then, all we can do is try to understand the rules and apply them as effectively and as efficiently as possible.

This brief discussion of the expensing of deal-related costs is a good example of the major changes to be effected by the new Fair Value rules.

MANAGING EARNINGS: THE POTENTIAL FOR MANIPULATION

Further adoption of FV accounting is being pushed by academics, some security analysts, and the FASB members and staff. There is at least one thing holding back the rush, however. The determination of FV is inherently imprecise. Values can be determined only within a range of perhaps 5% to 10%. This means that two equally competent appraisers, given the same assignment and the same assumptions as to outlook and competition, should come within 10% of each other. They will not arrive at identical answers.

Reasons for disparities among appraisers can arrive from different economic and political outlooks (can anyone agree on what the stock market is going to do over the next six months, much less the next six years?). Which party will control Congress and the White House after the next election? Is the United States going to become more, or less, competitive relative to China and many third-world countries? The problems with foretelling the future will never be solved, yet every valuation *must* make some assumptions about the future.

The real wonder is that two valuation specialists can come within even 10%. Valuation is not the same as calculation of a lapse schedule on future depreciation. Two accountants, told to forecast depreciation expense on a new building and to use accelerated depreciation for book and taxes, should come out with the same answer. Two appraisers asked to determine the FV of the same building will not have the same answer. They may arrive at answers that are reasonably close, but they won't be identical.

The real issue is that valuation requires professional judgment. Appraisers may require ten or more years before they are truly competent to value most types of financial assets. (Real estate, machinery, and equipment appraisers are two subspecialties within valuation.) But regardless of the length of experience and the quality of an appraiser's judgment, the fact remains that every valuation assignment requires professional judgment. Fair Values do not come out of a "black box" or a computer.

Every single appraisal report has one or more areas within the analysis where the valuation specialist has to make a choice based on judgment. And that judgment call cannot be audited. If a physician feels your belly and says, "I think you have appendicitis, and we should operate right away," he is exercising professional judgment. You can get a second opinion, but at some point you have to trust someone. And, occasionally, a physician will be wrong and you do not have appendicitis. Can the first physician's judgment call be audited? No. Based on seeing many similar cases, and comparing your belly to previous cases, he comes to a conclusion and expresses his opinion.

Now some readers may be surprised to hear that appraisers and physicians have very much in common. They do, in relation to the application of both judgment and experience being applied to a specific case.

Getting back to the heading for this section, how can Fair Values be manipulated? We disregard incompetence on the one side, and deliberate cheating on the other. (Remember the savings-and-loan [S&L] crisis of the early 1990s where fictitious valuations were prepared by "appraisers" who really did engage in fraud.) Recall that the professional designation for qualified real estate appraisers is MAI, which stands for Member of the Appraisal Institute. Unfortunately, as noted, many wags in industry refer to the MAI designation as standing for "Made as Instructed."

As with many witticisms, there is a kernel of truth here, and that is exactly what we referred to in terms of manipulation of Fair Value. It is a dirty little secret of valuation practice that clients often tell appraisers how they would like the report to come out. A borrower on a new building needs an FMV determination in excess of X, in order to obtain a loan. A probate attorney wants a block of stock valued at an amount less than Y in order to minimize estate taxes. And so forth. In practice, approximately 90% or more of clients know, in advance, what they would like the answer to be. This desire for a specific result sometimes is communicated to the valuation specialist, in a more or less direct form.

Most appraisers are aware of their client's wishes but can help only within a fairly narrow range, essentially the $\pm$ 10% that was mentioned earlier. But within that range, appraisers do have discretion. It would be unrealistic to assume that any professional is going to deliberately choose an answer at one end or the other within the range that will make the client most unhappy. Physicians want patients to return. Attorneys succeed through repeat business from a group of loyal clients. Auditors expect to work for the same company for many years as long as they provide good service. So, common sense suggests that appraisers, too, will try to provide a service to their client that encourages further business.

The question boils down now to the following: If appraisers have a narrow range, and within that range no point answer is better than another, then does coming up with a final Fair Value near one end of the range or the other represent "manipulation"? In one sense it does, because if the appraiser had no idea what the client was looking for, the odds are that he would have chosen something close to the middle of the range. However, as long as the final point estimate is supportable, and is within the range of acceptable answers, there is no manipulation.

The problem ultimately boils down to (1) inherently there is a lack of precision in valuation; and (2) clients have to have a point answer for recording in the books of account. While presenting a range would totally eliminate manipulation, who should choose the single point estimate within that range? Should it be the client, or should it be the appraiser? We vote for the appraiser, who, at the end of the day, has to be totally comfortable with his own professional judgments and has to be prepared to support them in a court of law, against an adverse party, or with the SEC.

Essentially, what one person is going to look at and call manipulation to achieve a predetermined answer, another person will say that trying to turn what is really a range into a single point answer simply is trying to square the circle and cannot be done without the exercise of judgment.

In terms of earnings management, management of a company is paid to produce certain economic results. Ideally, those results come from operations and not from earnings management of accounting results. But if you have a chance to put your best foot forward, within the rules of the game, why shouldn't you try to present a favorable picture. As Lord John Maynard Keynes once said, "In the long run we are all dead," and many accounting textbooks equally proclaim that "In the long run accounting treatment has no impact of real cash flows." The problem is that, unfortunately, financial reporting deals with the short run, and the imprecision inherent in accounting and valuation simply cannot be overcome if companies must report quarterly and show a bottom line that is a single number. In short, all accounting presents a false sense of precision, and valuation only makes it worse.

The moral here has to be this:

Do not believe that just because an appraisal shows a value to the nearest dollar, or thousand dollars, that the real answer is exactly what is shown. Any time Fair Values enter into the bottom line the real answer is in a range, not the single point value presented.

CHAPTER 2

Valuation of a Business: What Is It *Really* Worth?

When the Financial Accounting Standards Board (FASB) talks about Fair Value (FV), they are assuming that readers of financial statements want to know what something is worth—and this can best be thought of as what someone is willing to pay to acquire a specific asset. In this chapter we discuss how appraisers go about developing the FV of a business enterprise.

First, a brief diversion. Readers are thoroughly familiar with the purchase and sale of equity securities on the New York Stock Exchange (NYSE) and on Nasdaq. The buyer of 100, 1,000, or even 10,000 shares of a publicly traded security like AT&T is not buying a business. A mutual fund that is buying even one million shares of AT&T is not buying AT&T as a company, with the responsibility to run the company.

Security analysts, both those on the sell side (like Merrill Lynch) and on the buy side (like Fidelity mutual funds) make their own determination of "value." If their analysis is that the true value of shares of AT&T is $50 per share at a time when it is trading for $45 on the NYSE, they will recommend purchase of the security. Conversely, if their analysis leads them to the conclusion that the true value of AT&T is $40 when it is trading at $45, they will recommend a sell of the security.

Security purchases on the NYSE and Nasdaq, while involving valuation, do not involve the same type of valuation or analysis as that performed by appraisers or valuation specialists in valuing total business enterprises. There are two major differences.

First, purchase of one million shares of AT&T does not provide any degree of control over the company. A mutual fund that owns even ten million shares of General Electric or Microsoft does not control the company. Investors in traded equity securities are passive investors who, for practical purposes, can only hold or sell their shares to some other investor.

The second difference is that shareholders in publicly traded securities usually have a fairly high degree of liquidity (liquidity being defined as being able to sell the stock at short notice at a price close to the most recent trade). But they have no control over the company in which they are investing in terms of deciding policy, making capital investments, product decisions, outsourcing, and so forth.

Now compare an investment in Microsoft with that of the sole owner of a fairly large privately held software company, albeit one much smaller than Microsoft. The owner controls the company, but has very low liquidity. The only practical way the owner of a privately held company can obtain liquidity is to sell part or all of the company to a buyout firm or a competitor and effectively exit the business. Alternatively, he can enter into an initial public offering (IPO) and sell shares individually to investors. In the latter case, he has now assumed all the responsibilities of a public company (compliance with the Sarbanes-Oxley Act and the Securities Acts, supervised by the Securities and Exchange Commission) plus the burden of public oversight of what he does as a manager. The latter oversight includes the potential for class-action lawsuits by disgruntled shareholders, the requirement for holding annual meetings, virtually mandatory dealing with security analysts, and disclosing the most intimate details of overall compensation.

In short, buying and selling equity shares in the public securities markets is quite different from either the occasional sale of a total company or an IPO.

The reason for this brief discussion is that, at times, there is confusion between the value of a business enterprise and the amount that one can calculate by multiplying the latest per-share price of a stock by the total number of shares outstanding. Many analysts do make this calculation; if Microsoft has 10 billion shares outstanding and the latest quoted price is $30, they will say that Microsoft is a $300 billion company, implying that is the FV of the firm.

From a valuation perspective, the FV of a total business may be more than, or less than, the amount derived from simple multiplication of price per share times the number of shares. Control of an entire company provides scope for setting policy, compensation, and so forth, but also has costs. A privately held company, in contrast, has the benefit of control in few hands, but lacks liquidity.

Appraisers are often called on to value shares in privately held companies, and the major issues involve these concepts of control and liquidity. It is outside the scope of this book to discuss gift and estate tax valuations in detail. It is very common, however, for most taxpayers to argue with the Internal Revenue Service (IRS) that minority holdings in closely held firms should provide a discount for both lack of marketability *and* lack of control. This desire for low values is to minimize taxes. The IRS acknowledges the concepts of lack of marketability and lack of control as inherent in shares of closely held companies, but the Service fights furiously to keep the discounts low. The lower the discounts, the higher the taxable values of the stock, and the more taxes that will be collected. Consequently, most tax valuations involve discussions of control premiums on the one hand and discounts for lack of marketability on the other.

This discussion highlights that valuation is *not* a simple matter of multiplying two numbers together and assuming that the product of that calculation in some way represents FV. A great deal of judgment is required to arrive at the true FV of any asset, particularly so when there is a dispute about the value, and the dollar amount of the value in turn will affect one party or the other.

Unfortunately, the FASB in Statement of Financial Accounting Standards (SFAS) 157 does not fully acknowledge the types of judgments that have been discussed. Many observers believe that if you own a large block of a thinly traded stock, and want to sell it you may have to accept a discount from the last quoted per-share price. Yet the FASB explicitly prohibits recognition of what appraisers and stock traders call a blockage discount. The real world acknowledges that a large block of stock may sell for more, or for less, than the last per-share price quoted on the NYSE. The discount, or premium, depends on the current wishes of prospective buyers and sellers, so at times a large block of stock can sell for more than, or less than, the quoted price. The FASB, however, denies this aspect of economic reality. In short, the world of FV for accounting is made up of too many rules and too little judgment.

Value is created in the marketplace. The responsibility of a valuation specialist is to try and estimate just what an asset would sell for, or could be acquired for, *if* a transaction were to take place. Such determinations involve judgment and experience and cannot be derived by some simple computer program.

The remainder of this chapter will discuss just how appraisers actually value total businesses that are not publicly traded. These can be operating units of a larger company or self-contained privately held firms. The principles and approaches are the same. The purpose of this chapter is not to turn the reader into a do-it-yourself appraiser. Rather, it is to explain what we, as appraisers, do and why we do it.

FUNDAMENTAL BASIS OF ALL VALUES

The value of an asset is what someone else will pay for it. To put it even more concretely, how much cash would you get if you sold the asset, given a reasonable amount of time that the asset was exposed to the market?

If you are the owner of a business, you can try to sell the business. You will then find out exactly what it is worth when you accept the highest and best offer. However, at times, it is important for a business owner to get a very good idea of the value of the business, but it is totally impractical to actually try and sell the asset. A good example is a gift tax or estate tax return. The IRS requires the donor, or deceased's executor, to value the assets being transferred. But even the IRS does not require the donor or executor actually to sell, or even try to sell, the business. Rather, all parties are willing to accept the results of independent valuation specialists. Appraisers are in the business of valuing assets, for a fee, and it is important to remember that the fee is not related to the value of the assets, but rather to the time taken to perform the work.

So, the question becomes: How do appraisers value a business that is not actually being put up for sale? Valuation is actually a very simple process. As one of my colleagues once said, "Any three year old—with thirty years' experience—can value assets!" That may be a slight exaggeration, but certainly a high school graduate, with ten or more years of experience, can deliver a credible valuation report.

In fact, readers of this book are already appraisers, even if they are unaware of it. Do you have an idea of the value of the car in your driveway? What would your home sell for if you had to move? These are two questions to which readers can relate, and for which they probably have pretty good answers.

You would determine the value of your 2006 BMW by going to the Internet at www.cars.com, by looking at ads in the Sunday paper, and by calling a BMW dealer and seeing what he was asking for a more or less comparable car. Similarly, for your house, you would know what one or two of your neighbors had recently sold their house for and then make an adjustment—up or down—for features and amenities that differentiated your house from theirs.

Would you be able to precisely determine the value of your car or your house? Probably not, but you could estimate it closely enough to allow you to make good business decisions. If your estimate of value came within 5% to 10% of the true value, you would be unlikely to make any serious mistakes. The fact is that for assets with which you are familiar—and that includes collectibles that are a hobby—it is not all that difficult to estimate value within a realistic range.

Appraisers use *exactly* the same thought process in determining the value of a business as you do in estimating the value of your car or your house or your stamp collection.

Appraisers look at three distinct, yet interrelated, bases for determining FV.

Comparable Assets Can Determine Fair Value

Both the FASB and professionals in the valuation field believe that if you know the price at which specific assets have recently sold, then you can arrive at a reasonable estimate of the value of your asset by making any necessary adjustments. A real estate broker will tell you what she thinks your house would sell for if you listed it with her; her suggestion (when not motivated by a desire to obtain a listing by giving you a high estimate) will be based on her experience in selling comparable houses in your neighborhood. Your estimate of the value of your BMW is based on looking to see what other comparable BMWs are selling for.

There is only one problem with determining FV by looking at comparable assets. No two assets are identical. There are always differences. Your BMW has 30,000 miles, while the dealer's has only 22,000 miles. Your house has four bedrooms and three baths, while your next-door neighbor has a finished basement but only three bedrooms.

Determining value by reference to comparable assets is only as valid as are the comparisons one can make. Since there never are totally comparable or identical assets, judgment is required to make the necessary adjustments, whether for mileage and condition, size of lot, or type of construction.

In valuing businesses, no matter how large your database, no business out there is just like yours. In fact, the most frequent comment appraisers receive in starting to value any business enterprise is, "Our business is different!" And that comment is invariably accurate.

The secret in using comparable transactions to value a specific asset is to understand both the similarities and the differences. Then it is necessary to identify the value of those other firms, considering both pluses and minuses. You then have to add or subtract for the differences between the subject property and the comparables. How much each adjustment should be in dollar terms is no more or less than the application of judgment.

In the case of your own home in your own neighborhood, your personal experience usually suffices. If you were asked to value a regional shopping center—also real estate, but very different in scope and style—you probably would not know where to start to get information of comparable transactions, much less to make necessary adjustments for the differences among shopping centers. By the same token, an experienced commercial real estate appraiser works every day with this type of asset and knows exactly where to go for information and how to make appropriate (and supportable) adjustments.

It is easy to see why the FASB has suggested that, where available, the best indication of FV is from markets with comparable transactions.

Valuing a business in its entirety, however, calls for so many adjustments, in terms of both historical results and outlook, that very specific methodologies are usually applied by valuation specialists.

Valuing a business through comparables may have almost as many weaknesses as strengths.

But there are two other approaches which appraisers can utilize.

Discounted Cash Flow—The Income Approach

Virtually all finance and accounting majors have studied the discounted cash flow (DCF) methodology at one time or another. Whether they have actually used it in practice, the basic concept that a dollar five years from now is worth less than a dollar today is well accepted. Budgeting for capital expenditures uses a DCF methodology, as does the valuation of businesses. We assume readers are either familiar with the approach or can obtain necessary instruction in their own firm from financial analysts who do this day in and day out.

All DCF analyses rest on two very critical assumptions. The first is the accuracy of the projected income or cash flows. The second is the choice of the appropriate discount rate. The value of a U.S. government bond is the simplest example. There is 100% certainty that both the future interest payments and principal will be paid on the date due. This follows from the fact that the government can always print money to pay its debts, an alternative not open elsewhere. The discount rate is based on market forces, and at any one point in time the effective interest rate assumed by investors in discounting the future cash flow is widely publicized in the *Wall Street Journal* and elsewhere.

The determination of the FV of a Treasury bond today has no uncertainties–other than that future interest rates may go up or down, thus affecting the future value of the bond. But as of today, the FV is truly determinable without controversy.

Having said this, unfortunately, government securities are the *only* assets for which such unqualified statements can be made. For every other asset, the future cash flows are more or less uncertain. A corporate bond issued by a AAA firm still has some risk of future default. There are more and more risks as one goes down the ratings scale from AAA to CCC junk bonds and below.

But no matter the business risks of corporate securities, they are still much easier to evaluate than are self-contained businesses. There is no business for which the future cash flows (revenues less all expenditures) are certain. Competitors, suppliers, and customers are all unknowns at the date of any valuation. Further, economic events, international disturbances, and political factors make every forecast of business activity subject to more or less uncertainty.

We just stated that there are two problems with the DCF approach: the future projections of cash flow and the appropriate discount rate. The determination of the appropriate discount rate sometimes is developed from an analysis of the weighted average cost of capital (WACC). Literally, entire books have been written on the subject of calculating the WACC. For purposes of this discussion we can simplify the overly esoteric formulations of WACC put forth by some analysts and academics. Discount rates of 9% to 11% can be supported for most large *Fortune* 500 companies. Privately held firms that are established often are valued using a 12% to 15% discount rate. Somewhat less secure firms are often valued with a discount rate of 16% to 20%. Private-equity investors typically look for 20% or more returns, and hence that is the appropriate discount rate for a private-equity transaction. Finally, venture capital (VC) investors look for 25% to 35% rates of return, so start-up firms are usually valued using this range of discount rates.

Frankly, while many appraisers and those who review the appraisal reports of others spend an inordinate amount of time developing, supporting, and then questioning the exact discount used in a DCF analysis, the real key is the projections themselves. For every inappropriate discount rate we have seen applied, we have seen 10 to 15 more where it is the future projections that really should be questioned.

It may be difficult to come up with a good income projection, but that does not obviate the need for *someone* to make the assumptions, and then defend them against skeptical questioners.

Developing Supportable Cash Flow Projections

Most books on valuation spend a lot of time on the mechanics of DCF analysis, and there is an implicit or even explicit assumption that "someone else" has prepared the forecast and that it is safe to use it. In valuing a business using DCF—and this may well be the most popular valuation technique—developing the projection is critical.

In some instances the valuation specialist will himself develop the projections. More often the client develops the projections. In a prospective business combination, both the buyer and seller will independently develop their own projections. Differences here often lead to arrangements for contingent payouts; the valuation of such arrangements is discussed in Chapter 6.

Often, an appraiser will use projections prepared by his client as part of their annual profit planning cycle. Typically, these are reviewed by the board of directors, and the budget itself becomes the basis for performance evaluation and even future compensation. The development of sound budgets and forecasts is outside the scope of this book. Suffice it to say that developing good forecasts and budgets requires objectivity on everyone's part, in contrast to the all-too-common "gamesmanship" utilized in many companies' budget process.

The most difficult situation in valuing a company is what the appraiser should do if he receives projections—even a budget reviewed and approved by the board of directors—with which he does not agree. There are no appraisal standards that deal with this situation, even though it is very common.

Because the valuation answer using the DCF procedure is virtually 100% dependent on the financial projections, getting reliable projections is a challenge in the best of circumstances. When companies want, for whatever reason, to make things look better, it is easy to adjust the cash flow projections, particularly in the years further out. So if the company has lost money and done little more than break even this year, it is usually totally ridiculous in the next year to assume profit margins at 10%. But a gradual improvement over a three-year time frame can be supported by assertions that "we know what our problems were, and our plan will work and get us there."

How does an appraiser react to optimistic thinking that *could* turn out well, but on the surface appears highly optimistic? Appraisers first have to ask the tough questions of management, and ask management to reconsider. If management then reiterates its assertions, the appraiser usually applies a higher discount rate, thus reducing the net present value. How much of an adjustment to the discount

Observation: It is critical that readers of a valuation report actually *read* the entire narrative. Most appraisers tell "the story, the whole story, and nothing but the story" in their report. But any exculpatory language alerting the reader may not be shown on either the first page or the last page of the report. Unfortunately, too many users of valuation reports turn only to those two pages. There is a reason why the entire report has been prepared. Please review the sample report shown in the Appendix that supports this book as described in Chapter 1.

rate is appropriate is ultimately a matter of professional judgment. In one case of some truly egregious forecasts, the writer applied a 60% discount rate, which had the effect of obviating virtually all results beyond years three and four. Further, in the narrative of the report, the valuation specialist said something to the effect that "we accepted management's projections."

If you receive an appraisal report that indicates in some way that the appraiser himself questioned the projections, then you should review the underlying assumptions *very* closely. If the appraiser was uncomfortable, so should be the reader.

For a first-time valuation, the appraiser is at a disadvantage in challenging projections because there is little prior history. But, in many cases, appraisers periodically update previously developed values. For example, by law, employee stock option plans (ESOPs) must have an annual appraisal. It is far more economical for a company to engage the same appraiser in subsequent years. Thus, the appraiser can compare this past year's actual results with the forecast for last year submitted a year ago.

Again, missing a forecast for a year does not inevitably require an appraiser to disregard management's projections. It does, however, call for more intense scrutiny of the new forecast and asking even more penetrating questions. As with management's relations with independent auditors, unless the professional is comfortable with management and management's representations, it may be necessary to resign the engagement.

EARNINGS BEFORE INTEREST, TAXES, DEPRECIATION, AND AMORTIZATION (EBITDA)

In valuing a business in certain industries, or certain types of transactions, there are often rules of thumb assumed by the participants. A flower store may sell for one to one and a half times current revenues, or a car wash may sell for eight times EBITDA.

These rules of thumb can be truly dangerous to the economic health of participants. The underlying assumption in these shortcut approaches to valuation is that "all other things are equal." For the flower shop, one has to assume a certain standard gross margin percentage holds true. For the car wash, one has to assume that unusual maintenance or further capital expenditures will not be necessary.

EBITDA is particularly dangerous because it is based on a static measure, the *current* cash flow results. As a valuation method, EBITDA cannot handle growth or declines in future results. It does not handle unusual working capital requirements that affect cash flow. EBITDA says absolutely nothing about required capital expenditures. Finally, the nominal amount of EBITDA implicitly assumes that taxes and interest somehow are either irrelevant or in some manner will not have to be paid with actual cash disbursements.

EBITDA multiples are frequently used by investment bankers and business dealers, not to mention prospective buyers and sellers. But using EBITDA in place of a more rigorous analysis has the potential to provide incorrect answers for one party or the other. Some questions that should always be asked when EBITDA multiples are thrown around should include:

- Will next year's EBITDA be higher or lower than this year's?
- How much, and with what timing, will income taxes be paid?
- How much, and with what timing, will interest have to be paid?
- Will capital expenditures be equal to depreciation, in which case there is no net cash flow?
- How does this company differ from other companies from which the EBITDA multiple was derived?
  - Revenue growth
  - Margins
  - Operating expenses

- New product development
- Customer relationships
- Supplier relationships
- Competitive conditions
- Economic conditions

Unless these questions can be satisfactorily answered, one should ordinarily give EBITDA valuations a wide berth unless they are accompanied by other analyses. And even if the questions can be answered, at that point you probably have sufficient information to perform a proper valuation using a DCF approach.

MYTH OF COMPARABLE COMPANIES—MAKING ADJUSTMENTS

Most appraisers, and certainly the FASB, love to find comparables, usually companies, but often royalty rates, building costs, or debt-to-equity ratios, to name three examples.

Appraisers can and should adjust the financial results of both the subject company and the comparables to strip out unusual and nonrecurring results. Certainly, security analysts do this with the latest quarterly reports of NYSE companies. Actually, because of this tendency to disregard nonrecurring items, management often tries to bury unpleasant results by calling them nonrecurring. The author one time wrote the CEO of a major NYSE firm, chiding him for three consecutive years about the *same* supposedly nonrecurring item. Needless to say, when the CEO personally called to agree that they

Warning: There are never truly comparable assets. No two businesses are alike. No two buildings are alike. No two investors are alike. This does not mean that valuations should dispense with comparables. It does mean that it is incumbent on the valuation specialist to analyze closely the similarities *and* differences, and make the necessary adjustments. Without such adjustments there is a false sense of precision in simply comparing Company A with Company B, or Building C with Building D.

should not have done it and would not do it again, this confirmed the wisdom of communication with firms you are invested in. The same type of thought process is absolutely vital on the part of a financial analyst performing preliminary work for a valuation study.

No matter how many adjustments the analyst makes, no matter what is considered normal and what is considered nonrecurring, one can never make two companies with different cultures, different histories, or different product lines look the same and be truly comparable.

In the final analysis, what many appraisers do is to make a reasonable approximation of normal operating results for a number of companies, say six to eight that are in the same industry group. Then one can take the average or preferably the median of all the companies as the basis of comparison for the subject company. In other words, you do not compare your Company A just with more or less comparable Company B on its own. You compare Company A with a *basket* of companies, and simply hope that there is no bias in the way the six to eight companies each prepared their own financial statements.

DEFINITION OF A BUSINESS

To many readers, the topic of how to define a business may seem either overly esoteric or a "no-brainer." In financial reporting, however, the definition can make a significant difference. In 1998, the Emerging Issues Task Force (EITF) issued a ruling that if an acquisition was of "assets," and not of a "business," then the total purchase price had to be allocated to the individual assets, and there was no room for goodwill. In practice, this meant that what the buyer perceived as a business, and paid a premium to acquire, turned out to be only a "purchase of assets." The consequences could be severe.

The true FV of all the acquired assets might be less than the price paid, but under the accounting rules the "values" of each asset would be written up because the total purchase price had to go somewhere other than goodwill. But if the amounts assigned to the acquired assets were actually in excess of true FV, then the next consequence could be an impairment charge, writing the assets back down to FV.

Had the transaction been accounted for as the purchase of a business, however, the excess purchase amount would have been labeled as goodwill. The impairment test for goodwill, discussed in Chapter 9, is far less strict. This disparity between companies and auditors intent on following the letter of the law resulted in unnecessary arguments, with the valuation specialist often in the middle.

A further consequence of the EITF rule occurred with start-up or development companies. These often are acquired for large premiums over book value. Buyers thought they were acquiring a business and expected the premium to go into goodwill. But the old definition of a business, according to the EITF, required that it "must contain all of the inputs and processes necessary for it to continue to conduct normal operations . . . which includes the ability to sustain a revenue stream by providing its outputs to customers."

Now, most start-up firms in the software and biotech fields are often acquired *before* they have a product ready to sell, much less any customers, so by definition they were excluded from being considered a business. Rigid application of the EITF rule meant then that these acquisitions were treated as asset purchases, not a business combina-tion, with the consequent potential for massive impairment charges.

The new SFAS 141 R has language that dramatically reduces the differential between an asset purchase and a business combination. Without going into detail, the new rule will allow a much broader definition of a business. The consequence is that the accounting and valuation problems with the old rule, at least when narrowly applied, will no longer be a problem. Acquisition of a start-up or development business will actually be treated as just that—a business combination.

VALUING A START-UP (EARLY-STAGE) BUSINESS

One of the most difficult valuation problems deals with early-stage companies. A lot of time and resources are involved in developing, for example, a stem-cell approach to healing damaged heart tissue. But before the proposed product can be sold and generate revenue, it is required to meet a long series of Food and Drug Administration (FDA) requirements. These requirements, quite reasonably, deal with patient safety and the ultimate efficacy of the product.

In practice, completing all required FDA steps can easily take upwards of ten years, and involve literally millions of dollars in three separate phases of testing. The valuation issue deals with what the company is worth, say, at the end of the first three years. The research looks promising. All the lab tests indicate potential success, but the product has not as yet been tested on animals for safety or people for efficacy.

What is such a company worth? This is a very real problem, because start-up companies need themselves valued generally for two separate yet related reasons. They must be valued in order to raise additional capital after the initial resources of the founders have been exhausted. Too low a value means that the new investors capture a disproportionate amount of the value of the company—at the expense of the founders, who fear being diluted. Too high a valuation means that prospective investors are likely to be scared off and the company can literally die for lack of financial resources.

But wait, there is a further complication in valuing start-up businesses. Because they are often short of cash to pay large compensation, many employees are willing to settle for stock options. Under current accounting rules (SFAS 123 R) the expense of options granted must be recognized in the financial statements. So the value of the options, at date of grant, become critical both to the financial well-being of the employees and to the profit-and-loss (P&L) statement of the company.

Unfortunately, there is still one additional player in options, and that is the IRS. Under Internal Revenue Code (IRC) section 409A options, if granted, must be granted to employees at their true Fair Market Value (FMV). If the IRS can prove that options were granted at less than FMV, the penalties for both the company and the employee(s) are very serious.

The outline of the problem should be clear. A development company wants a high, but not unreasonable, valuation in order to attract new rounds of financing. They want a correct valuation for the IRS. And they want a low value for the granting of employee options, since the lower the exercise price, the greater the potential gain for the employee if the company succeeds. One solution to this dilemma would be to have three separate valuation reports: the first for the outside investors, the second for the IRS, and the third for granting options and recording expense.

A moment's thought quickly consigns this solution to the waste basket. Theoretically, as an appraiser, one could develop three separate valuations, each with its own assumptions and projections. But one has to believe that outside investors, the company's auditor, the Securities and Exchange Commission (SEC), and the IRS might not be very happy to have three separate valuations floating around at the same time. The concluding section of this chapter discusses this in more detail.

If three separate reports are not possible and one report has to accomplish three separate tasks, this now puts a premium on absolutely clear communication between the company and the valuation specialist. The only real solution is for the company to acknowledge that they cannot "play games" with valuation reports; the company should simply ask the valuation specialist to do his best and "get it right."

But asking for the right answer and obtaining it may not be as easy as it sounds when dealing with development-stage companies. The reason is that no one—not the company, not the FDA, and certainly not the valuation specialist—has any idea whether a new pharmaceutical product will succeed. The same holds true, of course, for start-up ventures in electronics, software, and any other field.

The future is uncertain, but valuation inevitably involves some sort of projections; those projections implicitly or explicitly *must* make assumptions about the future success (or failure) of the start-up firm. The problem is that the management itself is almost invariably optimistic about its prospects. The appraiser may not share that optimism, but it is highly unlikely that any appraiser is going to know as much about the technology, and the prospects for that technology, as the management. Further, estimates as to future developments, costs to complete, and customer acceptance are almost always tinged with faith and hope. Such feelings are normal for managers who may have invested years of their career, not to mention a significant part of their own net worth, in building the firm to its present position.

Look at this from the appraiser's perspective. If he accepts management's optimism and things do not work out, investors who relied on the report may be unhappy. If they do not work out, then the SEC will never get involved, and any stock options granted to employees essentially become worthless so whatever the strike price was becomes irrelevant.

On the other side, consider if the appraiser shows true "professional skepticism" and effectively lowballs the valuation and the company meets or exceeds management's expectations. Investors will be happy, employees holding options will be happy. But the IRS, with the benefit of hindsight may argue the options were granted below FMV and go after the individuals and the company for failing to comply with section 409A. Perhaps even more disturbing to the successful company that is either acquired or has an IPO is that the SEC will argue that the company issued *cheap stock*, a term used by the SEC to indicate options granted below what the SEC staff considers to have been the appropriate FMV.

Under the SEC's interpretation, if a company issued cheap stock, the company has to take a compensation charge for the difference between the actual option price and the value as determined by the SEC. Many people are unaware of the SEC's being in the valuation business. And they are not, except in the cheap stock situation.

The SEC argument is that if a company has an IPO at, say, $15, and options were granted 18 months earlier at, say, $2, it is *prima facie* evidence that the company issued cheap stock. The fact that of 10 companies 18 months ago that might have issued options, and now only one has been successful carries little weight with the SEC. They do not go back to 18 months ago, rather they simply assume that if you have an IPO today that you knew, or should have known, that a 7.5 times increase in value in a year and a half is unreasonable. Truly, this can be a Catch-22 situation.

The only answer, and one that that both the American Institute of Certified Public Accountants (AICPA) and the SEC bless, is to have a contemporaneous valuation every time options are going to be issued. If performed objectively, with all assumptions clearly spelled out in the valuation report, such a contemporaneous valuation report will probably suffice to stop both an SEC charge of cheap stock and an IRS assertion of a violation of section 409A.

MISUSE OF VALUATION REPORTS

Several times, it has been mentioned that it is incumbent on the recipient of a valuation report to read the total report. Most valuation reports dealing with the determination of FV for financial reporting are prepared in accordance with the Uniform Standards of Professional Appraisal Practice (USPAP). Standard 9 explicitly requires that the report include a complete description of the asset(s) being valued, the effective date of the valuation, identification of the client, and the intended use of the appraisal opinions by the client. Standard 9 recommends that every appraisal report include a statement to the effect that "This report is intended only for use in (*describe the use*). This report is not intended for any other use."

Thus, a business enterprise valuation undertaken to support the issuance of stock options to comply with IRC section 409A would so state. It might also state that the report is intended to comply with SFAS 123 R, covering financial reporting of stock options.

There would potentially be problems if the client then used the *same* valuation report for the purpose of convincing prospective lenders or investors that such an investment were justified. Lenders, in particular, want values based on potential sale or liquidation of the asset(s) used as collateral. An appraisal developed for valuing stock options might or might not be appropriate for a lending institution.

An egregious example concerned a client who obtained an appraisal for insurance purposes. Such a report is required to show the cost of reproduction or cost of replacement because, in case of loss, the insurance company has to make whole the insured. So an insurance appraisal does not develop FMV, the price at which the property would exchange between a willing buyer and a willing seller. The purpose of the insurance appraisal is to tell the insurance company what the assets are worth if those specific assets are lost, say in a fire or earthquake. Whether the assets were earning a return sufficient to invest in them today is irrelevant. The insurance company has a contingent liability in case of loss, and in exchange for standing by to reimburse a loss, it charges a premium directly related to the replacement cost of the assets. In other words, there is not really a financial analysis of economic feasibility as there is in most other valuations.

It is safe to assert that, uniformly, insurance appraisals have as high or higher dollar values than appraisals for any other purpose. At the opposite end of the value spectrum are appraisals for banks showing forced liquidation and orderly liquidation. Forced liquidation assumes an almost immediate auction, while orderly liquidation provides more time to find a buyer who will pay the highest amount for the asset(s). In forced liquidation auctions the bidders are usually used equipment dealers, while in an orderly liquidation the seller would try and find someone who could use the assets for the purpose for which they were assembled. The difference between forced and orderly liquidation can easily be between 15% and 20%; for an entire plant facility the difference could be even greater, perhaps up to 35%.

In one memorable situation, a client in the contracting business obtained an insurance appraisal on construction equipment, with the values essentially being the cost of new equipment and possibly a small reduction for physical wear and tear. Unknown to the appraisal firm, the client took the same report to his bank and told them, "See, this is the value of my equipment, according to a well-known appraisal firm." His use of the term *value*, in the context of his loan application, might in hindsight be considered slightly optimistic. But the point is that the bank officer either did not read the report or did not think that there could be a difference between insurable value and liquidation value.

Six months later, the construction market had cratered in that community, the contractor had gone bankrupt, and the bank was trying to recover its loan from selling the equipment. Needless to say, the market for used construction equipment at that point was soft and the bank was facing a large loss. So, the American way is to call someone and threaten to sue. The bank called the appraisal company and suggested, very politely, that the two firms might want to share the loss to avoid a nasty lawsuit for professional malpractice. After all, didn't the values in the appraisal report vastly exceed what the assets could be sold for today?

The appraisal company representative gently asked the banker on the other end of the phone call if he had actually read the valuation report. The representative pointed out that the date of the valuation was some six months earlier, during which period the market had collapsed. Further, the values were developed for insurance and not for liquidation. The report, having been prepared in accordance with USPAP, stood on its own, and the bank officer somewhat sheepishly retreated, having learned an important but expensive lesson.

BUSINESS ENTERPRISE VALUATIONS (BEVS)

The usual valuation report, sometimes referred to by appraisers as a BEV, ordinarily will have two types of valuation. First is the DCF analysis, relying on projections of the company. These projections are usually prepared by management and can, at times, appear optimistic. Appraisers can, and often will, allow for this optimism by increasing the discount rate. The argument is that there is more risk than usual in having the company attain the projections. While relatively infrequent, a very conservative projection would justify a lower discount rate (higher value).

A good BEV would also utilize the market comparable approach, comparing the subject company to publicly traded firms in the same industry grouping, and hopefully of similar size. As mentioned, there are never totally similar firms, so an appraiser must use professional judgment in adjusting, as necessary, the public firms chosen for the comparison.

Economic theory suggests that one should arrive at very similar, if not identical, results using different valuation techniques. Theory posits that there is *the* value and, if all the analyses and all the assumptions are correct, that this true value will be determined.

Practice, unfortunately, seldom seems to follow theory. In the real world, if an appraiser tries to value a company by the income approach, the answer will certainly differ from the value indication derived from the market comparable approach. So, if you have two indications of value from utilizing different approaches, which one is correct? The answer is that neither is probably the true value of the company. What appraisers have to do is ask themselves: What are the factors that influence each of the two value indications?

A simplistic solution, one that is not recommended, is to average the two answers and assume that we now have the correct value. Experience suggests that in most cases one or the other of the approaches will appear more robust, based on better assumptions. One cannot generalize that the DCF is always better than the market comparable approach, or vice versa.

We have often assigned a 75% weight to one of the approaches and a 25% weight to the other. Then, in the narrative report, we specify why we made the choices we did. That leaves it up to the reader to recalculate the final determination of FV if they disagree with the appraiser's weighting.

This leads into the final aspect of developing an FV for an appraisal report. We tell clients that we can determine the FV quite quickly, primarily based on our experience. So, on an oral basis, the client will have a pretty good idea of what he is looking for.

The trouble is that an oral indication of value has very little credibility in the real world, where other parties may have diverse interests. Just because the appraiser says it is $X does not make it so. Both the client and others affected by the value need support for the value conclusions. That support appears in the narrative report.

It is sometimes hard to get across to clients that preparing the draft report will take more time and require more effort than the initial determination of FV. Nevertheless, that is reality.

In this chapter we have laid out the framework under which appraisers determine the Fair Value of a company. In the next chapter we discuss how valuations are tested in the real world of litigation, where real money may depend on the supportability of the valuation specialist's professional work product.

CHAPTER 3

Litigation and the "True" Determination of Value

T here are only two ways to prove that a determination of Fair Value (FV) is correct. The first is for an actual arm's-length transaction to take place. In this case, one hopes that the exchange for the subject assets takes place at or close to the previously appraised value. This can happen if the appraisal was well prepared and, in fact, did approximate a marketplace transaction. Related is the possibility that the appraisal itself is in effect a self-fulfilling prophecy. The amount determined by the appraiser is then used by the parties to consummate a deal—at the appraised value.

If actual market transactions are one way to validate the work of a valuation specialist, the second is for the values to be tested in court. The determination of a judge and/or jury becomes dispositive. In other words, the true value then becomes what the judge or jury says it is.

In this chapter we offer an insider's perspective on valuation issues within the legal system and present some lessons learned that can help readers anticipate valuation within the context of an actual or potential legal dispute.

VALUATION FOR DIVORCE PROCEEDINGS

Perhaps the simplest type of dispute to discuss valuation issues is in the divorce arena. We discussed earlier in the book the necessity for an appraiser to utilize realistic and supportable projections. It is in exactly this area of valuation that the wheels come off the correct valuation process.

In a typical divorce situation, the husband and wife jointly own a closely held company, which the husband runs. The marriage starts to disintegrate, but the business itself keeps operating, albeit perhaps a little less well if the boss—in this case, the husband—is distracted and doesn't devote sufficient attention to the business. A moment's thought will suggest that it may even be in the husband's interest to let the business slide. The poorer the prospects for the business, the lower the values will be. And a lower value means the wife receives less.

In this typical divorce setting, the wife has not been actively involved in running the business. Her lawyer and her appraiser have to utilize the discovery process to obtain the documents they need. But no series of produced documents will ever substitute for personal knowledge of the business. This is why appraisers always insist, whenever possible, on talking to a company's management as part of the valuation process. In the unique setting of a civil lawsuit, where the parties probably aren't speaking to each other, the wife's professionals will not be able to obtain an objective perspective on the business's prospects from management—in this case, the husband.

First, we discuss what usually happens, and then we will discuss what *should* happen. In most divorce valuation cases, because the principal asset is shares in a privately held business with no market, each side hires an appraiser. The husband's appraiser takes a very pessimistic view of future prospects, and will essentially assert that the business is only a half step away from having to file for bankruptcy under chapter 11. Consequently, if the business has any value at all, it is purely nominal. To put it in the vernacular, the business is headed straight south.

The wife hires her appraiser, and his outlook is that with good management (usually assumed to be anyone other than the husband), the company has a potential exceeded only by Microsoft in the mid-1990s and Google in the 2005–06 period. To put this argument in perspective, the wife's valuation specialist is absolutely convinced the business can do nothing but head straight north.

In this situation, the judge now has two appraisal reports in front of him, and he does one of two things. He either splits the difference, which only encourages others in the future to go ridiculously high or ridiculously low. Alternatively, he will have the parties hire a neutral third appraiser, on whom the judge will rely.

Because the above description is all too familiar to appraisers, many appraisers will not accept a divorce assignment, while, occasionally, a practitioner will specialize solely in divorce work.

Now, what *should* be done? The parties should agree in advance and select one appraiser who will have two clients, each paying half his charges. The parties agree in advance, as in an arbitration, to be bound by the selected appraiser's opinion. For an appraiser, this is the hardest assignment to accept because, in the best of worlds, both parties are probably not going to like the answer.

This gets to the subject of bias. How can a wife like her own appraiser's high value, while the husband likes his appraiser's low value? Can they both be right? Are they both wrong? Why should we consider the report of the single neutral appraiser to be more reliable?

The answer deals with the philosophy of valuation. Value is *always* dealing with the future. Perceptions today as to future results determine today's value. There is no way around this, as long as the results of a valuation specialist's work are to be useful for some sort of decision. And a valuation report that is not useful to someone is never going to be requested or paid for.

Bias can creep in because we do not know the future. Therefore, whether one takes an optimistic perspective or a conservative perspective, nobody else can call the resultant value wrong. Anything can happen. As a colleague once said, talking about the chances of a particular outcome, "If I stepped out of the second floor window in this room, I *could* go up." Most people, however, are uncomfortable *relying* on remote possibilities. So while a very optimistic outcome or a very pessimistic outcome *could* happen, most of us would not count on its happening, and certainly would not want to trust a lot of money or our health to a remote possibility.

When appraisers take positions that are extreme, you cannot say that they are wrong, but you can ask, "Realistically, what are the *probabilities* of this actually happening?" Most appraisers will respond, "Well, it is not my job to predict the future. I take my client's projection(s) and use it in my report, and that leads to my answer. Therefore, I (the appraiser) am absolved, and it is the client who made me do it."

My personal view is diametrically opposite. It is my firm belief that an appraiser has to take responsibility for all aspects of his work.

Observation: One appraiser can work for both sides in a conflict situation. It is important that the individual be paid equally by both sides and meet independently with the parties. After all, the definition of Fair Value, or Fair Market Value, actually implies that there is just one correct answer at any point in time.

If he is given projections about future events that do not make sense (i.e., have a very low probability of occurrence) the appraiser must "step up to the plate" and clearly state whether or not he agrees with the projections. In the next section we discuss a legal case where the appraiser ducked behind his client's ridiculous projections and claimed his erroneous answers "weren't his fault." We submit that erroneous values in an appraisal report are totally the responsibility of the valuation specialist. There are, however, several ways of handling such disagreements, and we will discuss them below.

Any time you, the reader of this book, see an appraisal report that on the surface just does not make sense, it is easy to trace back where the bad answer came from. Unless the appraiser is totally incompetent (less often than you might think) or has made a mathematical error (more common than you might think), a bad answer can always be traced back to faulty assumptions about the future.

What is critical here is the routine valuation that simply provides an unexpected answer. It is true that every valuation requires, at some point, the exercise of professional judgment. And some people have better judgment than others. The point, however, is that an unacceptable indication of value is in all likelihood due to explicitly utilizing projections of the future that are not borne out by past experience or realistic future changes.

Consequently, if two parties are fighting it out in court (e.g., in a divorce), it is no surprise that each side obtains an answer favorable to their own position. But two conflicting appraisals do not really help a judge, much less a jury of your peers, to arrive at the truth. What is needed is a reasonable answer, and the most cost-effective approach is to put the burden on an appraiser who is totally neutral and is paid only to come up with the most supportable answer possible.

APPRAISAL REPORTS THAT ARE "MADE AS INSTRUCTED"

One of the greatest myths surrounding valuation is the often-spoken statement that an appraiser "will give you any answer you want (or need)." The implication is that appraisers are for sale, essentially working in the same type of marketplace as used cars and patent medicine. Those of us doing our work in a highly professional manner resent the statement and the implications.

"Where there is smoke, there is fire" probably sums up the real issue. As we noted earlier in the chapter, in many litigation situations each party will produce valuation reports that are essentially diametrically opposite in the value indication. Most observers, in this situation, draw the following conclusions:

- Both appraisers and appraisal reports cannot each be correct.
- Therefore, at least one is wrong.
- Maybe both are wrong.
- How did the appraisers come up with such wrong answers?
- They must have been asked to provide a report that supported a predetermined answer.
- They each accomplished their assignment, and in fact, the appraisals were "Made as Instructed."

It happens that the professional designation for real estate appraisers is "Member of the Appraisal Institute" and is often abbreviated as "MAI," just as a master in business administration is commonly referred to as an MBA. Real estate appraisers are required to have at least five years of experience performing real estate appraisals before they can even think of sitting for the required tests. In my own experience, MAI-certified appraisers do a topnotch job in a tremendous variety of real estate situations. My only complaint with our firm's own MAIs, as well as our noncertified real estate appraisers preparing to meet the requirements, is that their reports are too comprehensive, too long, and take too much time. The response is always, "Well, that's how we do our work." Virtually every real estate appraisal this author has reviewed has been well researched, comprehensive, and persuasive in its conclusions.

If our observation is accurate, then how does the myth persist? Very simply. Not all real estate appraisers have earned the MAI designation. Further, the experience of most businessmen with appraisal reports has come solely from applying for a mortgage on newly acquired residential property. Depending on when you buy in the real estate cycle (i.e., whether values are going up or are going down), the ability to get a mortgage that will pay for your purchase is dependent on only one thing: the appraised value of your new property.

In the residential real estate field, there are very few MAI professionally designated appraisers. By and large, the typical MAI will deal primarily with industrial and commercial property, as well as major real estate developments. Professional investors and real estate investment trusts (REITs) represent a substantial portion of the client base for MAIs. The billing rates for an MAI may be five or even ten times that of a local residential appraiser. Billing rates will range upwards from $300 an hour.

A typical home real estate appraisal for a mortgage might cost only $500. Because the appraiser knows the market personally, he does not have to do much research and can provide good answers quite quickly. An MAI, working in a broader geographic area and with a diverse property base, has to do a lot of research of comparable sales to support the values on properties that are unique. Appraising a standard four-bedroom, three-bath, two-car garage home in a subdivision will take perhaps half a day at most; in comparison, an MAI will spend upwards of 10 to 15 days valuing a regional shopping center.

Further, the local residential appraiser often has very close relationships with the local lenders, banks, and savings and loans (S&Ls). These close and often symbiotic relationships, both personal and business, over time can lead to performance by the appraiser that may not rise to the point of best practice. Both borrowers and lenders are under pressure to get the deal done. The borrower wants to move into his new home, and the lender wants the fees generated by a mortgage transaction. To get the deal done, the bank needs support in its file that the "loan to value" is at or below a certain percentage. Since the amount of the loan is a function of the purchase price of the house, plus the savings resources of the borrower, often the only way the mortgage application can pass is if the appraisal is at a certain minimum number.

Here is where the trouble begins. The borrower or the bank, or both, communicate to the appraiser, "You have to come in at $450,000 or the deal craters." If the appraiser obtains 80% to 90% of his work from one bank or S&L, and the bank wants to make the loan, it is not hard to feel empathy for the appraiser if, in his heart, he feels the top value is only $425,000. But it is relatively easy to justify by saying, "Well, every appraisal is accurate to a range of ± 10%, and $450,000 is less than 10% above my best figure, so I will go along and give them what they want." The further rationalization on the part of the appraiser—said only to himself—is, "Well, prices are going up in this neighborhood, the house won't come on the market for a couple of years, and by that time it will be worth $450,000." The idea is that while an appraisal is a professional estimate of value, it likely will not be tested in the rigors of the real marketplace.

And then comes disaster, as in the form of the S&L crisis of the 1980s and 1990s or real estate in 2007. Real estate values go down, not up. Old appraisals are taken out of the file, and questions are raised both about the competence of the appraiser and, often, about his ethics. Sales prices, if the borrower can't pay the mortgage and the house is foreclosed by the lender, are very low because prospective buyers know this is a distress sale and bid accordingly.

Now it is easy to see how skepticism about appraisals persists. Two appraisers come up with diametrically opposite views. Real estate appraisers appear to have come up with ridiculous valuations. The reasonable assumption of normal observers in these instances is that "of course, these valuation reports were indeed Made as Instructed."

Were they really Made as Instructed? Without trying to play on words, we would argue that what happened within these situations may well have been within the normal range of appraisal methodology. Indeed, the real problem is caused by *misuse* of the appraisal report.

AUDIENCE FOR APPRAISAL REPORTS

The report of a pathologist on a biopsy is written for other physicians. A legal brief is written for a judge. A structural analysis of a bridge is written for engineers. Most professional and technical documents are written for audiences that are both knowledgeable and quite specialized. So engineers would not read a pathologist's report on a biopsy, nor would judges usually be the audience for a technical structural analysis.

Appraisal reports do not fit in this mold. Appraisal reports are directly written for decision makers. A client who wants to know the value of an asset first hires the appraiser and then must read the subsequent report. Appraisal reports are not one-liners, "The value of this asset is $1.2 million. Period."

Appraisal reports are usually prepared in accordance with the requirements of the Uniform Standards of Professional Appraisal Practice (USPAP). Issued by the Appraisal Foundation, which was chartered by Congress after the S&L fiasco, USPAP is a fairly general set of practices and procedures that appraisers (who subscribe to USPAP) must follow. It is beyond the scope of this chapter to delve into the details of USPAP, and, frankly, it is not necessary for users of valuation reports to be familiar with the requirements. The fact is that most qualified appraisers do follow USPAP, if for no other reason than a well-prepared valuation report will automatically meet USPAP requirements. Put a different way, USPAP does little more than formally state what good appraisers were doing all along.

Any appraisal must specify the following:

- The asset(s) being valued.
- The as-of date when the values were determined.
- The definition of value being used.
- The purpose for which the appraisal was prepared.

This latter requirement is, for example, to preclude an insurance appraisal from being erroneously used for financing.

Appraisal reports will usually provide in some detail a description of what the assets are and how they are being used. The business outlook and risks for the assets, the company, and the industry are often presented, so that the reader can see whether he or she agrees with the appraiser's overall assumptions. The various valuation methodologies used, as well as those *not* used, are discussed, with an explanation as to why certain approaches were used, while others may have been omitted. Finally, the appraiser will usually describe what he did, whom he spoke to, what he relied on, and so forth.

In summary, a well-written appraisal report allows the reader to fully understand the thought process that the valuation specialist used. Then, in describing the historical financial information and any necessary adjustments made, the reader will understand the full background. The appraisal report will then clearly delineate the projections used in forecasting future results, and sometimes will provide the appraiser's perspective on the reliability of those projections. Remember, at the end of the day, today's value is based on the anticipated outcome of future events. If you disagree with the appraiser's evaluation of either the past results or the anticipated future, you will disagree with the value conclusions. It is both that simple and that complex.

Appraisal reports are written to be read, not put away in a file and pulled out only in the case of a future legal dispute.

Unfortunately, 40 years' experience suggests that, except for auditors who review my work for financial reporting (to see if what I did comports with their understanding of Generally Accepted Accounting Principles [GAAP]), very few clients really try to read and understand my thought process. Almost everyone takes the easy way out; goes to the last page of the report, which shows my final answer; and says, "Okay, I can live with that. Thank you very much, Mr. King. If I have any future valuation requirements, I'll call you." Many days and even weeks of work have been summarized and used in a flash. My 15- to 40-page report is filed away, hopefully never to be seen again.

But, as many cogent observers have noted: "Bad things happen!" Valuation reports do matter.

The following are two case studies of legal engagements where the author acted as an expert witness. To avoid disclosing nonpublic information, the background descriptions have been modified. The valuation issues are presented as they were found.

CASE STUDY 1

A large conglomerate had been built up over a number of years through the strategic acquisition of old plants at low prices. The management team was skilled in coaxing additional volume out of the old facilities and, through good cost control, was able to increase market share. A single major overseas investment, which was unsuccessful, put the company in a cash crunch. Further, many of the older plants from which most of the profit potential had been squeezed were no longer profitable, particularly at a time when selling prices in the industry were at an all-time low. In short, the company needed cash and needed it badly.

Some aggressive Wall Street dealmakers brought to the management team a brilliant strategy proposal. They suggested that the company set up a new subsidiary and transfer a number of the older plants to this new company on a tax-free basis. Stock in the new company was distributed pro rata to existing shareholders, again tax free; the shareholder now had two pieces of paper instead of one.

The brilliance of the strategy came to light when the new company issued massive amounts of debt and paid *all* the cash it received from the newly issued debt back to the parent in the form of a dividend. It was the best of all possible worlds. In one master stroke, the parent had rid itself of all the losing plants (the profitable plants had been retained) and, in addition, received back enough cash to completely offset the crunch that had arisen from the bad foreign investment. Management publicly congratulated itself for having been smart enough to see the wisdom of the Wall Street proposal.

But, as a sage once stated, "If something is too good to be true, it's too good to be true." What was good for the parent turned out to be a disaster for the newly formed public company that was spun off, as well as the investors who bought the junk bonds issued at the time of the transaction. Stand back and reflect a moment. How could the new company, with plants that had consistently lost money, suddenly support a whole lot of debt? Maybe the question that should have been asked was: How would the new company conceivably benefit when the cash proceeds had actually been dividended upstream and the new debt provided zero benefit to the debtor in terms of new working capital? In other words, the newly formed company now had massive interest expense and debt repayment obligations, and no corresponding assets.

The real issue should be how the Wall Street geniuses were able to sell the debt; the major investors in the debt truly represented a litany of informed and knowledgeable lenders, every one of whom is a household name. How did these sophisticated lenders get convinced to buy debt that within less than three years was worthless?

Unfortunately, from the perspective of a professional in the valuation field, the lenders were convinced to buy because the parent company hired a valuation firm, on behalf of the future borrower, and obtained a "solvency opinion."

A solvency opinion is a document that purports to analyze the anticipated financial performance of a borrower. It is supposed to demonstrate that the borrower, at the time of the transaction and after the debt is sold, is solvent. Without going into legal niceties, this means that the borrower's assets are greater than the liabilities, and that the anticipated cash flow will be sufficient for the company to operate *and* to repay the debt as it becomes due—in short, that the company can keep its head above water.

How did the valuation firm arrive at this conclusion? Even a high school graduate might wonder how a company losing money, and with huge new debt piled on, could remain in business, and the answer was that it couldn't. But that was not what the valuation firm's opinion stated.

The report relied on "management's projections," and these projections were made by the very management of the parent company that was going to gain from successful completion of the transaction. No wonder the management came up with projections that, *if* they came to pass, would permit the debt to be paid. These projections made some of the most optimistic assumptions about the future course of events we have ever seen, in effect projecting a 180-degree turnaround from past performance. When asked what was going to cause this to happen, they came up with generalities like "efficiencies" and "cost reductions" and "price improvement," obviously implying that for the past years management had not been working on these items.

In any event, the valuation firm accepted these bogus predictions. They then, in a feat of financial legerdemain not seen by the author in his entire business career, put together a cash flow projection that somehow left out all of the future interest expense to be incurred from the new borrowing. Obviously, with optimistic business assumptions and no interest expense to worry about, the new company appeared solvent. The investors in the debt accepted the word of the Wall Street underwriters, the Wall Street underwriters accepted the word of the valuation firm, and the company did nothing to challenge what was truly a "done deal."

After selling every asset they could, and never being able to show positive cash flow, the newly spun-off company entered chapter 11, and the entire house of cards collapsed. In the best American tradition, the losers sued everyone in sight, but the valuation firm—due to a technicality we still don't understand—was not sued. Nonetheless, the whole deal would have collapsed, with no money lost by the investors, were it not for the solvency opinion prepared by the valuation firm on the basis of bogus projections and a sleight of hand that somehow disregarded the interest expense.

The subject of this chapter is the true determination of value. In this case, nobody bothered to read the solvency report or question it. Almost everyone involved wanted the deal to succeed, and nobody asked the pertinent questions. Even the lenders viewed this as nothing more than a "portfolio problem." As investors, they were buying junk bonds from many issuers and just expected the high interest rates to be offset at some time by losses on some of the issues they bought. The truth was that the lenders did not perform Due Diligence—they trusted the lawyers, the accountants, the underwriters, and the valuation firm. In this case, the trust was totally misplaced.

The root cause of this fiasco was a management under pressure, advisers (underwriters, attorneys, accountants, and valuation specialists) who wanted to move on to the next deal, and a newly formed corporation whose future course was dictated not by its own management but by former management who were no longer going to be involved. Ridiculous projections about future sales and earnings were blindly accepted by all parties, including the valuation firm. Everyone seemed to trust everyone else to perform "real" Due Diligence. As a result, *nobody* performed meaningful Due Diligence, and hundreds of millions of dollars were ultimately lost. The writer blames the valuation firm as much as anyone, because the solvency report was supposed to be the last line of defense. Like the Maginot Line, the defense failed.

CASE STUDY 2

Like marriage, sometimes even the friendliest joint ventures and partnerships fail. At that point, some method has to be found to split the then-current value between or among the parties. Some joint ventures and partnerships utilize a formula approach as discussed below.

In this instance the two parties to the agreement originally had agreed that one side would put in mineral leases, and the other would put in cash. For a number of reasons that are irrelevant here, several years later the parties split up and the many issues, including both legal and valuation, were to be determined by an arbitrator. Essentially, the arbitrator had to find the "Fair Value" of the joint venture. One of the parties was, according to the agreement, going to have to pay the other side 50% of the arbitrator's determination. The prospective buyer had a strong incentive to minimize the value, and the prospective seller wanted to reach the highest possible value, thus maximizing their return.

Each party put forth its case to the arbitrator, whose decision was binding.

The mineral leases had never actually been developed, although the original plans had called for them to be developed quite rapidly. Nonetheless, even though the leases had never been exploited, they had greatly increased in value, as the market for the underlying asset had exploded. The party contributing the leases felt wronged because the partner had failed to exploit the leases. The financial investor complained that the other party had grossly hindered smooth operation of the partnership and had "interfered" with sound management. It is beyond the scope of a valuation specialist to try and determine the rights and wrongs of the business issues. It did fall to two separate appraisal firms to develop their respective valuations and present their best case to the arbitrator.

Party B, the prospective buyer, hired a firm that specialized in the specific industry, and the resulting report could at best be described as nontraditional. In order for the underlying asset to be exploited profitably, a number of sequential steps had to be undertaken, each step having its own cost and probability of success. The valuation specialist for B constructed a decision tree with the probabilities shown for each possible step of the development process. One crucial factor in the equation was that if the asset could be developed physically, the sale of the product was absolutely insured.

The risks, therefore, lay in the probability of successful drilling and exploitation of the resource, not in the joint venture's ability to receive cash for any output actually produced. Contrast this with Ford, which can produce physically many more cars than they can sell. Here, there was a guaranteed market for the product irrespective of how much could or would be produced, and the selling price per unit of output was also guaranteed at a level that would cover many times over all variable production costs. The risks lay solely in the up-front capital expenditures and the probability of successful exploitation.

The Seller, S, actually hired two appraisers, who worked jointly. In a combined 70 years of experience, neither of S's appraisers had ever seen a decision tree used as the basis of determining Fair Value. Nonetheless, the arbitrator was given the decision tree valuation report with the explicit statement that the resultant value (very low, indeed) represented what the buyer, B, thought the company was worth.

The very low value was derived from a series of cumulative probabilities involving drilling, capital investments, and expected tax treatment. Assigning relatively low probabilities for success, and then carrying out the decision tree for about five levels, the result was that the most profitable outcome showed a very low probability of occurring, while the most likely outcomes were at the front end, where the payoff was relatively low. By adding in the anticipated losses at each node to the potential payoff if things worked out well, the net expected value was indeed low.

The prospective seller, however, utilized a straightforward discounted cash flow approach discussed in detail in the author's earlier book on valuation.[1] Utilizing slightly more realistic assumptions for successful exploration (the U.S. government had conducted numerous successful explorations of the area), the seller's appraisers came up with an FV that was literally 35 times the amount put forth by the prospective buyer.

Interestingly, each party offered to transact a deal at the other side's valuation. The seller offered to buy the half of the project they did not already own at the other party's very low amount, while the buyer offered in turn to sell their half at the high amount determined by the seller.

Pity the poor arbitrator, or judge, when faced with two diametrically opposite valuation reports. The outcome of this specific case was not available at the time of writing, but the likelihood is that the arbitrator will probably find that, in his opinion, the FV is above the low estimate and below the high estimate. But because the two estimates are so far apart, even splitting the difference would make both sides unhappy.

---

[1] Alfred M. King, *Valuation: What Assets Are Really Worth*. Hoboken, NJ: John Wiley & Sons, 2002. Chapter 6 (pp. 91–106) covers discounted cash flow analysis.

This leads to our final recommendation in this chapter.

BUY AND SELL AGREEMENTS

As evidenced from these two cases, differences of opinion regarding value are all too frequent. Obviously, in the normal course of business, buyers and sellers will have differing perspectives on the value, or the price, of some product or service. Buyers always want to pay less, and sellers always want to obtain more. Economists refer to this as the "law of supply and demand," and transactions occur at a price where supply and demand are equal, where the buyer and seller are equally satisfied (or dissatisfied, as the case may be).

So, in normal business transactions, there usually is a small amount of negotiation, and one side or the other concedes simply for the purpose of getting the deal done and being able to move on. It is this state that appraisers try to replicate in determining their professional estimate of Fair Market Value. As mentioned more than once, valuations prepared by competent valuation specialists will probably fall within a ±10% range of where the actual negotiations lead. So, when one wants to obtain a reasonable answer, at a reasonable cost, normal valuations will usually do the trick.

But when two parties are fighting with each other, each trying to obtain an advantage over the other, valuation reports suddenly become a litigating tool, designed to accomplish an objective. No longer is the appraiser trying to find the right answer—what the asset in question is really worth. Rather, the appraiser is requested to come up with a valuation that will move the client's case forward.

Unfortunately, the lawyers for the other side have a similar objective, and *their* appraiser also has to move his client's case forward. In this scenario, it is no wonder that judges and arbitrators often throw up their hands in despair and are heard to mutter, "I knew I couldn't trust these damn appraisers."

The root of the problem is that when an appraiser is acting as an advocate, rather than a neutral determiner of "the value," bias can creep in. Assumptions that may be hard to sustain and methodologies that may be inappropriate suddenly seem like the answer to a prayer: "Oh, so that's how we can get a low (high) value. And even if someone questions our value, we know that the other side will be doing the same thing. So there!"

Lawsuits are very time consuming and even more expensive. If each party obtains *their* appraisal, and neither of them is unbiased, someone still has to make a determination of value, and that is going to be a judge or a jury. So each party's getting their own valuation report really just provides an equality of weapons, not a correct answer.

There is a solution to this problem, however, one that many readers may wish to consider. In one sentence, we recommend that both parties to any agreement spell out in advance that any differences of opinion regarding future values will be determined by an independent third-party appraiser, jointly hired by the parties and jointly paid by the parties.

With two clients, each on the opposite side of the issue(s), the appraiser then really has to develop the right answer. Even more important, he has to defend his answer, with appropriate support for both the assumptions and methodologies. The writer has been in this position, albeit less often than would be desirable. These appraisals are undoubtedly among the hardest to perform because you know that every assumption you make, every word you write, is potentially going to be challenged. As an appraiser in this situation of two clients, you know you have it right when both parties are unhappy with your answer. As long as there is no bias, no thumb on the scale favoring one side or the other, the system works. Both parties, having agreed in advance to abide by the answer, and both parties having paid for the answer, have the chance to ask the appraiser, "Did you consider this?" and "Why did you consider that?"

Appraisal reports, the valuation methodologies themselves, do not come out of a "black box." A good appraisal report is a very logical document, and the valuation specialist's thought process and assumptions should be crystal clear. Inherent in any valuation exercise is a projection about future events. The truth is that nobody can foretell the future. All you can do is make your best estimate and state why you have come to that conclusion. Past performance, combined with current business plans, can provide very good insight into the future. The unexpected can always happen, but if at the time the appraisal is made recognition is given to the inherent uncertainties, then the final indication of value will probably be as good as can be found. Both parties will probably agree that the recommended value is the best outcome that can be expected.

This recommendation—that both parties to an agreement jointly hire a single appraiser—really should be incorporated into partnership and joint venture agreements at the time the initial business is formed. Optimism reigns, things will turn out, and neither side really anticipates future problems. The history of partnerships and joint ventures, however, suggests that a substantial number do come apart. Rather than fighting over value, if the prior agreement now spells out exactly what should be done, then a road map to dissolution without a lawsuit has already been set forth.

The author certainly would prefer that his firm be named in agreements as the independent third party to determine value at some future point of disagreement. The truth is that *any* nationally recognized valuation firm can perform this type of valuation. In practice, it probably would be best that the agreement be worded that the parties "will agree on a nationally recognized appraisal firm." If the parties are at such loggerheads that they cannot even agree on the choice of an independent valuation firm, then the parties will probably have to revert to the old tried-and-true approach of each hiring their own dueling appraisers and letting the court decide the value.

DON'T USE A FORMULA!

In valuing a business, one must take into account a variety of factors. But the factors that are important one year may not be vital the next year. Business changes, circumstances change, the economy changes, competitors and customers change.

This sounds just like plain old common sense. Of course, the old French saying, "The more things change, the more they stay the same," implies constant change.

One very easy way to prove this point is to take out a budget or long-range business plan prepared no more than three years ago, and compare the then projection of the current year with today's reality. It is guaranteed that today's actuality is a far cry from what was anticipated only a few years ago.

Why belabor this point? Many business agreements call for valuing a business at some future point based on a formula built into the agreement. Such formulas might involve a multiple of earnings or of cash flow. They might involve book value or some multiple thereof. They could combine elements of current earnings and net worth. The range of formulas is almost unlimited, but they all have one thing in common: *Formulas cannot be used to determine value!*

There is no formula, developed in advance, that will properly value a specific business at a specific point in time. No formula can anticipate economic conditions, competitive conditions, governmental regulations, taxes, and so forth.

Valuations have to be made in the context of *today's* business environment, not that from the past. The business environment changes in many aspects. Industries rise and fall. Customer tastes change. New competitors (think China and India) arise. Services are outsourced. New forms of finance are developed. The list is almost endless.

We have never seen a formula that works after more than about 18 months. If there will ever have to be a valuation of the company in the future, base it only on then-current conditions. No formula can anticipate changes in the overall environment. The last section recommended that parties agree to hire a single appraiser, in case of disagreement. Relying on an outmoded or inappropriate formula will cause far more discord than it is worth.

If there is a single "take-away" from this book, it should be this: Valuation involves professional judgment. In concept, professional judgment is the diametric opposite to any predetermined formula. Appraisers bring their knowledge of economic and business conditions to every valuation assignment. There is no way for any formula involving "X times EBITDA" or "Y times book value" to consider what was unusual about the past and what can reasonably be expected about the future. Appraisers have to understand any anomalies about reported past results and take into consideration anticipated changes in the future. Formulas are like robots—they do what they are told but have no initiative and no judgment.

PERIODIC VALUATIONS OF PARTNERSHIPS, JOINT VENTURES, AND CLOSELY HELD COMPANIES

While it may seem a self-serving statement, the author truly believes that closely held nonpublic businesses should be valued periodically. The law requires that companies with an employee stock option plan (ESOP) have an annual valuation. This valuation, while mandated for purposes of employee benefits, has great benefit in many other areas.

Management of closely held companies cannot measure their own performance, or that of the firm itself, by looking at today's *Wall Street Journal* and seeing what the stock price did yesterday. Certainly, the top management of most companies has a good idea whether things are going well or going poorly. But just as kids in school get an objective report card from their teachers, so should a closely held company get some third-party evaluation on a periodic basis. Shareholders of closely held companies like to know how their investment is doing.

The economics of valuation are very straightforward. Appraisers charge clients on the basis of the time involved in the assignment. Common sense suggests that if appraisers were paid on the basis of the values they develop, the credibility of the report would immediately be suspect. Consequently, the only variable affecting fees is time spent. Different appraisers may have different billing rates, but even here an experienced appraiser with a high hourly rate may take fewer hours to perform an assignment, thus ending up with a similar fee.

If the cost of an appraisal is related to time spent, then it should be obvious that doing a second valuation will take less time than the first. Our experience in this area is primarily in ESOP valuations. A rule of thumb should be that a second valuation, say no more than a year later, should probably run at 50% to 66% (one half to two thirds) of the original; subsequent annual or quarterly valuations should require little increase in professional fees, absent major inflation or a significant underlying alteration in the business enterprise.

We recommend that companies, and the principals who invest, make provision for periodic valuations by an independent valuation specialist. The cost is usually low, and the benefits of obtaining a third-party view of the business are high. The biggest advantage of periodic appraisals (perhaps once a year is optimal) is that if one side or the other has to sell, then the likely price is not going to differ materially from the last valuation report. There will be few surprises, as long as valuations have been performed periodically.

CHAPTER 4

Accounting For Merger-And-Acquisition Transactions

At the current time, Fair Value (FV) is most likely to impact corporate executives in the context of mergers and acquisitions (M&A). While the Financial Accounting Standards Board (FASB), if it had its wishes, might like *all* financial reports to be at FV, in the short run they have compromised by requiring FV primarily when there is either an M&A deal, or a testing of previously recorded Fair Values.

The basic accounting rules that deal with the accounting for M&A transactions are found in Statement of Financial Accounting Standards (SFAS) 141. The revisions to the original SFAS 141 are made in the "Revised" version, now referred to as SFAS 141 R. These changes are rather far-reaching and will be covered later in this chapter. But, first, we cover the basic rules that have been in effect since 2001.

SFAS 141: ALLOCATION OF PURCHASE PRICE

As time goes on, fewer and fewer people will recall the pandemonium that was predicted to occur when the FASB banned pooling-of-interests accounting. In SFAS 141, issued in 2001, the Board required *all* M&A transactions to be accounted for as a purchase of one company by another, and abolished pooling once and for all. Because pooling has now been relegated to books on the history of accounting, we spend no time on it. Even this brief refresher on purchase accounting can be skipped by those familiar with the subject.

The basic concept of SFAS 141 is that the purchase price paid by the buyer, including the assumption of any debt, has to be allocated, or spread, over all the assets acquired. This requires a determination of the separate components that make up the target company, ranging from working capital through property, plant, and equipment (PP&E) and into each identifiable intangible asset. Then the analyst, usually a valuation specialist, determines the FV of each asset that was acquired.

There is usually a difference between the value of all the identifiable assets and the total adjusted purchase price. By definition, that difference between the sum of the asset values and the total purchase price (including assumption of debt) is denominated as goodwill. The new Fair Values of the assets now go on the Balance Sheet of the buyer and are subject to depreciation and/or amortization based on the expected lives.

In a compromise related to the abolishment of pooling-of-interests accounting, the FASB mandated that goodwill need not be amortized (prior to SFAS 141, goodwill had to be written off in less than 40 years). In exchange for giving up periodic goodwill amortization, companies were now required to annually test the dollars assigned to goodwill for impairment, which is covered in Chapter 9.

Under SFAS 141, the buyer's costs related to the transaction were included in the adjusted purchase price. This had the effect of avoiding a significant charge to the profit-and-loss (P&L) statement, inasmuch as investment banking, legal, and accounting fees for a major transaction can be in the many millions of dollars. Effectively, since there is no asset associated with such expenditures, the deal costs ended up in goodwill, never to be charged to expense or amortized unless there was a subsequent goodwill impairment charge.

SFAS 157 has totally reversed this position. Now, deal expenses must be charged off as incurred. This follows from the FASB definition of FV, that one use an exit value. If you are going to sell a business, then the next buyer does not care what you originally paid in the way of legal and accounting costs to buy the company you are now trying to sell. From the perspective of the current owner, however, its own deal costs are absolutely required and were incurred solely to buy the target company. Just as freight and installation are added to the basis of a milling machine, so it is argued that deal costs should be included in the basis of an M&A transaction. The FASB's position on deal costs strikes many people as illogical—and wrong. However, they write the rules and show no sign of wanting to change.

The way SFAS 142, dealing with impairments, handles goodwill effectively minimizes the likelihood of impairment unless the business dramatically underperforms expectations. This is not to say that there are no impairment charges for goodwill, but that they are few and far between. Essentially, both management and investors (shareholders and creditors) will have had plenty of warning about a deteriorating line of business prior to an actual impairment charge.

The treatment of contingent liabilities under SFAS 141, in theory, was supposed to have them individually valued at FV. That is, the buyer was supposed to estimate the ultimate cost of settling lawsuits and environmental liabilities, even though the probability of any payments being made was less than 50%. In addition, sometimes the parties to a transaction cannot agree on the future profits of the seller, and the deal provides for additional payments if the goals are achieved. Such contingent payments are added to the purchase price and goodwill, as they are made after the deal has closed. In effect, under SFAS 141, only liabilities on the seller's Balance Sheet were carried forward. The new SFAS 141 R will possibly change this reporting.

Finally, two minor issues exist. All in-process research and development (IPR&D) expenses that were acquired from the seller had to be written off immediately to expense. Now the IPR&D will be capitalized. Second, if the purchase price was less than the value of the assets acquired, sometimes referred to as a bargain purchase, goodwill would be written down to zero, and then any additional values assigned to PP&E would also be written down. Now, in a bargain purchase, there will be a credit to income, while all the assets will continue to be shown at true FV.

For six years, companies, auditors, and appraisers lived with SFAS 141, with few calls for change. Certain methodological issues arose among appraisers, auditors, and the Securities and Exchange Commission (SEC), and for the most part these were usually resolved, although almost always with a solution that increased the amount of recorded corporate expense. It will not come as a shock to most readers that the FASB and the SEC, when faced with a choice, almost invariably come up with a solution that increases expense and reduces reported earnings.

FAIR VALUES IMPACT FUTURE REPORTED INCOME

Amounts developed for the FV of assets—and liabilities, for that matter (covered in Chapter 6)—have a significant impact on reported income. In an M&A transaction, if dollars are currently assigned to IPR&D, the P&L is hit immediately. Residual dollars that remain in goodwill to the contrary have zero impact on current and future P&Ls, although there is always a potential for a future impairment charge.

One example will show this very clearly. Under the FASB's SFAS 141 rules, the buyer has to assign a dollar amount to the FV of customer relationships. This reflects the economic reality that whenever one company buys another, it is essentially acquiring, products, customers, and a workforce. Thus, the FASB argues, and they are correct, that part of the purchase price for any acquisition represents the value in place of the existing customer base. Without the existing customers, the buyer would have to take time and incur expense to develop such customers. Put another way, a company without any customers for its products or services might have little value.

So, requiring the buyer (through the appraisal specialist) to assign part of the purchase price to the FV of customer relationships is noncontroversial. What is controversial, however, is the *amount* of such FV. Depending on how you calculate customer relationships, and the inherent assumptions you make, this intangible asset could conceivably have a very high value, or in some cases a very low value.

The best example of this tension between a high and a low determination of FV comes about when one company in an industry buys a direct competitor in the same industry. Consider two companies that each make parts for the major automobile manufacturers. Such firms are often called original equipment manufacturers (OEMs), and they sell to the 10 or 12 companies, such as Toyota, Volkswagen, or General Motors, that produce all of the world's cars.

In the OEM business, there are only 10 or 12 customers. Other than perhaps China or Indonesia, virtually no new automobile companies are starting into production. Consequently, every one of the OEM firms has a very limited customer base, albeit one with fairly high unit and dollar volumes. Two brake manufacturers or two axle manufacturers are each calling on the same identical list of customers.

Thus, if axle Company A buys axle Company B, a natural question arises: Did Company A buy a *new* customer base, or did it simply acquire a broader product line to sell to the *same* customer base? The answer to this question directly affects future reported profitability.

If you argue that Company B's customer base has a value independent of whether it was Company A that bought B, or some third-party private-equity firm that bought B, then the relationships with GM, Toyota, and VW are quite valuable. If, however, you argue that from A's perspective it already had those relationships and that B's sales efforts are simply going to be replaced and the product sales added to A's existing marketing program, then B's existing relationships have little value.

Now step back and look at the P&L impact of this choice. Under current SEC interpretations, all customer relationships must be amortized, or written off, over their anticipated future life. Even though every business continues to have customers, the SEC argues that the specific customers acquired on the date of the merger are going to turn over. The fact that they will be replaced with new customers does not, in the SEC's eyes, mean that the customer relationship asset has an indefinite life.

Assigning a high value to B's customer base, and amortizing it over ten years, will adversely impact profits for the next ten years. On the contrary, if you say that B's customer base has little value to Company A, and virtually no dollars are assigned to this asset, the same dollars go into goodwill, and reported profits for the next ten years are enhanced. Accounting rules on FV do impact reported earnings very directly.

How you allocate the purchase price, how much you assign to each category of identifiable assets, and how much goes into nonamortizable goodwill can determine whether future earnings from the acquisition are accretive. Inasmuch as most buyers want any acquisition to be accretive, the allocation of actual price made is important. This is discussed further in Chapters 7 and 8. For purposes of this chapter, we merely want to show that application of SFAS 141 and its offspring, SFAS 141 R, is critical. The same argument here about customer relationships also applies to the determination of the FV of every other asset acquired. *FV determinations do make a difference in financial reporting.*

MARKET PARTICIPANTS

Two of the most controversial and difficult aspects of the FASB's new definition of Fair Value in SFAS 157 are related to "exit value" and "market participants." Recall that in our discussion of Fair Value, the same asset may have a specific FV to the owner, as long as it is being utilized for the purpose it was designed for. But that same asset has a different, and far lower, FV if it is actually going to be sold to a used equipment dealer. The dealer has to pay a lower price because he will be incurring storage and financing costs up until he is actually able to resell the asset. Thus, to the existing owner, the item (e.g., a milling machine) has two separate FVs, depending on what assumption you make as to its future state. Continue in production and the value could be $100,000. Consider selling the same milling machine to a dealer and the FV is now going to be, say, $40,000. The latter value is usually referred to as "exit value" or "orderly liquidation value."

In writing SFAS 157, the FASB had to define Fair Value, and in their wisdom they chose exit value, based on actual decisions that would be made by market participants. As noted earlier, this choice in large part was made as a result of trying to prevent a recurrence of the Enron fiasco. But the consequence of this decision to financial reporting is far-reaching.

The value of almost every asset will differ, depending on who you decide is the most likely "market participant." If you think the value of a milling machine should be determined by what used equipment dealers would pay, that such dealers represent the "market," then the reported value of the machine is low. If you consider that the value should be determined by what someone would pay to continue to use the milling machine for its current output, then the reported value of the machine is high.

In short, choice of the appropriate market participant will drive the valuation and accounting and, in the final analysis, the future reported earnings per share (EPS). While the FASB provides some limited guidance in the choice of the appropriate market participant, in practice reasonable people can, and do, differ. Why are there disputes over what at first seems to be such a noncontroversial decision? The answer is that the choice of market participant directly and irrevocably affects future reported EPS.

CHOICE OF LIFE FOR AMORTIZATION AND DEPRECIATION

In any allocation of purchase price, we not only have to determine the appropriate FV, but once we have established the amount of the asset, we then have to assign a useful life to the asset. There is a dispute within the valuation profession as to whether appraisers should be determining lives for financial accounting. One school of thought says that the choice of life, the period over which the asset will be written off, is strictly an accounting issue. In this view, appraisers are not experts in accounting and should stick to developing and supporting *values*.

We do not subscribe to this view. First of all, appraisers do look at and consider the condition of tangible assets, real estate, and machinery and equipment. You cannot value a building or a milling machine without looking at the asset. You have to determine its condition and estimate its remaining useful life because these are integral to the actual value today. Two milling machines otherwise identical in age and model will have significantly different values if one is well maintained and has at least an additional ten years of use, and the other is in such condition that in practice it will have to be scrapped within two years.

By extension, then, appraisers can—and in our judgment, should —help clients determine the most appropriate remaining life for intangible assets. Take the life of a patent. While there is a legal termination for a patent, in practice the development of new technology could well make a specific patent have little value today, even though technically it does not expire until 2014. Because the effective life of an asset directly impacts its value, it is incumbent on the appraiser to tell the client over what period the asset should be written off. True, this is an accounting issue, but, in effect, so is the determination of FV itself.

Financial statements are the responsibility of management, not the auditor, and not the appraiser acting as a professional adviser. Having said that, why should management hire a professional valuation specialist and then not take advantage of his or her professional expertise? This does not mean that the client is bound by the appraiser's recommendations, either on value or life.

ASSET LIVES

This leads directly into a discussion of one of the most controversial aspects of SFAS 141 and 142. All other things being equal, the longer the assigned life for an asset, the lower the immediate impact on reported P&Ls. Most companies, and virtually all chief financial officers, want to be able to report higher rather than lower income. This assumes that the accounting choices made are (1) in full compliance with Generally Accepted Accounting Principles (GAAP) and (2) will be sustained by independent auditors.

It is a fact of life for appraisers that clients often want longer lives assigned to intangible assets, and this is usually because of the impact on P&Ls. As mentioned several times in this book, appraising involves professional judgment, and the judgment made regarding useful lives can be considered accurate only within a fairly broad range. If an appraiser says that a milling machine has a remaining life of ten years, he does not mean that at the end of 120 months the machine will disintegrate. It really means that the machine may no longer be able to hold tight tolerances, it may be obsolete technologically, and/or maintenance costs may have become excessive.

It is very important here to distinguish economic lives from accounting or tax lives. Over the past 50 years, the tax code has progressively provided for more rapid depreciation. This makes good tax policy because the shorter the life for tax purposes, the higher the depreciation expense, the lower the taxable income, and the higher the after-tax cash flow. Carried to its ultimate, some politicians (and tax practitioners for that matter) have argued in favor of the ultimate solution: total expensing of all capital expenditures. That it would encourage capital spending is beyond doubt. Whether the negative impact on tax receipts in the first years could be handled in terms of fiscal restraint is a separate issue. Somehow, every time there is an economic recession, one of the first suggestions, in order to encourage capital expenditures, is that lives for tax purposes should be shrunk. The alternative suggestion is for an investment tax credit to be provided, which has virtually the same economic impact on actual cash flows.

Ever since the end of World War II, there has been a gradual trend for shortening tax lives. A collateral advantage of this has been that there are now relatively few disputes with the Internal Revenue Service (IRS) over depreciation. This is a dramatic change from 40 to 50 years ago, when an IRS agent would routinely challenge tax lives for capital asset additions.

As tax lives for capital assets got shorter, and to avoid potential arguments with IRS agents, many companies have simply chosen to adopt IRS lives for financial reporting. To the best of our knowledge, there is no requirement that tax and book lives be the same, compared to mandatory use of last in, first out (LIFO) for books if LIFO is used for taxes. Most fixed-asset software programs can easily handle different lives and different depreciation methodologies for books as compared to taxes. However, many companies do choose the same lives.

The consequence of such a decision is that tax lives currently are far shorter than economic lives, at least for almost all asset categories other than automobiles and computers. When appraisers perform a detailed inspection of many production facilities, it is not surprising to find many fully depreciated assets still in use. Almost by definition, the accounting lives (usually based on tax requirements) were too short if the asset still provided significant economic benefit.

In an allocation for a typical merger transaction involving physical production, we often find many fully depreciated assets. However, offsetting this "pickup" in value is the opposite situation. Assets that cannot be found are on the books. The reasons for these "ghost assets" disappearing are numerous, including theft, but more often, poor record keeping as assets are transferred to other facilities, traded in on new equipment, disassembled for parts to repair other machines, and prior expensing rather than capitalization to get around corporate capital expenditure paperwork requirements.

It is outside the scope of this book to discuss detailed controls over capital expenditures. Our experience suggests that the prevalence of so-called ghost assets is substantial, but often offset by fully depreciated assets still in use.

In many M&A allocations the buyer will simply carry over the carrying value of PP&E and treat the old book values as the new FVs. Auditors will usually pass on this shortcut as long as the book value of PP&E is a relatively small percentage of the total acquisition price. In other words, a judgment on materiality often precludes the need for expending resources on a detailed appraisal. Such an assumption is often justified. Very frequently, there is a more or less approximate offset between missing or ghost assets, on the one hand, and assets with zero book value that still have significant economic value, on the other hand.

LIVES FOR INTANGIBLE ASSETS: INDEFINITE VERSUS FIXED

When SFAS 141 was written, the FASB in effect said that lives should be assigned to all intangible assets unless it was difficult to identify the useful life. So, as an example, a trademark or trade name can retain its value to a company as long as the product continues to be sold and sufficient marketing resources continue to be applied. For example, Ivory™ soap has been sold for more than 125 years using the same name. Over time, the value of the tradename has undoubtedly been *increasing*, not depreciating. But not all trade names go on indefinitely. How many people remember Ipana toothpaste? Yet at one time it was a leading brand.

Some intangible assets, such as the Coke™ name, are among the world's most valuable assets. At the other end of the spectrum from popular consumer goods are the trade names associated with commodity chemicals. Buyers choose one supplier over another based on price, convenience, quality, and so forth, but industrial chemicals, for the most part, do not sell to professional purchasing agents on the basis of brand name. We really have two separate, yet related, factors in valuing intangible assets. One is the value, and the other is the life. Typically, high-value trade names go on for a very long time, while low-value intangibles may or may not continue in use—in many cases based on management decisions on the costs versus benefits of marketing under many different trade names.

In valuing a specific trade name, appraisers talk to management about their plans, competition, and buying patterns among customers. All other things being equal, companies almost always prefer that appraisers apply as much of the purchase price to trade names as can be supported.

The reason for this preference is based on future EPS. Under current rules, intangible assets with an indefinite life do not get amortized. Rather, they are tested for impairment each year. As long as the value is maintained at a level equal to its acquisition cost, no accounting entry has to be made; in fact, no entry can be made.

Only if a company plans to discontinue a specific brand name would a prior value have to be written down. But what if, at acquisition, the buyer knows he won't use the seller's trade name? Here is where the accounting gets interesting.

Indefinite life can be assigned to an asset only if you truly cannot determine its life. But this assertion cannot be made if the buyer knows on day one that the seller's name will be phased out or even discontinued. Under current rules, therefore, a specific value has to be assigned to the about-to-be-discontinued trade name. Obviously, the life is going to be short and the value should be minimal.

Under the FASB's definition of FV in SFAS 157, what if "market participants" *would* continue to use the trade name. If the market participants would be deemed to be private equity firms, then they would have to continue to use the seller's trade name because the buyout firm would likely not have its own competing (and better) trade name. Again, we face the conundrum that the same asset—in this case, the seller's trade name—can have a high value to a *theoretical* buyer and a low value to another *actual* purchaser. In this case, not only are the values different but so will be the lives: high value, long life; low value, short life.

Recall that there can be an interaction between the assigned lives and the value itself. An example would be customer relationships. If the existing customer base or the product(s) sold to the customer base are deemed to have a very brief life (e.g., three years), then the FV of the customer relationship asset is going to be relatively low. This is because the value of the intangible is a function of the profits to be earned from the future sale of the products to the existing customers.

If, however, one concludes that the product sales would continue to the existing customer base for perhaps ten years, then the present value of the future net income and cash flow from those sales would be relatively high. Put a different way, if the cash flow stream goes out only three years, there will be relatively little of it—but that amount, low as it is, must be written off over three years. If the cash flow stream will continue for ten years, however, the present value will be much higher, and it will have to be written off over the ten-year period. At times, the annual charge to expense for amortization may be the same for the first three years irrespective of the total. Of course, in the case of the ten-year time frame, the amortization charge will go on for an additional seven years.

MINIMIZING REPORTED INCOME

One final bit of bad news: SFAS 141 and 142 specifically require that the FV of any intangible be amortized in accordance with its *real* economic diminution in value. This means that an accelerated amortization would often be required as contrasted to a straight-line method. If the anticipated loss in customer sales would be expected over the early part of the ten-year time horizon, then a straight-line amortization would be incorrect. Many companies, in practice, use a straight-line amortization, albeit often with little support. This is of particular interest to the SEC and they are starting to review closely both assigned lives and amortization methods.

The SEC, and by extension the FASB and auditing firms, has a predilection for requiring whatever accounting treatment will have the greatest adverse impact on reported earnings. Thus, at times, companies will be forced to use an accelerated method of amortization for intangible assets just because it will reduce reported income in the early years.

Another example of the SEC bias is in the area of distinguishing an intangible that should be recognized from goodwill. For example, many people think that an assembled workforce has great value in terms of avoiding hiring and training costs. Yet the FASB says you cannot put a value on such an asset, and any such value is to be included in goodwill. The wording of SFAS 141 says that an intangible asset should be set up only if it is *separable* and *contractual*.

Take just one example, customer relationships, which has just been discussed. Most people believe that the relationship between a customer and its supplier is very valuable to the buyer, but it hardly ever is contractual. Compaq may have been selling computers to Wal-Mart for years before Compaq was acquired by Hewlett Packard (HP). When HP bought Compaq, could HP insist to Wal-Mart that the retailer must now continue to buy Hewlett Packard personal computers (PCs)? This is not very likely. Wal-Mart's decision on HP as an approved vendor for PCs after the Compaq acquisition would be made at that time and on its merits, not because Wal-Mart had to continue buying from Compaq because of a contract.

This logic, absolutely inherent in both the words and spirit of SFAS 141 and 142, led many valuation specialists to the conclusion that in the absence of a take-or-pay contract, enforceable at law, there were, in fact, very few customer relationships that met the SFAS 141 and 142 tests. When the SEC saw how few dollars were being allocated to amortizable customer relationships, and how many dollars remained in nonamortizable goodwill, they insisted that the FASB change the rules of the game.

In one of the most tortured decisions we have seen in financial accounting, the Emerging Issues Task Force (EITF) came out with a new interpretation of the term *contractual*. The FASB noticed that companies usually use a purchase order to acquire goods and services. A purchase order is actually a contract. By extension, if the target's previous sales to a customer had been entered into with a purchase order, this now, according to the FASB, represented a "contractual relationship." Further, if there had ever in the past been a purchase order (i.e., a contractual relationship at that time), then one was to assume that there would be an ongoing customer relationship into the future. In other words, one purchase order in the past equaled a continuing customer relationship in the future.

The fact that such relationships were neither separable nor truly contractual did not seem to bother the FASB or the SEC. Rather than formally change SFAS 141 and 142 (which would have required a full due process), the powers that be fell back on the convenience of an EITF decision to totally change the rules defining customer relationships. We now have the anomalous situation that current accounting rules for some intangible assets are predicated on a myth, the mysterious assumption that a past purchase order now causes a current contractual relationship. The usual definition of a contract or contractual relationship assumes that one party or the other can go to court and enforce the terms of the contract. Can anyone seriously believe that HP could go to court to force Wal-Mart to buy its computers? Merely stating this provides its own answer.

The total irrationality of the EITF position is further contradicted by the FASB's insistence that the value of an assembled workforce is *not* a recognizable asset. The grounds for this position are that a workforce is neither separable nor contractual. Technically, that assertion is probably true, absent employment contracts with a few top executives. And since the time of Abraham Lincoln, people cannot be "sold," which means that the assembled workforce cannot be treated as would be a trade name or a patent.

Most businessmen would believe that it is unlikely that the majority of employees would leave a company simply upon a change in ownership. Companies often will try to reduce future employment costs, but this is only if employees usually do not voluntarily quit.

In short, one would believe that the economic factors in both customer relationships and in employment relationships have a great deal of similarity. Neither is technically contractual, and neither is separable in the legal sense. But the accounting treatment of these two intangible assets is very different. The impact from amortization also is different because if you do not set the assembled workforce up as an asset, you do not have to amortize anything.

That an established employee base has value is absolutely beyond question. The only reason that Company A buys Company B is to acquire its products, its customers, and its employees. Otherwise, what is there? If the FASB and the SEC require that the purchase price paid be spread over the assets acquired, how can one explain the divergence between customers and employees?

For tax purposes, prior to the adoption of Internal Revenue Code (IRC) section 197, for all purchases, companies routinely and regularly valued the assembled workforce. In turn, companies were permitted to amortize the value of the workforce and obtain a valid tax deduction. This position was totally supported by the courts. It is true that tax accounting and financial accounting are separate, yet it is hard to believe that the very definition of an asset can be different in these two systems.

GOODWILL

Goodwill is the simplest of concepts. Goodwill is the most complex of concepts.

First, the simple concept. For financial reporting, the FASB has simply defined it as the residual between the purchase price of a business combination and the sum of all the identifiable assets that have been valued. Very simplistically, if you paid $100 million for a company and the sum of all the tangible and intangible assets (working capital, PP&E, and intangible assets) add up to $85 million, then, be definition, you have $15 million of goodwill. In the same acquisition, if the purchase price had been $85 million, there would be no goodwill and if the purchase price was $115 million you would record $30 million of goodwill. In other words, the dollar amount of goodwill is simply a residual that depends on (1) what you paid for the new business and (2) what the FV of the assets comprising that business turn out to be.

Looked at this way, goodwill is simply an artificial accounting construct, developed by the FASB and subject to any changes they may wish to make.

There is another way of looking at goodwill, and that is the way the dictionary defines it:

The established custom or popularity of a business, etc.; (a sum paid for) the privilege, granted to the purchaser by the seller of a business, or trading as the recognized successor of the seller.[1]

This dictionary definition, even if slightly stilted, is what the man on the street thinks of as goodwill. Some courts tended to look at goodwill as the tendency of customers to return to a business, and this would go on perhaps irrespective of who owned the business.

The measurement of goodwill, on its own, is impossible under the FASB definition inasmuch as it is a residual of two other things. The common-sense definition of goodwill might be difficult to measure, but it could be done in terms of the avoidance of marketing expense on the one side and the ability to make higher operating profit on the other. If an accountant or a barber sells his practice, the buyer reasonably expects that many clients and customers will continue to trade with the new owner. That is the goodwill that the new owner has purchased.

We doubt that any prospective buyer of a business ever actually estimated, even mentally, the expected goodwill other than in the dictionary sense. While a buyer cannot prove how many customers or clients will return, reasonable estimates can be made. Such an estimate enters into the negotiations, leading to a final deal. Looked at one way, prospective buyers (and sellers for that matter) estimate how much repeat business there will be and settle on a purchase price accordingly. Looked at in terms of financial reporting, the

---

[1] *The New Shorter Oxford English Dictionary.* Oxford: Clarendon Press, 1993.

prospective buyer adds up all the values he can identify, and then the final purchase price is simply a function of negotiating skill. The lower the purchase price, the lower will be the amount of goodwill.

The reason for this discussion is simple. Under the FASB definition, the amount of goodwill on the balance sheet represents nothing specific, other than an arithmetic resultant. In common parlance, goodwill represents something real, albeit intangible, that was explicitly bargained for at the time of the sale of the original business.

Many people try to assign a meaning to the dollar amount of goodwill on a company's financial statements. While a logical effort, it is doomed to failure. There is only one way to understand goodwill on a Balance Sheet, and that is to accept that the amount is totally artificial and bears no relation to any outside reality.

As discussed in Chapter 9, testing goodwill for impairment is a complex procedure. You cannot "value" goodwill as you can a patent or a trademark. The only way to value goodwill at any point subsequent to the initial purchase is to estimate the FV of the overall business, determine the FV of all the assets (both those on the Balance Sheet and those not on the Balance Sheet—e.g., value of a new trade name developed subsequent to the original purchase of the business) and subtract the latter from the former. You then compare the new number to the old, and if the new number is lower, then you have impairment by definition.

Because under current accounting rules goodwill is not amortized (although tested for impairment at least annually), management almost always wants the maximum amount of any purchase price assigned to goodwill. In turn, this means minimizing the value of working capital, PP&E, and intangible assets, and maximizing the dollar amount of all liabilities. The common mantra among acquirers is "The more goodwill, the better." Never mind that you cannot touch, feel, or taste goodwill on its own. Just make it as large as possible in accordance with the accounting rules.

SOLVENCY OPINIONS

In many transactions involving the purchase or sale of a business enterprise, there is a question as to whether or not the new business will be solvent, using the technical or legal definition of solvency. In simple terms, a company is solvent if it has more assets than liabilities and can pay its debts when they become due.

The issue of solvency arises when a substantial amount of debt is incurred to finance the transaction. Such new debt, and the related interest requirements, will substantially change the cash flow going forward, as contrasted with previous results prior to the transaction.

Under the legal doctrine of "fraudulent conveyance," if a business incurs debt when it is insolvent, the new creditor can go to court and undo the loan. The principle is that an owner, knowing he faces financial distress, may try to borrow money from a bank and use it to pay off loans to himself, in effect giving himself a priority position. The law looks unkindly on such a transaction and says if the company was insolvent when the payment was made, the payment can be recouped. The same reasoning applies in an arm's-length business transaction. If the new owner pays off the former owner and then runs into financial difficulty, the new creditors can go back to the old owner and recoup the payments. Needless to say, the former owner does not want this to happen.

The solution is to obtain an opinion that the debtor company is solvent at the time of the transaction. This precludes a subsequent claim that the business really was insolvent thus negating the original transaction. A solvency opinion is often provided by either an investment banking firm or a professional valuation firm. The concepts applied, the procedures utilized, and the assumptions made are identical between an investment banking firm's solvency opinion and that of a professional valuation firm. The only difference will be the fee. Investment bankers often charge $500,000 for expressing their opinion, while many solvency opinions by valuation firms are billed at less than $100,000. The only difference is in the name on the letterhead of the opinion.

The process that a valuation specialist goes through to develop a solvency opinion is very similar to that of developing a business enterprise valuation (BEV). Emphasis is placed on the FV of the assets and liabilities and the income projections, including interest expense from the new debt. From the perspective of a professional performing this service, the business risks are perceived as substantial. If some information was not taken into account, and the subject company fails within a year or so, the professional firm that prepared the solvency opinion may find itself liable to the injured parties (i.e., those who lent money to the business and now cannot recover their loan). Even if the professional firm wins such a lawsuit, the legal cost of defense alone can be substantial, often way in excess of the fee charged for the opinion.

While to the client it may appear that the fee for a solvency opinion is far in excess of that charged for an equivalent BEV, the extra fee probably does not fully cover the legal exposure.

Whenever significant debt is incurred during the course of an M&A transaction, most corporate attorneys will recommend obtaining a solvency opinion. In the majority of cases it will be worthwhile to have the peace of mind that comes with any insurance policy. And a solvency opinion is just that—an insurance policy protecting against the claim of fraudulent conveyance.

CHAPTER 5

Due Diligence: What Is the Real Value of the Target's Business?

"Due Diligence" is defined as: "The process of investigation, performed by investors, into the details of a potential investment, such as an examination of operations and management and the verification of material facts."
—www.investorwords.com

This chapter is written for those directly involved in the acquisition process. The sequence of events in any specific business combination (to use the words of the Financial Accounting Standards Board [FASB]) or merger-and-acquisition (M&A) transaction may differ slightly from case to case. Perhaps an investment banker or a business broker is involved. Invariably, the attorneys for both sides will be intimately involved. Accountants will be called on to evaluate the financial soundness of the target and to provide an opinion on the adequacy of the financial statements.

What is often overlooked in the Due Diligence process that precedes an acquisition is that current accounting requirements may result in surprises in the subsequent financial statements. What was assumed to be an accretive acquisition may actually have to be reported as having a negative impact on earnings per share (EPS). These EPS surprises need not occur if those responsible for the Due Diligence process go one step further and try to estimate *in advance* (1) what the final allocation of purchase price will look like; and (2) the subsequent EPS impact of required depreciation and amortization on the newly acquired assets that now must be carried at Fair Value (FV).

Many acquiring companies hire outside expertise to perform the Due Diligence. This is often a major accounting firm, a management consultant, or an organization that specializes in performing Due Diligence. A detailed Due Diligence report, when properly prepared, will go into detail concerning such areas as human resources, employee benefits, customer relationships, supplier relationships, competitive conditions, productive capabilities, financial policies, and any other aspect of the target that might affect the future success or failure of the combined companies. If the target is active in several different industries, then a separate section of the Due Diligence report will probably be devoted to each product line.

A really well-done Due Diligence report will usually provide a basis sufficient for management, and ultimately the board, of the acquiring company to make informed decisions both on whether to proceed and to influence the final purchase price. There is one area, however, that most professionals who provide Due Diligence reports do not cover. That deals with the "Fair Values" of the acquired assets and liabilities. We are using the term *Fair Value* in quotation marks. We specifically are considering the amounts to be reported on the new combined Balance Sheet, computed in accordance with SFAS 157. In other words, the dollar amounts that will go on the Balance Sheet will be computed in accordance with current Generally Accepted Accounting Principles (GAAP) and do not necessarily reflect the "true economic value" to the purchaser.

This latter statement may be hard for some readers to swallow. Why should the amounts that will appear on *their* Balance Sheet differ in any way from the real value of those specific assets to *them?* The answer follows directly from the way the FASB developed SFAS 157. The Board's definition of Fair Value is simply an arbitrary construct that they themselves developed. Further, the FASB's definition of Fair Value, while perhaps satisfactory for financial instruments and derivatives, simply provides misleading answers for tangible and intangible assets.

For 115 years, valuation specialists have been developing Fair Market Values (FMV) for clients on an arm's-length independent basis. The concepts and ideas that made up FMV had been considered, discussed, debated, and ultimately agreed upon by the courts and the taxing authorities. This is not to say that differences did not exist between taxpayers and the IRS, or between insurance companies and people who had suffered a loss. There have been disputes about value ever since there was property to be divided or sold.

What wasn't in dispute was the *definition* of FMV. The determination of the FMV in a specific situation could easily lead to a difference of opinion regarding such things as the quantity and quality of the assets in question, or the future performance of the business. If a woman lost a diamond ring, the insurance company might question the color and quality of the diamond. In a divorce, the husband might argue that the outlook for the business was grim, while the wife could argue that things had never looked better. So, while there were always disputes about the specific value of a specific asset, the accepted *definition* of value was straightforward:

> *Fair Market Value is defined as the price for which property would exchange between a willing buyer and a willing seller, each having reasonable knowledge of all relevant facts, neither under compulsion to buy or sell, and with equity to both.*

Reasonable people differed on the attributes that contributed to value. But as long as an appraiser was truly independent and applied his professional knowledge and experience objectively, it was rare indeed for his values not to be accepted. To this appraiser the ultimate test as to whether a determination of value was reasonable was common sense: "Would I myself pay such and such an amount for this asset, or would I sell this asset for that same amount?" If I could answer in the affirmative, the answer was probably correct.

As we have seen in earlier chapters, the FASB in issuing SFAS 157 adopted a totally *new* definition, and in the process adopted new terminology. Instead of "Fair Market Value," the Board substituted the different, albeit similar "Fair Value" (FV). But the Board went further and adopted its own definition of FV:

> *Fair Value is the price that would be received to sell an asset, or paid to transfer a liability, in an orderly transaction between market participants at the measurement date.* [SFAS 157 ¶5]

> **Observation:** Without a detailed estimate of FV prior to the consummation of a business combination, buyers may be unpleasantly surprised at some of the accounting and financial reporting consequences. The solution, while self-serving for appraisers, is simple: Ask an appraisal firm to participate in the Due Diligence process.

The purpose of this chapter on Due Diligence is to suggest that many current Due Diligence reports do *not* appear to take into consideration the financial statement impact of the business combination as it is implemented under SFAS 157 and SFAS 141 R. Looked at from a different perspective, there is usually an unstated but explicit assumption in many Due Diligence assignments that dollar amounts on the seller's financial statements are "likely" to be carried over to the buyer's financials.

Thus, many potential acquirers in effect add the seller's Balance Sheet to their own in making their preliminary analyses. Interestingly, this was the exact approach actually utilized in the old pooling-of-interests accounting that was explicitly outlawed when SFAS 141 and SFAS 142 were adopted in 2001. Readers will recall that in exchange for giving up pooling, goodwill no longer had to be amortized, although it still has to be tested annually for impairment.

The trouble is that the new FV requirements of SFAS 157 will most likely give quite different answers to the buyer than were on the seller's financials.

Further, as asset and liability amounts change from the seller's book value to the buyer's new FV, so will the impact on future Income Statements as depreciation and amortization is recorded.

In short, you cannot project the financial statement impact of an acquisition without going through the same analysis that an appraiser does in actually performing the final purchase price allocation. For purposes of Due Diligence, it is not necessary to perform a complete valuation study. Quite close estimates can be developed quickly and at low cost. These estimates of what the final allocation will look like will probably be accurate for at least 90% to 95% of the final numbers.

The reason why this can be done quickly and at low cost is simple. There are two aspects to every valuation. The first is the determination of the FV. The second is the support needed to prepare and write the final report. Final values that go into financial statements will be audited, and in the current Sarbanes-Oxley environment, auditors scrutinize all FV information closely. Auditors demand supporting detail. Development of that support is time consuming. Additional work is usually necessary to meet audit requirements, but almost never does the answer change because of work required to prepare the final written report.

An experienced appraiser, based on his professional experience and professional judgment, can estimate values very quickly and with a high degree of confidence that his estimate will approximate the final detailed valuation study. It is really similar to an experienced physician who can almost always diagnose appendicitis over the phone from a description of the symptoms, but would operate only after a detailed examination of the patient in person. Similarly, a buyer can make sound decisions based on estimates of value, but they can be booked and audited only after the complete study is performed.

FINANCIAL PROJECTIONS

As discussed in Chapter 4, it is critical that the buyer have a clear idea of the expected financial results to be derived after the transaction closes. Occasionally, there are instances where the buyer did not make such projections, at least on a formal basis. Usually, however, the board of directors of a company will insist that management outline the expected financial outcome of the proposed transaction. The number one question is almost always, "Will the transaction be accretive to earnings per share? If not immediately, then how long will it take to break even, to get back to current EPS?"

The only way this important question can be answered is for the buyer to make his own projections. Typically, the seller already has made financial projections of future operating results, and almost invariably those seller projections show a very favorable trend line. This is natural, because if the seller were projecting that operations were going south, few would be interested in buying the company. So it is a safe assumption that, from the seller's perspective, the future is bright.

Many buyers have learned not to totally trust seller projections and therefore make their own. The reason for stressing the necessity of making your own projections as a buyer is simple. In addition to common-sense caution, appraisers actually need those projections to complete the allocation process. As described in Chapter 4, appraisers will calculate the internal rate of return inherent in the transaction, and compare that with the weighted average cost of capital.

While there is nothing an appraiser can do after the fact if it appears that the buyer paid too much, this information is vital to support the allocation of the purchase price among the intangible assets. And as discussed in this chapter, whether an M&A transaction has a positive EPS impact rests in large part on how the purchase price has been allocated.

It is important for the appraiser, and the auditor in reviewing the appraiser's work, to know what management is expecting. Now those expectations may be optimistic or conservative, but as long as management committed to them with the board of directors, they become a more or less official document that the appraiser and auditor can rely on. Reasonable management projections will eliminate a lot of second guessing by auditors, the Securities and Exchange Commission (SEC), and the Public Company Accounting Oversight Board (PCAOB). Projections can be wrong, but as long as they were prepared in good faith, those projections can be used to support values for the intangible assets that must be valued and amortized.

The following are four categories of assets and liabilities that should be reviewed as part of every Due Diligence process.

1. Hard Assets:
      Working Capital
      Property, Plant, and Equipment (PP&E)
2. Liabilities
3. Intangible Assets
4. Contingent Liabilities

ESTIMATING THE VALUE OF WORKING CAPITAL

In looking at working capital during a Due Diligence exam, the usual approach is to test the receivables for collectability and the inventory to make sure it is there and properly valued.

Evaluating the collectability of receivables is pretty standard in the area of financial management. Aging of past-due receivables will be requested and the oldest items on the list scrutinized carefully for ultimate collectability. Under the rules of SFAS 157 and the proposed rules in SFAS 141 R, the buyer must set up the new FV of the receivables, rather than carrying the gross amounts forward with an offsetting reserve for noncollectability.

Depending on the size of the accounts receivable ledger and the number of accounts, it may be possible to evaluate each separate account; however, with a large number of consumer receivables, it will be necessary to apply some sort of statistical approach, marking all receivables down by perhaps 0.5% or 1%. The concept of FV as it applies to receivables is to look at what the specific asset (receivable) could be sold for to a third party. Since the buyer would not want any bad debts, and a reserve cannot be set up, it seems that the easiest way is simply to deduct an appropriate amount from each account to assure that there will be no shortfalls.

In terms of strategy, an acquisition represents a terrific opportunity to clean up the target's receivables, in effect writing down or writing off all balances that could cause trouble. Here is a case where the FASB's new definition of FV will actually help the buyer. Obviously, auditors and the SEC and the PCAOB will be looking to see that "built-in gains" are not being created simply to maximize future income. Nonetheless, a conservative approach can hardly be faulted.

With regard to inventories, a lot more work may be necessary in the Due Diligence process.

First of all, it is a safe statement that virtually every company that has inventories has items that are not moving and may never sell at the current carrying amount. Most financial managers know of this "surplus and obsolete," because every firm has it. Often, little is done about it for two reasons. To obtain a tax deduction for inventory that has lost its value, the IRS requires that you physically dispose of it. You are not allowed to write it down to a nominal amount, store it on the back shelf, and then pull it out at some point in the future when you suddenly find a customer asking for that part. So discretion, in terms of customer satisfaction, suggests you keep the items and forgo a potential tax deduction.

The second reason for not getting rid of surplus and obsolete inventory goes to the heart of financial reporting and the pressure for current earnings. Disposing of worthless inventory will free up storage space, reduce property taxes and insurance, and lead to more efficient operations. However, to accomplish these laudable goals, GAAP requires you to take a current charge to earnings. Such a charge reflects poorly on current management; there is a natural desire to postpone any bad news as long as possible. So, in many firms, surplus and obsolete inventory continues to expand, with the promise made that "someday soon we will have to take care of this problem." Someday, however, often seems to be postponed.

Now in a potential acquisition the prospective buyer truly gets a free ride. None of the bad inventory must be thrown out physically, although in practice that might be a good idea. Instead, the FV of each portion of the acquired inventory is determined; in the case of surplus and obsolete inventory, only a nominal amount need be applied. Since the true FV probably is close to zero, this represents both good accounting and good financial management.

In the case of inventories, the actual determination of FV for work-in-process, raw materials, and finished goods has to be determined on a facts-and-circumstances basis. The FV of finished goods currently is determined on the basis of expected selling prices, less cost to sell and a profit margin. For work-in-process, you estimate the selling price of the finished good less the "cost to complete" plus selling expense and profit. The FASB does not go into the fine points of cost accounting and allocation of factory overhead or selling, general and administrative (SGA) expenses, so careful scrutiny is needed here. Finally, raw materials currently are to be valued at replacement cost, although the definition of FV in SFAS 157, with its emphasis on exit price or selling price, might call for a write-up or write-down of raw materials in certain instances.

Cash and marketable securities usually will present few difficulties in a Due Diligence environment, as long as the auditors have confirmed the balances. Prepaid expenses and other assets can be reviewed for accuracy of calculation but are unlikely to cause any valuation problems.

The FV of current liabilities again probably poses few problems. Accounts payable are likely to represent actual liabilities at face value. Certainly, accruals for liabilities such as vacation will be scrutinized and, if necessary, adjusted upward. The allocation process does not put any penalty on increasing liabilities on the seller's books because "liabilities assumed" go into the net purchase price; any increase in recognized liabilities ultimately shows up in nondeductible goodwill, hence the need for the buyer to scrutinize the current liability side of working capital to minimize future charges and thus maximize future profit. Again, the warning must be sounded that the buyer does not have a free hand just to increase liabilities in order to help manage future income. But any and all supportable liabilities should be fully developed and disclosed.

ESTIMATING THE VALUE OF PROPERTY, PLANT, AND EQUIPMENT

For many businesses, other than manufacturing, most buyers will *not* spend money on obtaining a professional appraisal in order formally to comply with the FV requirements. If the PP&E consists mainly of personal computers and office furniture and fixtures, the probability is fairly high that the current "book value" on the seller's books approximates FV. Book depreciation, usually based on tax rules, by and large is too aggressive for furniture and fixtures, and too conservative for computers. If personal computers are a major asset class, then perhaps they could be valued separately. We do not often see that in practice.

On the basis of materiality, most auditors will pass on carrying forward the prior book value. If this is the case, then there is little to be gained from a more accurate figure derived from a formal valuation study.

For manufacturing companies, where PP&E is a major asset, prospective buyers performing a Due Diligence exam should look at the physical facilities, of course. This is almost always done by the buyer's engineering and manufacturing staff. What is not as often performed is an examination of the property record system.

It is beyond the scope of this book to go into detail as to how valuation specialists actually perform a detailed valuation of PP&E. Basically, there are two ways, one expensive and the other less so.

The expensive way to perform a fixed-asset appraisal of what appraisers call "machinery and equipment" is to visit the facility; list a description of each asset, including condition; and then go back to the office and "price" the complement of assets in place. This "pricing" can range from detailed correspondence with vendors to examination of current auction results, quotes for similar assets from used equipment dealers in the industry, and indexing of original costs.

There are a lot of machinery price indexes, some public and some proprietary. Those indexes, if carefully constructed and applied, can help an appraiser determine the cost today of assets acquired in the past. What indexes cannot do is either adjust for technology and quality differences or allow for physical condition. So, depending on the industry and the current state of manufacturing processes, indexes can provide usable values at far lower cost than the detailed inspection, listing, and pricing described above.

A moment's thought will lead to the conclusion that if you can index some of the assets, why not index them all. Competent appraisers can determine current values of machinery and equipment economically by indexing and still adjust for physical condition and technological improvements.

There is, however, often a major problem in indexing the historical cost on the seller's books to derive a current FV. The problem is simple to describe and hard to overcome. Price or cost indexes cannot be applied to anything other than the original cost of the asset when it was new. Therefore, indexing relies on the availability of *original* date of acquisition and original cost. For a facility that has never changed hands in the past, that data is usually available.

But if the subject facility was bought by the current owner from a previous owner, there will often be available only the appraised values as of the date of acquisition. Often, the original date and original cost will have been discarded or lost. It would be too strong a statement to say that previously allocated values cannot be indexed forward. However, there are some real conceptual problems that may be hard to overcome.

Prospective buyers, as part of Due Diligence, should examine carefully the detail contained in the fixed-asset register. If original date of acquisition and original cost are available, the determination of the FV of PP&E will be relatively simple. However, if the information is not available, if there is only allocated costs from a prior acquisition, then there will be added cost for valuing the PP&E.

A word about real estate. In many companies, there can be a substantial amount of land, often much of it purchased years ago at relatively low cost. Land is never depreciated, but by the same token land cannot be written up to current FV while still held by the purchaser. There then can be a real discrepancy between the dollars shown on the target's balance sheet for land and the current real FV.

The issue deals with the cost of determining the FV of the land. Real estate valuation professionals perform much of their work for lenders. Many lenders, particularly banks, have strict legal requirements for appraisals that they use in granting loans against real estate. Consequently, many real estate appraisers are used to providing very comprehensive reports. As you can imagine, such comprehensive reports, with numerous photos and analyses of comparable properties, can be quite expensive and time consuming.

For financial reporting purposes, however, it is not necessary to have totally comprehensive real estate appraisal reports, reports that go into detail needed only by banks. (These legal requirements were put in place as a result of the savings-and-loan crisis many years ago and were never relaxed.) It is incumbent on a company to specify what kind of valuation it wants performed on acquired real estate. If, in fact, the buyer plans to mortgage some of the newly acquired real estate, then obtaining a comprehensive appraisal in advance will save subsequent duplication. But if the real estate will not form the collateral for subsequent borrowing, it may be possible to obtain approximate FVs at substantially less cost—but the onus is on the buyer to specify the detail and support needed.

There have been several instances where real estate made up less than 5% of the acquired assets, but the proposed valuation fee for the allocation had over 50% of the time applied to the real estate. Essentially, this would be a waste of resources since part of Due Diligence is to determine just what information will be needed about acquired real estate.

ESTIMATING THE VALUE OF LIABILITIES

Virtually any company being considered for potential acquisition is likely to have had full audited financials. It is indeed rare for auditors to miss any understatement of accounts payable and accrued liabilities. Certainly, detailed questions can and should be asked of the target's auditors, but it is unlikely that major misstatements will have occurred. Both short-term bank loans and long-term loans will definitely be on the Balance Sheet, and there could be only technical issues about measuring the FV of the liabilities in relation to the creditworthiness of the borrower.

The FASB wants liability measurements to take into account the credit of the borrower, but there is a perverse, even counterintuitive result. The worse the borrower's credit, the smaller the liability shown will be. If the company is bought by a stronger company, the liabilities, if carried at FV, might have to be revalued upward. But since few companies write down the liability for their own borrowings to FV, we consider this a more theoretical than practical problem.

Longer-term liabilities for pensions and deferred taxes, however, are another issue. Again, it is outside the scope of this book to deal with pensions and deferred taxes, both quite specialized areas that appraisers seldom get involved in. In the case of pensions, it is critical for the buyer's actuary to review the target's plans and make sure that all actuarial assumptions are in line with the buyer's policies. There is substantial scope within actuarial science for optimistic (high interest rates) assumptions to have been utilized. Since the ultimate cost of a pension plan actually depends on cash inflows and outflows, and not actuarial assumptions, it behooves the buyer, if at all possible, to maximize the reported liabilities through appropriate assumptions.

With regard to deferred taxes, this has become an extremely technical issue outside the scope of valuation specialists. Suffice it so say that, just as with pensions and actuaries, different accountants can end up with somewhat different estimates of both deferred tax assets and deferred tax liabilities. This requires close scrutiny by the buyer's accounting firm, again requesting they use the most conservative assumptions possible.

ESTIMATING THE VALUE AND LIFE OF INTANGIBLE ASSETS

In terms of where the most improvement is needed in the Due Diligence process, it has to be in evaluating the prospective intangible assets that will be put on the books after the deal closes. Working capital, and even PP&E, may change only slightly from the target's book value once the required SFAS 141 R allocation is made. Estimating the new dollar amounts of the assets and liabilities, and the consequent effect on income of amortizing or depreciating the new values, can be done by many experienced buyers.

Estimating the dollar value of intangible assets, their lives, and the impact on future profit and loss (P&L) is an order of magnitude more difficult. Finally, as discussed earlier, goodwill, although it cannot be calculated directly, is going to be a final residual amount; while not subject to amortization, significant amounts of goodwill may lead to a future impairment charge.

Other than operational problems in merging two disparate companies, the biggest surprises in many mergers revolve around unexpected amortization charges for intangible assets that were never on the seller's books. These surprises flow directly from the GAAP requirement that the total purchase price be allocated among the assets acquired. That buyers may want, even need, the targets' customers is without question. But the *value* of those customer relationships, no matter how great, has never appeared on the seller's Balance Sheet. The old adage "out of sight, out of mind" is particularly apt.

Most experienced executives are used to looking at a Balance Sheet and mentally making adjustments to what they believe may be the current values. But it is hard to make an adjustment for an asset that does not appear in any financial disclosure. There is an anomaly in present GAAP: certain assets *must* appear on the buyer's Balance Sheet when they have a business combination; those same assets *cannot* appear on their Balance Sheet absent a business combination.

It is impossible to answer the question why purchased intangibles are recognized on financial statements, but those same intangibles cannot be recognized on their own. To use a far-out analogy, the values of the respective Coca-Cola™ and Pepsi-Cola™ trade names do not appear on either company's financial statements today, no matter how valuable they may be. But, to make a point, if Pepsi bought Coke, then the value of the Coke trademark would have to appear on the Pepsi Balance Sheet.

We cannot resolve this conundrum. We simply have to look at today's rules, no matter how inconsistent, and apply them accordingly. In SFAS 141, the FASB provided a list of some 29 different identifiable intangible assets that could possibly have been acquired in a business combination. In the over six years since this list was issued, it may be surprising that valuation specialists have not identified any intangibles that the Board missed. The all-inclusive list has stood the test of time. There are about a half dozen intangibles that are extremely rare, like newspaper mastheads, song lyrics, ballet scores, and computer mask works. Many of the others are relatively rare. But there are ten that are very frequent, and each has to be sought in the allocation process. They are the following (in the order provided by SFAS 141):

1. Trademarks, trade names
2. Noncompete agreements
3. Customer relationships
4. Licensing agreements
5. Lease agreements
6. Employment contracts
7. Patents
8. Computer software
9. Unpatented technology
10. Trade secrets

Each of these will be discussed in a brief paragraph. For more detailed discussion, refer to the author's book, *Fair Value for Financial Reporting*.

That *trademarks* and *trade names* are valuable is self-evident. The valuation of this asset is very straightforward, and appraisers have well-established methodologies for the valuation. The key point here is that an indefinite life can often be ascribed to trade names, which means that there will be no amortization charge hitting the P&L statement. Companies generally like to have as much as possible of the purchase price allocated to trade names for this very reason. It should be noted that the SEC casts a skeptical eye on all assets with an indefinite life, but since many trade names have been in use for decades, this is a challenge that can usually be met.

Noncompete agreements are virtually universal in every purchase agreement as the buyer's attorney strives to "protect" his client. Only rarely, however, do these have significant value. First, with regard to individuals, they can usually run for only a brief time period and they are hard to enforce in court. Second, the FV of a noncompete is based on the probability that the seller would actually go back into competition. So, for example, Company B sells a product line to Company A "in order to focus on strategic alternatives." How likely is it that, having sold the business, Company B will suddenly want to return? The usual answer is that it is quite unlikely; in that case, little value will be ascribed to the agreement.

Because of their importance, customer relationships are covered in detail in Chapter 10.

Licensing agreements can go in two directions. Company A can license a trade name it owns to Company B and obtain royalties based on the sales of B's products that use A's name. Alternatively, Company A can license a patent owned by B in order to produce a product; in this case, A pays to B royalties based on A's sales. Licensing is a major business activity, with its own specialists and trade organizations, and in such fields as cosmetics and clothing, royalties are a major expense or income. Valuing these licensing agreements depends on how much the license adds to the income stream of the subject. Basically valuation specialists use a discounted cash flow (DCF) approach to obtain the current FV.

Lease agreements or contracts are prevalent in almost every industry, particularly for real estate and some types of equipment such as airplanes. The concept of FV with respect to lease agreements is clear. You value specific leases only if they are either *above* or *below* current rates. If a retailer has a ten-year lease at $22 per square foot and current rates in that shopping center are between $21 and $24, then an appraiser might conclude that it was neither a favorable nor an unfavorable lease and would not assign any value in a purchase price allocation. However, if current lease rates were, say, $30, then it is obvious that the buyer is going to be paying below-market rates for the next ten years. This saving has value, and the FV of the favorable lease is calculated on a DCF basis. A similar calculation is made to reflect the liability if the unbreakable lease is at above-market conditions.

Employment agreements are very common and undoubtedly would have been looked at as part of standard Due Diligence. But the fact that there is an employment contract with one or more key individuals does not mean that dollars of purchase price are allocated to the contract. The reason is that there is current value or liability only if the contractual terms are again above or below current compensation levels. A five-year employment contract for a sales vice president at $300,000 a year would be valued only if the real market worth of the individual was, say, $450,000 a year. But it is extremely rare for key executives to be underpaid as measured by current market conditions. Perhaps Warren Buffet's reported nominal $100,000-a-year salary would qualify for recognition if someone were to buy Berkshire Hathaway. Similarly, buyers usually will not want to keep an overpaid executive, and a settlement would have been reached prior to the deal's being consummated. In practice, we rarely find value, either plus or minus, in employment agreements.

Patents often have significant value to the owner, because they either provide a direct cost advantage or preclude competitors from doing the same thing. In the pharmaceutical industry, it might not be an overstatement to suggest that the majority of the value of a target company would relate to its patents and the sales potential of the patented items. For many companies, however, patents essentially are defensive in nature. It may be surprising, but in many allocations, quite nominal values usually end up being ascribed to patents. It turns out that competitors are pretty smart and have been able to work around the specific patents being valued. This does not suggest that companies should not file for patents, but when we cast a cold and impartial eye on them, very few patents are generating meaningful cash flows. There are exceptions, but these will be readily apparent in even the most cursory Due Diligence.

Computer software is present in 100% of companies involved in a business combination, but that does not mean that significant value will be assigned to this intangible. Software such as that produced by Microsoft is present on every personal computer, but it is not valued separately from the computer itself. There are really only three types of software that are separately valued. The first would be an Oracle or

SAP system, which is extremely expensive to install, and the valuation specialist will estimate the dollar amount that would be required to duplicate the installation. The second type of software is products developed by software firms for licensing to others. The value of such products is based on the DCF of the estimated future revenues, less required costs to maintain the existing software. This point is a special bone of contention because auditors often question whether a software company has a *legal obligation* to maintain the software during the life of the maintenance contract. Anyone contemplating buying a software company should look into this quite closely. The third and final type of software that has to be valued is internal software for billing or general ledger. The value of such software is often determined by the current cost to replace the existing software.

Unpatented technology is, as the name implies, know-how that enables the owner to manufacture or otherwise perform a function at a lower price. Many companies explicitly do not want to disclose what they are doing through the patent process and choose not to patent a technique or technology. The valuation is simple and based on evaluating the cost benefit to the owner of the technology. The only issue deals with the life over which the value should be amortized. By and large, one would assume that unpatented technology has a relatively short life. This will be due to the fact that employees change jobs, while suppliers and customers also "talk" about industry activities. Combined, this means that the cost advantage of unpatented technology may be fairly short. Keep in mind, though, that the dollar amount of the value is also a function of the expected life. So you may have a higher value going on for a longer period, or a smaller value going on for a brief period. The P&L effect per year *in the first few years after the deal closes* may not be all that significantly affected by the choice of life.

Trade secrets are hard to distinguish from unpatented technology, and the same valuation approach is applied.

LIVES FOR AMORTIZATION

Some appraisers will not provide their clients with an estimated life for specific intangibles, using the argument that this is an accounting function, not a valuation problem. We beg to differ, believing that the very process of determining the value of an asset provides us with insight into its likely life. The real issue is not developing a specific life in years. The issue is that companies want long lives, to minimize the current P&L impact of amortization. On the other side, auditors working on behalf of precluding SEC questions usually argue for shorter lives. It is well known that the SEC always seems to come down on any accounting issue by choosing the alternative that most impacts reported profits. Writing off a customer relationship in five years is going to have twice the impact of allowing a ten-year life if the value is the same for both periods.

As noted above, in some cases the use of a shorter life automatically generates a smaller value, because the future cash flows do not go out as far. Nevertheless, there almost always is tension between the company and its auditors, with the appraiser in the middle. A personal observation would be that the SEC often overreaches in arguing for a short amortization period, but at the end of the day, the SEC holds all the cards. Very few publicly traded companies are willing to go to the mat with the SEC over a choice of life for amortization.

One note of caution is necessary here. Most companies think of amortization of intangible asset values in terms of a straight line. Depreciation for PP&E is usually straight line for books and accelerated for taxes. Therefore, the initial thought pattern of corporate controllers is to assume that all intangible values developed for a purchase price allocation should be amortized straight line.

Unfortunately, when the FASB wrote SFAS 142, they thought of this. In paragraph 12 there is an innocuous sentence that reads: "The method of amortization shall reflect the pattern over which the economic benefits of the intangible asset are consumed or otherwise used up." This approach may not make any difference if reviewing how to amortize the benefits of a favorable ten-year lease. Straight lining the amount is undoubtedly correct.

But switch to the value assigned to unpatented technology or trade secrets. The chances are pretty high that one or more competitors will be trying pretty hard to work around the benefit you just acquired. Thus, the argument will be made that the majority of the earnings potential, the future cash flow, should probably be attributed to the early years, with less value assigned to the out years. When this argument is made, it is hard to refute—except that it adversely

> **Observation:** Part of Due Diligence involving intangible assets should be to examine carefully whether straight-line amortization will be permitted. Accelerated amortization will adversely affect prior assumptions about reported EPS as projections of whether an acquisition will be accretive.

impacts current P&L. The SEC is not particularly responsive to requests for an accounting treatment that pushes expenses out into the future and maximizes current income.

GOODWILL ON THE TARGET'S BOOKS

As mentioned earlier, most intangible assets that have to be recognized and valued in a business combination never appeared on the target's books. There is one exception, and that often causes some confusion. What about goodwill that appears on the books of the target before the acquisition and during the Due Diligence process?

The answer is very simple: Goodwill on the target's books is always ignored by an appraiser and, in effect, disappears. The appraisal process for a business combination will likely produce a *new* goodwill amount, but that amount is a function of the purchase price and *not* how much goodwill was on the prior company's books.

In explanation, the amount of goodwill on the target's books was based on an acquisition it made in the past. But you are now buying a total company and do not know, and do not care, what goodwill is on the books or where it came from. Your new financial statements will be based on the *current* FV of what you bought and what you paid, not what somebody else did in the past.

ESTIMATING THE VALUE OF CONTINGENT LIABILITIES

The new SFAS 141R is going to change, in a material way, how companies account for contingent payouts. Very frequently, the buyer and seller in an M&A transaction cannot agree on the future sales and profit potential the seller is bringing to the transaction. The seller thinks things will be great, and wants to be paid for this potential. The buyer is somewhat more skeptical and does not want to pay today for something that may never come to pass.

The solution, and it is common, is for the purchase documents to call for certain additional payments to the seller if stated goals or objectives are met. If the goals are achieved, it means the purchase was a good one, and buyers willingly pay up. If the seller was too optimistic, then the buyer congratulates himself on not having paid too much.

Under accounting in place for many years, any such additional contingent payouts have been charged to goodwill, with no impact on subsequent reported EPS. There is little chance of an impairment charge due to the increased goodwill since the company is fully meeting its profit and sales expectations.

Now, in SFAS 141 R, the rules have been totally changed. The buyer (or his appraiser) must estimate as accurately as possible what is the most likely contingent payout, if any. This amount is set up as an initial liability on the buyer's books, and the effective offset is to initial goodwill.

The question is often asked by one, or both, of the parties, "If we cannot agree on what is likely to happen, how can you (the appraiser) tell us?"

In this case, the answer is easy. Appraisers are objective, independent, and neutral without any vested interest in the outcome. Neither payment of dollars nor receipt of dollars affects us. Consequently, we can make our own assessment of the most likely outcome. In trying to predict an outcome, the parties to the transaction not only have a vested interest in the outcome, there is a real worry that somehow one's negotiating position may be damaged by agreeing to the other side's number. Appraisers don't have that problem.

Estimating the future results of combined operations is no more difficult than in any valuation that involves projections of the future. In fact, this situation is actually easier because we will have available the projections made by each side; this actually provides us with *more* information than we usually have.

The one downside to the new FASB position on contingent payments is that if the appraiser *under*estimates the final actual payout, the buyer will have to take a charge to income, reducing EPS.

If, however, the appraiser *over*estimates the actual payment, the buyer will have a credit to income, increasing EPS. It does not take a rocket scientist to see what type of estimate the buyer would like to receive from the valuation specialist. Of course, any determination by an appraiser of a potential contingent payment is going to be closely scrutinized by the auditor and, if publicly traded, certainly reviewed by the SEC. This will prevent truly ridiculous assumptions from being made. Nonetheless, it is hard to see how an auditor can question an appraiser's judgment if the valuation specialist truly believes that the seller's projections will most likely be met, thus leading to a high FV to be shown as a liability.

We are not predictors of doom and gloom. Anything can be made to work. But if we have to make a bet, we would put our money on the assumption that there will be very few contingent payouts in excess of the original assumption. Further, if some companies start to show large reported increases in EPS because the contingent payout is far less than originally assumed, the financial journalists will be all over this abuse. The FASB hates to admit they made a mistake, and they rarely change their mind on fundamental decisions. We would be surprised if this particular part of SFAS 141 R and SFAS 157 is not revisited very shortly. Potential abuse, which is all that can be considered today, has a low priority. Actual abuse—and we predict it will come—does draw close scrutiny and will have a high priority.

CHAPTER 6

Valuation of Liabilities

One of the key aspects of any Due Diligence investigation is to (1) determine what liabilities, if any, the target company may have; and (2) develop an estimate of the dollar amount of the potential losses or expense required to meet those liabilities. The Due Diligence analysis would include actual current liabilities as well as contingent liabilities. The issues to be examined may or may not have been disclosed in the financial statements or any other public disclosures. It is outside the scope of this book on valuation to provide guidelines on how to conduct a Due Diligence examination. Many of the larger public accounting firms, some valuation firms, and specialist consulting firms perform this type of service. Very few merger-and-acquisition (M&A) transactions, however, are undertaken without substantial due diligence. (Visit www.allbusiness.com for a Due Diligence checklist.)

The question is: What can we do if we find there are actual or potential liabilities that *cannot* easily be quantified? Irrespective of the difficulty in quantification, the Financial Accounting Standards Board (FASB) in its Statement of Financial Accounting Standards (SFAS) 141 R calls for buyers to quantify all acquired liabilities that are more likely than not and put them on the new Balance Sheet. This can turn out to be a major change from past practice.

For many years the valuation and quantification of liabilities has been governed by SFAS 5. In its own summary of Statement 5, the Board says:

This Statement ... requires accrual by a charge to income (and disclosure) for an estimated loss from a loss contingency if two conditions are met: (a) information available prior to issuance of the financial statements indicates that it is probable that an asset had been impaired or a liability had been incurred at the date of the financial statements, and (b) the amount of loss can be reasonably estimated.

Cutting through what might at first glance appear to be legalistic jargon, there are two key concepts in this description. Until the Board issues SFAS 141 R, liabilities don't have to be quantified on the Balance Sheet unless it is "probable" they will occur. In practice, *probable* has been taken to mean greater than a 50% probability. So a lawsuit that your attorney says you are likely to win—in fact, the plaintiff has only a 5% chance of success—would *not* be put on the Balance Sheet. Disclosure in the footnotes about the lawsuit is probably required. But as long as someone is willing to opine that it is unlikely (less than 50%) the company will lose the case, one need not, in fact cannot, put the potential loss on the Balance Sheet.

But SFAS 5 goes even further. Just because there may be a 50.1% (or greater) probability of a loss, you still do not show a dollar liability on the face of the financial statements unless you can "reasonably estimate" the magnitude. An example would be the numerous major class-action lawsuits faced by tobacco and pharmaceutical firms. Seasoned observers might agree there is a significant chance that the companies may lose one or more of the cases. But who is going to tell you *how much* the loss is likely to be, how much a jury award could be? The truth is that nobody knows, and if that is the case, then disclosure, but not quantification, is all that is currently needed.

SFAS 5 was issued in 1975, and in the more than 30 years that it has been the "law of the land," accountants and management have found the rule to be pretty effective. In fact, there has been virtually no clamor to change SFAS 5 from either preparers (who are scared of guessing wrong) or from statement users (who get the information they need from the footnote disclosures).

THE FASB'S MOTIVES FOR CHANGING SFAS 5

As indicated earlier, the FASB initially proposed to change the application of SFAS 5 in the case of business combinations. They have not answered the even more logical question: If you are going to require in business combinations quantification of *all* liabilities (disregarding probability and irrespective of how hard it is to perform the calculations), then why would it not similarly be required in the *absence* of an M&A transaction?

As with many other aspects of Fair Value (FV) accounting, the Board is considering new accounting for business combinations, but only on a piecemeal basis. They appear to be reluctant to go all the way with their own internal logic, since this would require them to withdraw SFAS 5 and mandate that all liabilities have to be valued.

This push by the FASB, starting with purchase price accounting, to value liabilities flows inexorably from the Board's most fundamental belief: A company's Balance Sheet is paramount; the Income Statement, therefore, is little more than a residual between the opening and closing Balance Sheets.

Many readers of this book may have thought they learned that periodic income was derived from a proper matching of revenues and expenses. In fact, today's profit-and-loss (P&L) statement starts on line 1 with revenue from sales, and ends, after subtracting all expenses and charges, with a net income figure. The fact is that (1) management compensation is often based on income; (2) taxes are based and paid on income; (3) security analysts routinely analyze anticipated earnings and calculate the ubiquitous price/earnings ratio; and (4) dividends can be paid only out of earnings and cash flow. Notwithstanding that all their constituents focus on revenue and earnings, the FASB theoreticians believe that assets and liabilities are *really* more important. To them, the primacy in financial reporting belongs to the Balance Sheet.

From this belief, with which one is free to agree or disagree, flows a major consequence. If you are really going to put assets and liabilities front and center, and put revenues and expense off in the wings, then it is important to first identify and then value correctly all assets and liabilities. From the Board's perspective, focusing on the Balance Sheet requires those asset and liability balances to reflect economic reality.

Today's accounting model, with its emphasis on the Income Statement, effectively treats the Balance Sheet as a residual. Thus, the amount shown today for net property, plant, and equipment (PP&E) essentially represents only the original cost of the asset, less accumulated depreciation charges. The PP&E balance does not show the true current value of the assets. In this case, current value can be defined as to either what it would cost to replace the assets or what the assets could be sold for to a third party. The current Balance Sheet amounts do not purport, nor do they actually reflect, current value.

The FASB argues, with some justification, that if the Balance Sheet is primary, then it has little utility unless the amounts shown are correct. The same argument for PP&E is then applied by the Board to all other assets on the Balance Sheet and to all liabilities.

Here is where the Board is changing the rules of the game. Currently, the only liabilities shown on a Balance Sheet represent future outlays that have at least a 50.1% chance of being paid. But under their new concept of "Fair Value Measurements" as enunciated in SFAS 157 with the same name, *all* the seller's liabilities would have to be valued and recognized on the face of the financial statements. What is the logic of quantifying a remote probability, much less a slight possibility just because a business combination occurred?

If there is a 5% chance that a lawsuit will be filed against a company for damages of $1 million, the Board originally argued that the "expected value" ($50,000) should appropriately be booked. The argument was that if there were, in fact, 20 such lawsuits, each with a 5% probability, then one would anticipate that at least one of the lawsuits would be lost with a payment of $1 million and 19 lawsuits would be settled with no payment. If the cost of losing one lawsuit out of 20 is $1 million, then logically any one of the lawsuits should carry a proportionate share of that liability. One twentieth of $1 million is $50,000, and the FASB says that is why, no matter how remote, some dollar amount should be on the Balance Sheet.

Critics have jumped on this approach with two arguments:

1. Putting $50,000 on the Balance Sheet for one specific lawsuit tells you nothing as to whether or not this specific case will result in either no loss (19/20) or $1 million (1/20). It is a binary outcome, either/or. So if the purpose of financial statements is to provide information about future cash flows, the one thing readers (and management, for that matter) know is that $50,000 will *never* be paid out. It is all or nothing, $1 million or zero.

2. The second argument against the Board's position on valuing contingent liabilities is that estimating probabilities, when the

outcome is uncertain, is no easier now than it was in 1975 when SFAS 5 was promulgated. As will be discussed more fully below, if the Board sticks to its guns, it is easy to see that income statements can—and probably will—be manipulated.

The FASB's position on expected value works beautifully when there are a lot of identical situations. Think of a roulette wheel at a casino. There are 37 chances (including 0 and 00) and the payoff is 35 to 1. The House has a 2/37 expected value, and if enough spins of the wheel take place, the casino will win its 5.4%. But on any one spin of the wheel, the house either wins everything that was bet or pays out $35 for each dollar bet. The house does have a 5.4% edge, but only over a long stretch. In the short run, it is simply chance.

Now let us apply this expected value concept to the real world. For most companies, there are not thousands of identical lawsuits, with the same odds of winning or losing each case. There is only a series of single cases, each of which will be either won or lost.

If companies were required, when buying another firm that has a lawsuit, to estimate the probabilities of each lawsuit, this was going to be difficult for two reasons. Corporate attorneys historically have been reluctant to provide estimates of winning or losing a lawsuit because trying to predict the behavior of a judge (much less a jury) is inherently risky. Lawyers, by training, simply do not like taking risks.

Even when a company holds the feet of its counsel to the proverbial fire, and says, "You have to come up with an estimate, or we will be forced to get another lawyer," the question from the lawyer then becomes, "Okay, I really don't know, but if I have to put down some number, should it be a high probability (conservative) or a low probability (optimistic)?"

Now we get to the heart of the matter. The FASB is setting Corporate America up for the greatest opportunity in the world to "manage" earnings. How is this possible?

Under the proposed accounting in SFAS 157 and 141 R, remember that if a company estimates a 5% probability of loss on the $1 million lawsuit, it will have set up on its books $50,000 on the liability side. That is the 'expected value.'

Now fast forward three years: The lawsuit has settled, the plaintiff has lost (as he will do 19 out of 20 times), and now the company has an unneeded $50,000 liability that has to go away. How does it go away? It gets written off to income! Yes, it gets written off to income, because in the eyes of the FASB, the Balance Sheet has to be correct. There is now no liability. The Balance Sheet has to be at FV. The FV of no liability is zero, and the Balance Sheet has to reflect this situation. As we used to say in geometry class: "QED."

The only way to get the Balance Sheet to a zero liability is to credit income and debit the liability. Debiting the liability wipes it out, and crediting income now shows up on the Income Statement as a favorable entry. What could be better for a chief financial officer who wants to report more income to the company's shareholders and analysts?

Now step back a minute to three years ago when counsel told the company that there was a "5% chance" of losing, which caused a $50,000 liability to be accrued. What if counsel decided that *really* there was a 10% chance of losing and the company should really set up $100,000 as the liability. Who in the world is smart enough to tell whether the probabilities of losing a specific lawsuit are 5% or 10%? As Don Adams used to say on *Get Smart*, Would you believe 15%?

If the Board insists on quantifying the FV of very uncertain items, then companies will be under pressure to maximize the dollar amount of those liabilities, absent a constraint placed by debt covenants relative to debt/equity levels and working capital requirements.

REGULATORY RESPONSE TO THE POTENTIAL FOR MANIPULATION

This potential for manipulation—by inflating the probability of loss—is fully appreciated by the members and staff of the FASB. In other words, the scenario we painted—of urging outside counsel to be conservative in their evaluation of potential losses—is known. The standard setters are under no illusions as to what incentive companies may have under their new approach.

When asked about this abuse potential, the response of the Board members seems to revolve around two areas:

1. Companies are responsible for their own financial reports and they have a responsibility to "get it right." Looked at a different

way, the FASB can "only write the rules" and it is up to companies to appropriately apply those rules.

2. Auditors will have to sign off on the company assertions, while auditors themselves will have the Securities and Exchange Commission (SEC) and Public Company Accounting Oversight Board (PCAOB) looking over their shoulder.

It is interesting that at times the FASB, despite the injunction to have "principles-based" rules, nonetheless adopts very specific antiabuse rules. An example of this is the absolute restriction on not using a blockage discount in valuing a large block of a single security. Economically, if someone wanted to sell a large block in the open market, the price would in practice go down. But, afraid of abuse, the new rule in SFAS 157 simply says "No blockage discounts, period."

In the case of estimating liabilities, however, the Board is shrugging their collective shoulders and saying, in effect, "Okay, you guys figure it out. We only write the rules." Trust me, companies *will* figure it out and, as a consequence, many academics and financial journalists will be pointing with alarm at the manipulation potential.

Even worse is going to be the ability of the SEC and the PCAOB when they audit the auditors a year or two later, to "second guess" the company for its contemporaneous judgments.

In every valuation report ever prepared there is at least one professional judgment that cannot be proven beyond a doubt. People can question an appraiser about his sources of information. One can choose to disagree with the professional judgments that were applied. But at the end of the day, it ultimately boils down to the issue as to whether the reader agrees or disagrees with the conclusion.

A reader cannot state that an appraiser is right or wrong. Absent intent to deceive, an appraiser's judgment, at the time it is made, is just that—an opinion or judgment. It ultimately is no different than two friends disagreeing on who is going to win the Super Bowl. Before the game, there are two separate opinions or judgment. When the game is over, one will have been right and the other wrong. But that does not mean that the loser's judgment, made before the game, was inappropriate.

The same thing holds true for estimating the future outcome of a lawsuit prior to trial. If the SEC/PCAOB review is made *after* settlement, it is easy to show that the company, appraiser, and/or auditor were wrong. But that is simply hindsight. The real issue is what should have been booked *prior* to settlement. And, in the final analysis, that has to be someone's judgment.

AUDITING OF VALUATION REPORTS

One of the most contentious areas in the professional practice of valuation is that a company's auditors review the work of an outside specialist. Auditing standards mandate that if the company has relied on an outside professional, such as an appraiser or actuary, then the auditor must satisfy himself as to the qualifications of the specialist. Further, if the financial impact of the appraisal is material to the company's financial report, the auditor has to perform substantive tests. So, for an actuarial report, the auditor would look at the rates chosen to assume future earnings on the assets, the future salary progression, turnover, and so forth.

In the case of an actuarial report, the auditor probably would not replicate the technical valuation formulas but would look to see if the interest and discount rates are market based and whether the company history supports the turnover rate and salary progression. If the auditor felt that the assumptions were reasonable, then he would assume that the client's use of the actuarial report was in accordance with Generally Accepted Accounting Principles (GAAP) and fairly presented the results of operations and future liabilities.

Of course, if the auditor disagrees with the actuarial assumptions, he is free to challenge the resulting pension expense. It is beyond the scope of this book as to how such disagreements ultimately get resolved. The choices are somewhat limited. The auditor can tell the client to go get another actuarial report; the actuary can change the assumptions; or, finally, the auditor does not sign off on the audit and the company has to engage a new auditor.

In one respect, actuarial reports and appraisal reports are very similar—in both, the professional exercises judgment, and the choice of variables or assumptions ultimately impacts the final answer.

In the author's opinion, the range of assumptions required to perform a valuation assignment is greater than those required for a pension report. There are different assumptions about the relevant market, the market participants, future operating results, risk factors affecting the discount rate, and overall economic events.

To perform a proper valuation, an appraiser has to make an assumption about future income tax rates. Who will be writing the tax rules in Congress four years from now? Who will be president, and will he (or she) sign that tax bill? What will happen to foreign tax credits? On any one of those issues and many others, reasonable people will disagree, yet a change in any of the assumptions will significantly affect the final indication of value.

Most readers will understand the issues discussed here, so there is no need to elaborate. The bottom line is that auditors and appraisers often find themselves disagreeing about the final FVs developed by the appraiser. And, more often than not, the differences in opinion have to be considered material by any standard of materiality.

In practice, auditors send appraisers a detailed list of questions regarding the report. The answers to those questions are then reviewed and a second list of questions and disagreements developed. Then there is a round of discussions on the telephone, followed by more questions and more responses. Meanwhile, of course, the client is paying for the time of the appraiser and the time of the auditor.

We have seen more than one case in our own practice, and anecdotally have confirmed this with numerous other valuations specialists that the client is billed *more* for the auditor's review than the appraiser billed initially. The former chief auditor of the PCAOB made a speech once that indicated that, at least in his opinion, valuations really could not be audited because so much of the answer is judgmental. Nonetheless, auditors continue to try and audit the work of appraisal specialists.

What happens in practice, after significant resources have been expended, is that if the auditor and the appraiser disagree, the client is left to make the decision. Of course, the auditor has the final threat; their ultimate argument is that they won't certify the financials unless their perception of FV is adopted. But few valuation arguments actually are so significant that an auditor would be compelled to resign if the client disagreed with their position.

> **Recommendation:** Any time a valuation report is needed for financial reporting, make sure that the auditors and the appraisers are on the same page. Financial reports are the responsibility of the company, and that means financial executives must take an active role in monitoring and supervising the work of outside consultants.

There is no perfect solution to this disagreement regarding professional judgment of two separate organizations. We have found in our practice something that alleviates many of the problems but does not make them go away. This is to have an initial meeting, prior to commencement of the valuation assignment, among the company, the auditor, and the appraiser. The purpose of the meeting is to get agreement on (1) the scope of the valuation work; (2) the methodologies to be utilized; and (3) the basic assumptions regarding sales growth, profitability, and so forth. Getting agreement in advance among all the parties does not preclude the auditor from undertaking his required skeptical approach to review. It does preclude many of the types of disagreements that in total require the work to be done over, and an often tripling of the total costs to the company.

VALUATION OF CONTINGENT PAYMENTS

In many merger transactions the two parties cannot agree about the future prospects of the seller, sometimes referred to as the *target*. In a typical scenario, of course, the seller will be very optimistic about its growth prospects. The buyer is usually skeptical about meeting those sales and earnings goals.

The seller wants to be paid on the basis of what he is sure will turn out to be true, while the buyer does not want to commit dollars today for something that has not yet occurred. The answer—and it is a common one—is for the buyer to pay a base price today and an additional amount in the future *if* the seller's projections are met. If the seller's projections are not met, then the original purchase price stands. If they are met, it means the deal turned out well; the buyer is happy to pay for the incremental revenue and profits.

Under the accounting rules in effect for many years, any payments made to the sellers subsequent to the original transaction were treated simply as goodwill. With goodwill not being subject to amortization, in effect there was no accounting impact as a result of such subsequent payments. In theory, after the payment, there was an increase in goodwill on the books, and thus a greater possibility of an impairment charge. In practice, this was not true because the better-than-expected results (which caused the additional payout) virtually precluded any potential impairment. Impairment testing is covered in more detail in Chapter 9.

Under the new rules set forth in 141 R, the entire ball game is changing. The magnitude of the change is about the same as if the NFL said that from here forward field goals scored 4 points and touchdowns only 5 points. You could still play the game, but the coaches' strategy would certainly change if the scoring were changed. Similarly, the FASB is now changing the scoring of business combinations.

Under the new approach, the FASB is requiring the buyer to estimate what the subsequent contingent payout is likely to be. This is set up as a liability. When the final amount(s) are determined, there will either be a credit to income (if the amount were overestimated) or a charge to income (if the amount were underestimated). How will companies estimate the future payout?

Clearly, there will be pressure to estimate a high potential payout, just as there is the same pressure in the case of legal liabilities. There is, however, one significant difference between estimating the dollar amount of contingent payouts and estimating the potential cost of possibly losing a lawsuit.

In the case of the lawsuit, essentially the only people qualified to provide an estimate are corporate counsel who are involved in the litigation. In theory, a company could go to an outside attorney and ask for his professional judgment about the odds of the company prevailing or losing. This would be equivalent to a second opinion, often sought by patients facing a serious operation. In any event, nobody expects management to have the requisite professional expertise to accurately estimate such liabilities.

When we look at trying to estimate contingent payments for a recently completed business combination, the burden of proof is on management itself. They participated in the negotiations. They had their own projections. They did not believe the seller's projections, hence the way the deal was ultimately structured, which involved the contingent payout.

Now the FASB is telling management "You couldn't agree with the sellers on the outcome over the next two or three years, but now tell us just what you think will really happen." The only reasonable answer, if management is to maintain creditability, is to say that their own projections were accurate and they don't think there will be a payout. But the sellers could have been correct, and a payoff is not only possible but perhaps even likely. In fact, the buyer may have used his economic position to cram down a pessimistic projection, with the seller agreeing on a lower initial price, hoping that the contingent payout formula will, in practice, work out favorably in total.

Management will appear to face an unpleasant choice. It can stick to its guns; management can say they do not believe there will be a further payout. If it does this and the seller does earn additional compensation, then the future P&L is going to take a big hit, as is intended under the new rules.

Alternatively, management can say, "Okay, there may be a future payment, but if we and the seller can't agree, how can anyone come up with a specific amount? The two parties to the agreement are the most knowledgeable in the world, and if we can't agree, who can tell us better?" In this case, the answer is simple and clear.

Appraisers can, and do, determine estimates of Fair Market Value (FMV) even when the parties to a transaction themselves do not agree. Many privately held companies have so-called buy and sell agreements, whereby if one party wants out, the other partners or investors have to buy him out. In many such situations the potential seller thinks the business is worth a lot, and the prospective buyers typically are pessimistic. In divorce situations this also holds true, with husbands who run the business coming up with low estimates of value, while wives believe the business has unlimited potential.

The fact that parties to a transaction disagree, however, does not preclude an independent third party from making an objective assessment and determining a supportable estimate of FMV. Appraisers do this all the time, and if the assignment is carried out professionally and objectively, then the final answer usually becomes the basis for resolving the disagreement. The two key aspects of this approach are that the appraiser is truly independent and the work product is

> **Recommendation:** In a business combination it is all right for the parties to agree to disagree about the potential earnings that the seller's business can generate in the future. A contingent payout makes good sense. For purposes of complying with GAAP, however, and to avoid unfavorable future charges to income, an independent appraiser should be retained, after the deal is consummated, to determine a supportable estimate of what the payout, if any, is most likely to be.

totally professional; that is to say, the appraiser does not favor one party or the other.

If an appraiser can determine FMV in a divorce situation or for a buy and sell arrangement, there is every reason to believe he can independently assess the likelihood of a contingent payout's being made; he can also determine what the magnitude of any such payment might be. How does an appraiser do this when, as we have seen, the parties themselves cannot agree?

Without going into too much detail about valuation methodology, suffice it to say that the valuation specialist would look at the projections prepared by each side, evaluate both, perform an independent economic and market analysis, and arrive at a professional judgment as to the most likely outcome. The answer might be expressed as a range, rather than a specific single value expectation. But that range would be far narrower than the extremes previously developed by each party.

In the situation where the parties cannot agree on the outcome, and despite negotiation there is still a wide disparity, the contingent payout approach is highly workable and can be recommended. But an accounting entry is still required, and the least supportable approach would be for the buyer simply to book an amount halfway between the two parties. It is unlikely that such an approach would stand up to SEC scrutiny, and hence most auditors would balk at a formulistic approach.

It may sound self-serving, but appraisers are in the business today—and have been for years—of resolving this determination of the true FMV.

ENVIRONMENTAL LIABILITIES

In terms of the valuation of liabilities, called for in SFAS 141 R, we have covered legal contingencies and contingent payments, which depend on how well the acquired company performs. There is a third type of liability that should be covered, and that deals with environmental liabilities. As we have seen, placing a dollar amount on potential legal liabilities requires the input of corporate counsel. In the case of estimating the costs of future environmental factors, both management and appraisers have to defer to professional environmental engineering firms.

There are two types of environmental costs that should be reviewed. The first is where, under current law, the company is considered a potentially responsible party. Here, it is clear that environmental damage has been done and will have to be cleaned up. What is not necessarily clear, however, is (1) how much it will cost to clean up; (2) who will pay what share of the ultimate cost; and (3) when the payments will have to be made. An example would be contaminated land where, over the years, several companies had manufacturing operations.

The second cost is related to future outlays required once a business operation ceases. An example here would be ultimate disposal costs for shutting down a nuclear generating plant.

We cannot go into the detailed accounting requirements that have been mandated for environmental liabilities, but we do discuss the valuation issues.

In dealing with pensions expense, companies have to use the services of outside consulting actuaries. For environmental expenses, most firms have used, or will use, independent third-party environmental consultants. Appraisers are not necessarily competent in this area and probably cannot, on their own, determine the FV of environmental liabilities. The ultimate dollar value placed on the environmental liabilities of a seller in a business combination will significantly affect the overall valuation. As with the case of the other liabilities discussed, any overaccrual will ultimately be reversed, while an underaccrual will cause future charges to income to be incurred.

Many people believe that, over time, environmental requirements are likely to grow stricter, causing the cost of remediation to increase. For this reason, very conservative assumptions about environmental liabilities are not likely to be challenged by auditors, the SEC, and the PCAOB, as long as there is a good written record, setting forth the assumptions. Keep in mind that you cannot accrue today for costs that possibly will be mandated in the future. Your estimate of liability has to be based on today's rules and today's knowledge. Within those parameters, however, there should be significant scope for conservatism.

One fear often expressed by companies is, "If we disclose today an estimate of our future payments, won't this tip off the other side as to how much we are willing to settle for? Aren't we laying out a road map for the government?" The answer is probably yes, if a company has only one environmental problem or one lawsuit.

Fortunately, or unfortunately perhaps, most companies are involved in numerous lawsuits at any point in time and will probably have more than one environmental issue. In such circumstances, the disclosure footnote probably can be written in such a way as to avoid tipping off the other side. Having said that, there will be circumstances occasionally where there is only one issue, and disclosure may be highly detrimental.

All we can say is that issue was thought of by the FASB in their deliberations. It was brought to their attention in numerous communications from business. The FASB decided on the current rules irrespective of adverse comments from their constituents.

We are not advocates of having the federal government set accounting standards and rules. Just look at what Congress and the IRS have brought us in the tax arena. Having said that, some complaints by business about the adverse impact of accounting rules, complaints that the FASB decides not to honor might receive *more* attention in the political arena. There are a number of observers who at least have speculated that perhaps accounting is too important to leave in the hands of the accountants at the FASB. While no definitive answer is possible, even having such a thought should provoke discussion.

CHAPTER 7

Fair Value; Property, Plant, And Equipment; And Sarbanes-Oxley

Financial executives and their advisers are aware of the greatly heightened scrutiny their financial statements are receiving. This is directly as a result of the Sarbanes-Oxley Act (SOX), which was passed by Congress following the series of financial reporting scandals including Enron, MCI, and WorldCom. While there are many good books that cover SOX in detail, and we recommend one specifically,[1] this chapter will cover a major aspect of SOX that relates to Fair Value (FV).

While sound internal controls have always been a requirement, with SOX these necessary controls are being scrutinized as never before. Not only do the controls have to be in place and management attest that the controls are working, outside auditors now must certify that, in their judgment, the controls are working. This, in turn, has led to some extraordinarily high expenses. Congress, the Securities and Exchange Commission (SEC), and the Public Company Accounting Oversight Board (PCAOB) have all been wrestling with how to reduce the resources devoted to SOX implementation, while still keeping the acknowledged benefits attributable to good controls.

In this chapter we cover only one limited aspect of internal controls, and that is property, plant, and equipment (PP&E). Many companies, and some auditors, tend to diminish the importance of controls over PP&E, with the notable exception of personal computers (PCs).

---

[1]Scott Green, *Manager's Guide to the Sarbanes-Oxley Act*. Hoboken, NJ: John Wiley & Sons, 2004.

With regard to auditing of FV, we draw on our personal experience as well as that of numerous other valuation specialists. Almost all appraisers have the same criticisms of how auditors review the work of a valuation specialist. That may not seem particularly important to financial officers, but it does impact them directly because of the excessive time charged and the consequent increased audit fees. Prejudging our conclusion, we believe that auditors, by and large, spend a disproportionate amount of billable time, and hence audit fees, on unnecessary work. We discuss how management can reduce such non-value-added effort.

REQUIRED CONTROLS OVER PP&E

The PCAOB, in its Auditing Standard AS2, had the following to say about fixed assets:

> ¶66. *For example, in a financial statement audit, the auditor might not consider the fixed asset accounts significant when there is a low volume of transactions and when inherent risk is assessed as low, even though the balances are material to the financial statements. Accordingly, he or she might decide to perform only substantive procedures on such balances. In an audit of internal control over financial reporting, however, such accounts are significant accounts because of their materiality to the financial statements.*

There is a very good reason why we are discussing PP&E in a book about Fair Value. This is because in a business combination, a merger-and-acquisition (M&A) transaction to use the common description, all PP&E is revalued. But the process of performing this revaluation comes up short, in many situations, because of inadequate property records related to the seller's PP&E.

Up until about 1995, accounting systems for property records were definitely a mainframe computer project. PCs had not yet developed to the point where they could comfortably handle the massive detail in a typical record. Mainframe fixed-asset software was expensive, difficult to manipulate, and often updated only once a year or once a quarter.

Starting out with a "clean" property record in the mainframe era was difficult because the original records typically were on index cards, posted by hand. Over the years, sad to say, the best and brightest accountants were hardly ever assigned to fixed-asset controls. Budgeting, cost accounting, and financial reporting all seemed to have a higher priority and be more important. Further, even if there were significant errors in the property record, most auditors did not really get concerned.

Errors in a property record do tend to self-correct over time. If an asset on the books was missing, no one might be aware of this. Yet the annual depreciation charge would be automatically calculated and reported until the asset was fully depreciated or written down to salvage value. So even if there were an underlying error, the profit-and-loss (P&L) statement from year to year was not impacted. Auditors typically, in their annual management letters, urged the company to "take a physical inventory of your fixed assets," but few companies were prepared to take the time and incur the expense. For most companies, the easy way out was to add new PP&E purchases to the record, calculate annual depreciation charges, and, if notified, remove from the records assets that were sold or retired.

As more and more companies became involved in M&A activity, and APB 16 and then SFAS 141 were applied, we had a different situation. The newly acquired assets in a merger would be valued at the then-current Fair Market Value (now Fair Value), while the old assets on the *buyer's* books would continue to be carried forward at original cost. Fixed-asset records were now more confusing than ever, with some items valued currently and others at whatever amount had been applied when acquired.

Further, controls over PP&E in most companies are weak. Assets can be moved, rebuilt, traded in, and abandoned, often with virtually no notification to the accounting department. Since the individual charged with the responsibility for fixed assets is often either the newest recruit to the accounting department, or good old Sam about to retire, accounting control over PP&E has generally received little attention.

Now a brief digression as to how appraisers value machinery and equipment: Appraisers often will determine from a manufacturer the cost today to acquire a piece of equipment with the same capacity and output. This "replacement cost new" is then lowered by the appraiser's best estimate of depreciation existing on the asset being valued. Appraisers essentially look at the physical condition of the asset, the functional or technological obsolescence, and at times on broader economic conditions affecting the asset's utility. This replacement cost new less depreciation appears to meet the FASB's market participant approach because the valuation specialist actually goes out to the market and determines actual transaction prices, exactly what the FASB puts forth as their Level 1 and Level 2 for FV.

This approach is the "gold standard" for valuation, but as with any item made with gold, it is costly. Appraisers have, over the years, developed shortcuts that involve the application of cost or price indexes to the original cost. Taking milling machines as an example, one can utilize existing indexes or develop a new index that is applied to the original cost and year of acquisition. If you know that a milling machine cost $175,000 in 1995, and 13 years later a new comparable machine sells for 137% of the 1995 price (assume, say, an index of 142% for a 1994 acquisition), then the replacement cost new would be shown as $240,000 (175,000 × 1.37). The appraiser would subtract an appropriate allowance for depreciation from all causes, and that would be considered the current FV.

Obviously, this approach *depends on the accuracy of the original record and the validity of the index*. Many indexes used by appraisers have been developed either by the government or by trade associations; hardly ever is there an indication of bias within the indexes commonly utilized.

The problem arises from the accuracy of the cost base and date of acquisition shown on the company's books. What often happens is that Business A acquires Business B and determines the then-current FV. Those amounts are now shown on the buyer's books with the acquisition date being the date of the merger, and the "cost" really being the then-current FV. Now if Business A in turn is sold five years later, an appraiser trying to use indexes is stymied. There are no known indexes that adjust for changes in FV. And a cost index or sales price index really can properly be applied only to an original cost and date.

Consequently, in many business combinations, it is impractical to try and develop FVs by indexing original cost, because the original cost is no longer available. The only date in the property record is the merger date, not the date when the asset was acquired from the manufacturer. Without an original cost and an original date, indexing really does not work.

That forces the acquiring company to do one of two things. Either they pay a relatively high professional fee for an appraiser to do a proper valuation, going to manufacturers as discussed above, or, if that is too expensive or not considered cost-effective, what many companies do is simply carry forward the dollar amounts on the seller's books.

The assumption being made is either (1) the old costs are close enough to current FV; or (2) if the old costs were good enough before, they are good enough today. Fortunately, there is some validity in this approach. As a broad generalization, often a detailed physical inventory followed by a proper valuation will develop overall totals for PP&E that are not all that far off from the carrying value on the seller's books.

The reason for this phenomenon is often quite simple. Many companies have significant amounts of fully depreciated assets on their books that have zero or, at most, a nominal book value. Inasmuch as they are still being utilized, they have significant FV to the buyer, so putting an appropriate FV on such assets essentially provides a gain for the buyer. It is not unusual for 10%, 15%, or even 20% of productive equipment still to be used even though the original life of the asset for tax and accounting purposes has come and gone.

Offsetting this gain is the fact that when complete physical inventories of fixed assets are taken, there are often significant dollar amounts that simply cannot be found or at least identified. It would be rare for a heavy machine tool to literally be stolen. Rather, sloppy paperwork over the years brings about a substantial disconnect between what is on the property records and what is actually out on the shop floor. Unrecorded retirements, trade-ins, transfers, and rebuilding by creative shop mechanics cause items no longer to be where the records say they are located.

Most experienced production executives do not worry about this, as long as actual production output is not adversely affected. Auditors usually do not worry about inaccuracies in PP&E accounts because the expiration of time, annual depreciation charges, will ultimately solve the problem. The only time management or auditors worry about fixed assets is when a PC goes missing. A hue and cry goes up, "Let's account for all our PCs." Over time, a lot of PCs do seem to have "walked out" with former employees or to have been traded in on new models surreptitiously.

A good recommendation for many clients is to have a minimum capitalization policy of $5,000 or $10,000 and expense everything acquired under those amounts. Under this policy, then, PCs would not even be in the PP&E record. You do not have to have an asset on the fixed-asset register in order to control it. It is possible to keep a separate inventory of PCs by serial number and person responsible if management feels the problem is sufficiently serious to commit out-of-pocket resources to this control. The old adage about being "penny wise and pound foolish" still applies to PP&E. The time saved in not attempting to control minor items can then be spent making sure that all entries are self-explanatory. For example, we all too often see huge building additions being entered as a single line item, "Building addition, 2002, $3,598,366.09." Five years later, we defy anyone to identify just what that represents and what is the true FV.[2]

Now to get back to the PCAOB and their requirement that auditors in fact should pay attention to fixed assets. A good property record system will accomplish a lot of goals. Among these are:

- Improved information for calculating return on investment (ROI).
- Lower property taxes.
- Lower insurance premiums.
- Optimized depreciation for income tax purposes.
- Correct internal controls.

BENEFITS OF A GOOD PROPERTY RECORD SYSTEM

Many companies measure operating performance utilizing an ROI analysis. While cost accountants can attempt to define the return part of an ROI calculation (usually some form of operating income), the investment part of the ratio relies on the Balance Sheet. Allocating

---

[2]To see the validity for yourself, ask your accounting department to sort in descending order all the items in the property register. Then obtain a printout of the first two or three pages and the last two or three pages. This exercise should convince most executives that property records have, over time, not received sufficient resources.

receivables and inventory to specific operating units is straightforward and requires little judgment. Allocating PP&E, which often is the major component of an asset base, requires accurate property records.

Further, it is desirable that the investment base is developed on true FVs. The reason is often pointed out by professors and other theorists. If you have two divisions essentially operating at the same revenue and profit levels, there will be significant differences in ROI if one unit has old and nearly fully depreciated assets, while the other is operating a recently acquired facility where all the assets on the books are already on an FV basis. The ROI calculation is very sensitive to the denominator, which is the investment base. If one general manager has old assets that were never revalued upward and the other general manager is operating with revalued assets, improper conclusions can be drawn. This is not a theoretical problem for companies using ROI as a performance measure.

Accurate property records are essential if one utilizes ROI to measure performance because, as we have seen, many companies have fully depreciated assets, while others may have what we refer to as "ghost assets." *Ghost assets* is the term that Marshall & Stevens, Inc., uses for missing assets. There can be any number of reasons, many quite benign, why ghost assets are still on the books and not part of current production. But for comparative measurement purposes, operating executives *should* be charged for all the assets they are actually using, and *should not* be charged for assets not there. If a company is really serious about relying on ROI for performance evaluation, then it behooves management to clean up the property register and, ideally at least, have all the assets at FV.

Keep in mind that most fixed-asset accounting systems have multiple columns, so you can show current FV in a column and still retain the information required for current GAAP reports. Since companies can write down assets but can never write them up, if one is going to use FV for the investment base, it is necessary to set up a memo column in the property record system.

To show that this is not some theoretical solution, searching for a problem to solve, readers should keep in mind that up-to-date insurance values and property tax values are each a (separate) measure of FV. Many companies update these FV information fields annually with the help of valuation firms.

Lower property taxes not only are a benefit to having good property records, but in some cases companies deliberately incur out-of-pocket costs to develop accurate property records at FV. Remember that FV for property taxes will differ from, and probably be less than, FV for insurance.

Most taxing jurisdictions rely on self-reporting of new capital assets. These new expenditures this year are then added by the county or municipality to previous acquisitions. Taxing bodies almost invariably each year apply cost indexes to the PP&E reported in previous years.

Consequently, if a company has ghost assets and removes them from the books, this information can be reported to the taxing authorities, with a consequent reduction in property taxes. The cost of an inventory of fixed assets, with consequent straightening out of the property record and removal of ghost assets, often pays for itself in a very short time period.

Going one step further, if a company has supportable property records at current FVs, this provides a sound basis for appealing the municipalities' assessment. The basic principle of property taxes, often referred to as *ad valorem* (literally, *at value)* taxes, is that the tax base for all taxpayers must be on a level playing field, and that playing field is supposed to be FV or, technically, Fair Market Value (FMV), the definition used outside of GAAP.

Cost indexes applied for a number of years cumulatively will probably overstate the current FV of assets. This is because no index can properly take account of technological changes. The true FV of a specific asset will be affected when "new and better" assets are developed and available for purchase. However, the cost index can reflect only the cost today to buy the *old* asset, not a new and improved model that reduces operating costs or increases productivity.

Any company wishing to challenge property tax assessments must present evidence of the *current FMV.* Obviously, if your FMV is *above* the assessment, most people stop right there and would not think of appealing. But how do you know what the FMV of PP&E is? Property records based on original costs, or recently allocated costs following an M&A transaction, will not tell you the relationship of FMV to book values. The only way to make the preliminary judgment whether to appeal has to be based on knowledge, or at least an informed estimate, of the potential savings from a successful appeal of the current assessment.

Insurable values, and hence property insurance expense, can be optimized only with full knowledge of (1) what is there and (2) what it is worth today (i.e., FMV). As with property taxes, keeping ghost assets on the book is dangerous to your financial health.

Few companies want to overinsure their assets. At least in theory, insurance companies will not reimburse a loss (e.g., caused by a flood or fire) for more than you lost. Actually, the appraisal profession started over 100 years ago specifically to develop insurable values and provide information for proof of loss in case of a disaster.

The one thing that has changed, particularly for very large companies, is the prior agreement between the insured and carrier on an agreed value. In effect, the parties are saying, "If we have a loss, you will pay us $X, and in turn we will pay premiums on $X." This obviates the need both for determining the FMV of PP&E and having on hand the data necessary to file a claim for proof of loss.

Smaller companies usually have neither the quality of records nor the financial strength to develop agreed values. Further, without serious negotiations, and a full knowledge of how insurance companies work, it is not a foregone conclusion that agreed values actually lower insurance premium expense.

Optimizing income taxes is one of the few universal goals among companies, and particularly among financial officers. It is interesting that when appraisal firms perform an allocation of purchase price (SFAS 141) for privately held companies, the owners always want to maximize the dollars assigned to PP&E and minimize the dollars assigned to intangible assets.

Privately held companies want to lower out-of-pocket cash disbursements for taxes and don't care nearly as much about reported financial income, particularly since they view GAAP as an artificial construct of the FASB and the SEC. By and large, privately held companies focus on cash flow, not reported income. By putting more dollars against fixed assets that can be depreciated fairly quickly, as contrasted with intangible assets that have a 15-year life for taxes, cash is saved.

To the contrary, publicly held companies, by and large, focus on reported GAAP income and pay their taxes as they come due. Public company treasurers and controllers, focusing on earnings per share

(EPS), always want the maximum amount that the appraiser can squeeze out to go to nonamortizable goodwill. While book and tax allocations, in theory, do not have to be the same, most companies use more or less the same allocation assumptions for GAAP income and for taxable income. Putting more dollars into goodwill may increase income taxes payable in the early years, but it certainly will have a beneficial impact on reported income and EPS.

In this book we do not urge private companies to focus on GAAP and EPS; neither do we want public companies necessarily to reduce reported income in order to save modestly on taxes payable. Virtually all finance and management professors and textbooks tell readers to maximize cash flow, disregard reported income, and let the chips fall where they may. This exhortation not only is interesting, but is probably correct—at least in theory.

For some strange reason, however, our clients in public companies, while giving lip service to cash flows, invariably are really focused on EPS. Wall Street and company management both have one goal in mind: to raise the stock price. As long as security analysts hyperventilate when a company misses the analysts' estimated EPS by even one cent, managers are going to go along with the game and focus on just that—EPS.

On a direct basis, the most perfect property records are probably not going to enhance EPS, other than for the potential savings in property taxes and insurance. So we are not encouraging companies that are fixated on EPS necessarily to devote massive resources to the controls over fixed assets, no matter what SOX says.

Yet there is one surefire way to both reduce taxes and increase EPS. This is to have a cost segregation study performed on one's buildings. The IRS allows companies to depreciate their assets over the useful life of the asset. For a building, taken as a whole, there is a 39-year life applied to the structure.

Many companies simply add up the total cost of a building and then depreciate that total amount over the 39-year period. The same is true of existing structures acquired at FV in a business combination or simply acquired in the marketplace in an outright purchase. Land, of course, is never depreciable for either books or taxes; sometimes it is necessary to allocate the total value of the land and building into the two distinct assets.

What is not generally known or utilized is that just as you can allocate a real estate purchase between land and the building, you can also allocate the *components* of a building. That is, you can break down the total cost of the building into such elements as heating, ventilation, and air conditioning (HVAC); elevators; and nonstructural partitions. Each of these elements is assigned its own tax life, in accordance with IRS regulations; these lives are invariably shorter than 39 years, thus accelerating the timing of depreciation charges.

The net savings and impact on cash flow and earnings comes from speeding up the timing of the depreciation charge, inasmuch as the total building cost remains fixed. The concept is that a dollar of depreciation today, reducing today's tax payments, is worth much more than the same dollar deducted only 15 years or even 38 years from now. In short, it is the time value of money that benefits from depreciation calculated under a cost segregation study.

Estimating the dollar savings from a cost segregation study can be performed rapidly and at virtually no out-of-pocket expense; professionals who specialize in this work and provide accurate estimates of the savings usually will do so as part of their business development. We strongly recommend that a cost segregation study be done for almost all commercial and industrial buildings. Further, while not usually included in a typical Due Diligence study, there is no reason to overlook the potential savings.

SUMMARY AND CONCLUSIONS

For all manufacturing firms and many commercial and industrial businesses, real estate and machinery are a major part of the Balance Sheet, comprising a substantial portion of total assets. Over time, these assets—machinery and equipment as well as buildings—have not received sufficient management attention. Companies put far more effort into controlling inventory and receivables, and auditors typically tend to assume that fixed assets will take care of themselves through the expiration of time and corresponding depreciation charges.

SOX and the PCAOB's interpretation in Auditing Standards 2 now require much more management attention to this asset base. It is only a matter of time before auditing firms, as part of their Section 404 review, start to test controls over fixed assets.

Historically, management attention has been elsewhere, with the consequence that property records often do not reflect the underlying assets they purport to cover. In turn, poor property records may lead to overpayment of both property taxes and insurance premiums.

A good property record system, properly maintained, with reference to both original cost and date of acquisition, as well as current FMV, will go a long way toward meeting the multiple requirements of owning and operating PP&E. The cost of putting existing poor property records into shape is far from a trivial exercise and requires the commitment of substantial effort and resources. The benefits are twofold. There will be direct cash savings in property taxes and insurance. Cost segregation studies will further accelerate the timing of depreciation expense.

The second benefit is the knowledge that the company is in full compliance with the internal control regulations of SOX. Given where the courts, the PCAOB, and the SEC are going, it will never be too soon to ensure that these controls are in place.

CHAPTER 8

Allocation Of Purchase Price in a Business Combination

This chapter discusses what accounting entries are required for a business combination. In order to comply with current Financial Accounting Standards Board (FASB) requirements, all of the entries are supposed to be at Fair Value (FV). We describe what has to be done and what the FV implications are. Those with knowledge of the subject can skip this chapter, always being able to refer back in case of a specific question. We do not attempt, in this chapter, to discuss *how* appraisers determine the FV of each type of asset. This material was covered in detail in our recent book, *Fair Value for Financial Reporting*.[1]

If a company buys an existing 100,000-square-foot warehouse on five acres of land for $2 million, then somebody has to determine how much of the purchase price should be allocated to the building and how much to the land. The reason for this requirement is simple. Land is not depreciated. Dollars assigned to the building's value will have to be depreciated over its remaining future economic life, probably 39 years, which is the period required for tax accounting and usually chosen by companies for their Generally Accepted Accounting Principles (GAAP) financial report. How much of the $2 million is applied to each of the two categories is supposed to be at the FV of each of the two assets.

In theory, and in a perfect world, the FV of the land and the separately computed FV of the building should both add up to

---

[1]Alfred M. King, *Fair Value for Financial Reporting: Meeting the New FASB Requirements*. Hoboken, NJ: John Wiley & Sons, 2006.

or total exactly $2 million. A moment's reflection shows that the chance of two independently determined values adding up to an exact predetermined amount is remote. In practice, appraisers would value the land based on current transactions and subtract that from the $2 million to determine the building's value. Or the appraiser would value the building, perhaps on a cost-per-square-foot basis, and subtract that total from the $2 million to determine the value of the land. With one purchase price, and only two items to be valued, this method of subtraction will work.

If, on the other hand, a business buys another business, then each and every asset category, and liability category for that matter, has to be valued separately. In this case, we know the total will never balance out exactly to the purchase price. For purchase price allocations, it is goodwill that absorbs the positive or negative balance; the final sum of all the assets and liabilities, including goodwill, must sum up to the adjusted purchase price of the transaction.

ADJUSTED PURCHASE PRICE

When one company buys another, the buyer, in effect, steps into the shoes of the seller. This means that the buyer effectively is now responsible for the seller's liabilities. Taking on liabilities is conceptually identical to buying assets. For assets, you buy first and then pay for it. By assuming liabilities, you agree to pay, and then the cash is disbursed according to the payment schedule, even though no asset changes hands.

In valuing a business, therefore, the assumption of the seller's liabilities adds to the final total cash outlay just as does the payment for the seller's shares of stock you buy from the former shareholders. When the business press reports the size of merger-and-acquisition (M&A) transactions, they will often quote the price paid for the stock and then provide a second and larger number corresponding to the "assumption of liabilities."

In practice, it is assumed that most ongoing businesses have a standard amount of working capital, current assets less current liabilities; the net balance stays more or less constant. Individual inventory items and customer accounts receivable are continually turning over on a day-to-day basis as sales are made and cash is received. Similarly, accounts payable are created when assets are bought, paid off, and new payables created when the next vendor shipment is received.

For this reason, in an allocation the accounts payable and accrued liabilities must be valued and shown on the new starting Balance Sheet. But, essentially, it is only bank debt and long-term debt that are considered in estimating the adjusted purchase price. This is because an assumption is made that receivables and inventory balances in total remain more or less constant, as do the offsetting payables and accrued liabilities.

So, while the absolute balance of net working capital does enter into the final computation necessary for the beginning Balance Sheet, common usage tends to disregard working capital as an adjustment to the purchase price.

Under Statement of Financial Accounting Standards (SFAS) 141, and the new SFAS 141 R, which present the accounting rules for the allocation of purchase price in a business combination, the buyer is required to value *all* assets, and *all* liabilities, at FV. The final end product of this process is a starting Balance Sheet of the seller at the FV to the buyer. This new Balance Sheet will contain a lot of items that were not on the seller's books and may omit one or two items that were on the seller's financial statements.

With this adjusted purchase price in place, in the remainder of this chapter we briefly describe what appraisers do, and why they do it to arrive at the detailed required entries. This process of allocating a purchase price requires a lot of judgment and, in many cases, there can and will be substantial differences of opinion.

Readers should keep in mind that the ultimate responsibility for financial reporting is always with management. Management can hire valuation specialists to assist in the allocation. Unfortunately, in too many cases, reasonable people can differ in the determination of FV. So while the company has hired a valuation specialist, who provides his best professional judgment, ultimately, it is the independent auditor who has the last word. See Chapter 11 for a discussion of what types of disagreements there are among companies, auditors, and appraisers and how such differences should be resolved.

FINANCIAL PROJECTIONS

Most buyers conduct Due Diligence before making a final offer. The subject of Due Diligence in an FV environment is covered in Chapter 5. But here we make a key assumption: Prior to closing the transaction, and as part of any Due Diligence, the buyer will have a detailed projection of the seller's expected operating results. The reason is clear. It is unrealistic to assume that financial projections prepared by someone selling his business will be conservative. The higher the seller's projections, the higher the price the seller will ask. A seller's financial projections inevitably presuppose that everything will turn out for the best: All problems will be solved, competitors will not take any annoying actions, the economy will be rising without inflation, and so forth.

Buyers, knowing this, can do one of two things. They can simply discount the seller's projections, or they can make their own projections as the basis for subsequent negotiations on a final price.

Appraisers have to use projections in valuing certain of the intangible assets, such as customer relationships and technology. Both the values and the expected lives of the assets are impacted by the projections. Since the values developed by the appraiser will be challenged by the auditors, and sometimes the Securities and Exchange Commission (SEC) and the Public Company Accounting Oversight Board (PCAOB), it is critical that the projections utilized in the valuation process are the same as those that the buyer's board utilized in approving the deal. The projections may ultimately turn out better or worse than anticipated. That is relatively unimportant in the context of developing FV at the date of the transactions. What is important is that the information used be both contemporaneous and supportable. When an appraiser uses the *same* information that the buyer's board used, it greatly enhances the credibility of the value determinations.

A final use of contemporaneous projections comes into play in the context of an unresolved disagreement between the buyer and the seller about the outcome of the seller's business. Obviously, the seller is optimistic, and often the buyer is skeptical. The solution to this difference of opinion lies in a contingent future payment, the amount of which is a function of actual future operating results. So, many purchase contracts contain a section that spells out how much additional purchase price will be paid depending on the nature of the agreed-upon formula.

This contingent payout, a potential future liability, must be valued at the time of purchase according to SFAS 141 R. By definition, the parties could not agree on the outcome, and a contingent payment is the answer. But if this contingent payment itself has to be valued, how can the appraiser do something that the parties themselves could not agree on?

The answer is actually very easy. The appraiser looks at the two sets of projections, one relatively high and one relatively low, and in that case will probably make his own projections using his best professional judgment. This is discussed in more detail in Chapter 6. What is important here is that there exist fairly detailed projections prepared by the buyer's management in good faith. At that point, appraisers are comfortable relying on those projections. Absent those projections, the appraiser is in an almost untenable position.

FAIR VALUE OF WORKING CAPITAL

Once an appraiser has the total adjusted purchase price, he must go through the exercise of valuing *all* the acquired assets and liabilities. The net sum of these FVs is then compared to the adjusted purchase price, and the difference is considered, by definition, to be goodwill.

The first place most appraisers start is with current assets and current liabilities, the two components of working capital.

Cash is easy to value, and in almost all cases is carried forward from the company's books. Similarly, *marketable securities* will usually already be on the seller's books at FV, and the appraiser typically will not spend much time verifying such values. Any verification is really an audit function, and appraisers are not auditors.

Accounts receivable in most companies are shown on the basis of the face amount of the invoice to the customer. To the extent that a certain portion of receivables will not be collected, and will have to be written off as bad debts, companies usually set up a reserve for bad debts (or uncollectible accounts). The net of these two numbers is the accounts receivable balance. The reason for

> **Observation:** The distinction between auditing and valuation is sometimes lost sight of. Appraisers explicitly state in their valuation report that they will accept historical financial statements as accurately reflecting the underlying information. Appraisers do not verify the title to assets, the quantities of inventories, or the accuracy of the accounts receivable and payables. These are audit functions that are never performed by appraisers unless explicitly so stated.

setting up a reserve is simple: On day one, the company expects to collect all of its receivables; experience, however, tells us that some percentage simply will not be paid, for whatever reason. If you knew on the day of the sale that it would not be paid for, you would never have made the sale in the first place. But, statistically, there are always a certain number of customers who will go bankrupt or who complain about the delivery and quality of the product/service they bought and simply will not pay. Turning such accounts over to a collection agency costs something, as does filing for a court judgment. By far the simplest method of evaluating the collectability of receivables is to do it statistically, based on past performance and anticipated future results.

Unfortunately, the FASB in SFAS 157 and 141 R requires that the FV of *each* separate receivable balance be determined individually. The consequence is that the FASB does *not* allow a general reserve for uncollectible accounts to be carried forward. The practical impact of this rule is that the company or the appraiser will simply apply the normal percentage separately to each receivable. That means that for the first six months after the deal closes, the company will probably be receiving more than the dollar amount of the receivable on its books from most customers, offset by those few customers whose accounts ultimately have to be written off.

Inventories must be valued at FV, and this may involve some significant adjustments. For example, if a company uses last in, first out (LIFO), the IRS has a conformity requirement; this requires that amounts shown for taxes must also be reflected on the books. It is not clear how complying with the GAAP requirement to show the inventories at FV will or will not be in conflict with the conformity rule that is enforced by the IRS.

Leaving that issue aside, the rules in SFAS 141 R are clear that the buyer cannot have any inventory valuation reserves carried forward. This means that surplus and obsolete inventories will have to be written down to true current FV. Since there will be no profit-and-loss (P&L) impact because of this write-down, companies will want to be conservative.

For raw materials that turn over quickly, the FV will probably be the most recent acquisition price. For work in process, the FV may be close to the amounts on the seller's books, depending on the complexity of the situation, and the cycle time of production. Finished goods inventories may have to be written up to an amount equal to the anticipated selling price less all the costs of selling, including a return on the assets employed.

The revaluation of inventories may be fairly complex and time consuming. The implications for future reported earnings, particularly in the first year, suggest that significant attention and resources should be devoted to this task, both in the Due Diligence phase and after the transaction closes. The reason should be obvious. The higher the FV of the inventory, the greater will be the cost of goods sold when the corresponding sale is recorded. A higher cost of goods sold equals a lower gross profit; consequently, under this revaluation of inventory, operating margins are likely to be depressed for the first three to six months after a business is acquired. This point, unfortunately, often comes as a surprise to the buyer.

Current liabilities present few challenges in terms of determining FV. Assuming the seller has not been hiding invoices in desk drawers, then few areas of current liabilities present FV problems. Accruals for vacation will have to be recalculated, but this is not a usual task of appraisers.

The one bit of advice here is to be ultraconservative in evaluating liabilities. It is far better to record every conceivable future payment on the opening balance sheet than it is to recognize a prior year's expense after the closing. Because there are relatively few judgment areas in current liabilities, other than tax accruals, this is not an area that should require significant time commitment.

Tax accruals and deferred taxes are beyond the scope of this book. The determination of the proper tax accruals and/or tax assets is not really within the purview of valuation specialists. Rather, it is either the company's tax department that should review the tax position or, for smaller companies, the outside auditors who perform this function.

While the FASB and the SEC believe that tax accruals are pretty straightforward and require little judgment, there could, in fact, be a wide variance between the lowest and highest estimates. It is hard to specify in advance, because taxes are very much a basis of facts and circumstances; generally speaking, one should aim for opening entries that are as conservative as possible. Erring on the side of caution can only help future reported results because any mistake must be charged to P&L when discovered. If, subsequently, you find an error in the allocation, you are *not* allowed to go back and restate an opening Balance Sheet. If you did err on the side of caution, it means that ultimately you may have a small cushion rather than a debit to expense.

PROPERTY, PLANT, AND EQUIPMENT (PP&E)

The FV of PP&E could take an entire book of its own, if we were to go into the detail of how appraisers value different kinds of assets. For this chapter we only outline the techniques used so as to understand the basic valuation principles.

In many M&A transactions the buyer is specifically interested in acquiring the seller's production facilities. One reason is to expand capacity quickly. An opposite reason would be to shut them down to get rid of excess capacity in the industry. Often, there are more or less duplicate facilities, and the buyer must decide what to do with the newly acquired production capability.

If the buyer knows, on day one, that a specific facility is to be sold, then the FASB requires that it be valued on the basis of what it could be sold for to a third party. This involves an understanding of the difference between *value-in-use* and *value-in-exchange*. Value in-exchange is what most people think of as FV. You value your house on what it could be sold for. You value your car on what somebody would pay you to buy it. So if you buy a factory and plan to sell it, the appraiser has to determine what a different buyer would pay just for that one plant. There are valuation techniques that will provide appropriate answers, including looking at other transactions and auction prices for comparable equipment.

Value-in-use is a different concept that can best be described in the statement, "The whole is worth more than the sum of the parts." A plant that is producing a product that sells at a profit is more than just an accumulation of assets. First, the assets had to be assembled, installed, tested, and debugged. Workers had to be hired and trained. Design problems had to be worked out between the blueprints and the actual required product.

If you simply added up the current value of the individual tangible assets, the machine tools, conveyor belts, electrical installation, and so forth, you would probably come up with a value indication significantly *below* what the assembled assets are really worth. How do appraisers get around this issue?

The usual way of valuing PP&E on an individual, stand-alone basis is to use the cost approach. Appraisers ask what the asset would cost new, and then subtract for physical depreciation and functional obsolescence. To capture the value of the intangibles inherent in a smoothly running production operation may involve a financial analysis using the income approach or discounted cash flow analysis. These concepts are discussed in virtually every book on valuation, including the author's own book on FV for financial reporting.[2]

The issue is fairly simple to explain. If an assembled group of assets is producing net cash flows of $300,000 a year, and investors in similar facilities are looking for a 15% return on their investment, then one way of valuing the plant is to say it is worth $2 million because an investor would pay that much. There may be only $1.5 million of hard assets in the facility, but if the product line produced therein would belong to the buyer, then the facility could be sold for $2 million.

The opposite also holds true. In valuing any assets or group of assets where discrete cash flows can be identified, it is always necessary to test the values derived by the cost approach. The income or cash flows that the assets will generate must be sufficiently high to provide an adequate return on investment (ROI).

---

[2]Id.

> Productive assets (e.g., machinery and equipment) are never worth more than the income they can generate, based on required rates of return.

The preceding example can now be reworked with a simple change in assumptions. The cost of the assets, allowing for depreciation, is still $1.5 million. But if instead of generating $300,000 of net cash flow, the facility generated only $100,000, then would any investor buy the assets for $1.5 million? The answer is clear. To obtain a 15% ROI, one would never pay more than $667,000.

You have a facility with assets that individually add up to $1.5 million, based on the cost of replacement. But would anybody actually replace those assets (i.e., buy them) if one could generate only $100,000 a year of income? There is a critical piece of valuation theory here.

Another way to look at it is the fad of hula hoops. You could build a truly state-of-the-art factory, including the latest injection molding equipment, to produce plastic hula hoops at an absolute rock-bottom selling price. Nobody could compete with you on selling price. The trouble is that the demand for hula hoops is pretty low, and the factory, efficient as it is, simply would be run at best at a small fraction of its capacity. Value ultimately is based on the present value of future cash flows. Consequently, every valuation of machinery and equipment for any purpose whatsoever *must* be tested by looking at future cash flows.

VALUATION OF INTANGIBLES

Most financial executives are used to dealing with receivables, inventory, and real estate, and those in manufacturing are comfortable with machinery and equipment. The hardest concept to grasp is usually intangible assets. The FASB requires the buyer of another company to value the intangibles that were acquired. That is understandable.

What is not understandable to many operating executives is the distinction made by the FASB between acquired intangibles and self-developed intangibles. What is the difference between a competitor's trade name that you bought and now own and your own trade name for a directly competitive product line? The FV of the newer, and presumably less valuable, trade name that you just bought is now going to go on your Balance Sheet. Your own trade name, which in your mind is more valuable, appears nowhere in your own financial statements.

There appears to be a mismatch, from one perspective. The less valuable asset is on your Balance Sheet, while the more valuable asset is ignored. From another perspective, having an asset heading on your Balance Sheet called "Trade Name" that is incomplete and, in fact, deals with something you may not continue to use, seems to tell your shareholders less than nothing about the real value of your business.

This dilemma is fully recognized by almost all appraisers, most accountants, and some security analysts and is totally understood by the FASB and its staff. We cannot resolve these issues here; suffice it to say there is no really good solution. Going to a basis of valuing *all* assets at FV would resolve the issue described above, but would cause a totally different set of problems for analysts and shareholders in trying to understand the basic operations of a business. Changes in FV would likely swamp the results of operation and would lead to calls to go back to the good old days before FV.

At this point, one just has to accept that the new FV accounting model set forth in SFAS 157 and SFAS 141 R is a "work in progress." It is easy to criticize, but much harder to come up with a solution that is better than what we have today.

The valuation of intangibles effectively requires an analysis of future cash flows generated by the business entity. The real problem is that there usually is only one stream of cash flows, derived ultimately from sales to customers. But the FASB wants separate values assigned, say, to the trade name, the customer relationships, and the technology. It is possible to make assumptions about the relative contribution each separate intangible makes to the whole. But those assumptions are often arbitrary, and what an appraiser assumes may be challenged by an auditor who has a different idea.

DUPLICATE ASSETS—EXIT VALUE AND MARKET PARTICIPANTS

Many M&A transactions take place between direct competitors. The buyer believes it may be less expensive in the long run to acquire a competitor, rather than spending years, and millions of dollars, trying to increase market share. Assuming the deal passes the scrutiny of the Justice Department and the Federal Trade Commission (FTC) when two companies in the same industry merge, the allocation provides some very real—and often unanticipated—problems.

The buyer typically wants to sell to the customers he just acquired, but does not want to support two brand names. So, quite often, the buyer will simply decide to retire the seller's brand name. To the buyer, who already has an established brand name, the seller's brand has little or no value, other than perhaps on a defensive basis that no one else can use it either.

In SFAS 141 R, and building on the definition of FV in SFAS 157, the buyer must ascribe value to the seller's trade name *even if he does not plan to use it*. Worse, ascribing value to a trade name that won't be used means that the FV of that name one or two years from now is going to be drastically diminished.

Under current accounting rules, the buyer must ascribe value to assets that he will not use. Then, in the supreme irony, those values will have to be tested for impairment in subsequent periods and probably written off. The FASB's logic is impeccable; the result is usually unacceptable both to the acquiring company and to security analysts.

"Why must a buyer ascribe value to an asset that will not be used?" is the question that appraisers always receive. At the end of the day, all we can answer is, "That's what the FASB makes us do." The FASB's logic can be explained, even if one totally disagrees with it.

SFAS 157 says that the definition of FV is based on what an asset would sell for to a market participant. If one competitor buys another, the appraiser has to ask, "In this situation, who is a likely market participant that would acquire the seller's trade name and how much would he pay for it?" If the only possible market participant is considered to be another competitor in the same industry, and that company also would not use the trade name, then it is permissible to ascribe little or no value to the trade name.

But if the market participant is considered to be a private-equity firm—one that does not have its own trade name in that market space—then it is highly likely that such a buyer *would* continue to use the seller's trade name. The trade name would have value to some buyers and have no value to other buyers. This confirms a statement made in Chapter 1 that the same asset can have different values for different people or for different purposes.

Getting back to the specific allocation of purchase price, it makes a tremendous difference in the subsequent P&L of the acquiring company whether the market participant is considered to be a competitor or a private-equity firm. Unfortunately, in this day and age, private equity is buying almost any type of company, in any industry, and of any size. So it is difficult to make the case in a specific allocation of purchase price that the market participant is *only* an industry competitor and *not* a private-equity player. In practice, proving a negative is impossible; proving that a private-equity firm could not have bought the company just acquired by a competitor is almost impossible.

When SFAS 141 R becomes effective in 2009, there will be a lot of impairment charges within a year of many, if not most, acquisitions. The only solace is that the FASB is aware of this problem of instant impairment. Whether they will do something about it or not remains to be seen.

This same dilemma just discussed with relationship to duplicate trade names also holds true for duplicate customers, duplicate technology, and so forth. If the reader is in an original equipment manufacturer (OEM) auto parts company, with only about a dozen potential customers, and already selling to those international auto manufacturers, it is hard to understand why the appraiser and auditor are requiring the buyer to place a large value on the seller's customer base. The argument is made, "Gosh, we are already selling to their customers, and we know the buyers at, say, Ford better than they do. We did not buy them for their entrée into Ford because we already have that opening. We bought them for their product line and manufacturing facilities and technology."

To this perception, the appraiser and auditor have to respond, "You are totally correct in your analysis and understanding of the business realities. What you don't understand or accept is that the FASB's definition of FV, involving exit prices and market participants, provides answers that don't make a lot of business sense. But those are the rules that you and we must follow and that the SEC and the PCAOB will be checking. Sorry about that!"

CHAPTER 9

Testing for Impairment

When the Financial Accounting Standards Board (FASB) adopted Statement of Financial Accounting Standards (SFAS) 141 and SFAS 142 in 2001, they got rid of pooling-of-interests accounting, which many companies had relied on as a way of boosting reported earnings. The main reason for the popularity of *pooling*, as it was known, was that there was no goodwill. Under the old rules, goodwill had to be amortized over 30 to 40 years, and this amortization affected reported earnings. Pooling, on the other hand, with no goodwill and no amortization, appeared to maximize the reported earnings of any company after it had made a major acquisition. The FASB got rid of pooling to "converge" with the International Accounting Standards, which did not permit pooling-of-interests accounting at all.

In exchange for abolishing the desirable pooling, the FASB now requires that *all* merger-and-acquisition (M&A) transactions be accounted for as a purchase, with the concomitant goodwill. In exchange for abolishing pooling, the FASB threw a bone to Corporate America. Under the new rules, goodwill need *not* be amortized at all; thus, there is no directly adverse impact on reported earnings and earnings per share (EPS) for changing to purchase accounting from pooling.

But even the most ardent advocate of zero amortization of goodwill has to admit that in some cases, sooner or later, the initial goodwill following a business combination might lose some of its value. After all, there are statistics that show a high percentage of M&A transactions do not meet initial expectations, and some transactions actually end up as a dead loss.

If goodwill is not to be amortized, and sooner or later may have to be written down or impaired, then there has to be a methodology for determining whether there is impairment. A further requirement is to determine what the new lower resulting Fair Value (FV) for goodwill should be. That is the subject of this chapter.

We first cover the definition of impairment because there are actually three different tests that appraisers and accountants use. Then we discuss how to anticipate whether there is likely to be an impairment charge. Finally, to the extent possible, we examine some strategies for avoiding or mitigating impairment charges. But, first, we have to ask an important question: Do impairment charges or write-offs really matter?

HOW DOES THE MARKET RESPOND TO IMPAIRMENT WRITE-OFFS?

Before we go into detail, it is important to examine whether there is a penalty for companies that report an impairment charge. Invariably, when announcing an impairment write-off, companies will emphasize that "this is a noncash charge," the implication being that since the company is not losing actual hard-earned cash, it is little more than a "technical accounting matter." And such a statement is undoubtedly true. The amount and timing of impairment charges do represent a response to required accounting rules in Generally Accepted Accounting Principles (GAAP). Further, at the time of the charge, no cash is changing hands.

Such statements by companies, attempting to minimize the significance of the reduction in net income and EPS because of the impairment write-down, are somewhat disingenuous. What the press release does *not* say is that "previously disbursed cash, paid out to make the acquisition, did not work out as planned." Buying another company for cash results in intangible assets being put on the books, as discussed throughout this book. Subsequent write-offs do not involve cash at the date of the charge, but they certainly did involve cash (or stock that has cash value) when the deal was made.

An impairment charge is a reflection that something about previous decisions turned out worse than expected. Saying "Yes, we made a dumb decision then, but now we are smart enough to correct for that mistake" is hardly a brilliant reflection on past decision making.

The stock market, despite its reputed flaws, is actually a very efficient mechanism for coming up with a consensus—for investors taken as a group. The reason the market does not penalize the company the month the impairment charge is reported is that the market is always looking ahead and puts bad news behind. The market actually looks through management's attempt to distance itself from past mistakes.

What is hurt, although hard to quantify, is the market's evaluation today regarding management's prospects going forward. One bad deal in the past, followed by an impairment charge, can be overlooked. If there is a second such mistake, however, the company's stock price will be affected.

The conclusion we reach, with which readers may or may not agree, is that a single impairment charge related to a past acquisition will be forgiven: Nobody bats 1.000. A second charge, either for the same prior acquisition or for a totally different acquisition, will result in management's competence being called into question: "Fool me once, shame on you. Fool me twice, shame on me." This sums up how we believe the market reacts to an impairment charge.

In summary, impairment charges implicitly or explicitly are a reflection of past management mistakes in paying too much for a business that did not do as well as anticipated. Because the market looks ahead, and will let bygones be bygones, every management is allowed at least one mistake without serious penalty. The conclusion, however, may not be obvious. If you are going to have to take an impairment charge, make sure it is the last one. There is little more disturbing to the market than a *series* of impairment charges, which will lead people to ask the question, "Do these people know what they are doing?"

CAN WE CONTROL THE TIMING AND AMOUNT OF IMPAIRMENT CHARGES?

The simple answer to the preceding question is a qualified "yes." The FASB rules for testing impairment are pretty straightforward in themselves. These same rules do allow substantial leeway; in effect, the rules require the application of management judgment in making the actual calculations. In this section we will summarize the three types of impairment testing, discussing the "flexibility" inherent in the rules. Then, in the next section, we will discuss the extent to which management can control the amount and timing of impairment charges. The three types of impairment calculations are as follows:

1. When the FV of an *intangible asset with an indefinite life* is less than book value.
2. When the FV of an *intangible asset that is being amortized* is less than book value.
3. When the FV of *goodwill* is less than book value.

Each of the three types of impairment has different rules and different required calculations. Whether this is necessary or even makes sense is irrelevant. The three separate rules are what they are and, in the author's judgment, are unlikely to be changed.

The rule for determining whether there is or is not an impairment for an *intangible asset with an indefinite life* is very straightforward. Remember that the FASB and the Securities and Exchange Commission (SEC) do not like intangible assets with an indefinite life that do not get amortized, so this is not a common occurrence. Trade names and renewable licenses are two of the most common categories that do not get amortized. The only requirement is that once a year the company determine the then-current FV of the intangible asset (e.g., a trade name).

The valuation requirement essentially requires the appraiser to use the *same* methodology as was applied initially, when the asset was acquired. Current assumptions and information have to be utilized, but you cannot suddenly apply a brand new *methodology* just because the old approach happens to give you today an answer you don't like.

Experience suggests that if the intangible asset (e.g., a favorable trade name or brand) continues to be used and the underlying business is doing well, there is very little chance of an impairment charge for indefinite-life intangible assets. Only when the company stops using a trade name, for example, or sales drop precipitously will an impairment result.

The ground rules for assets that are being amortized or depreciated are significantly different. Surprising as it may seem, you do *not* determine today's FV and compare it to the carrying amount of book value. Common sense suggests that this should be the approach, but the FASB rejected a test that would determine only today's FV. There was concern that there would be too many impairment charges if this approach were adopted. If you stop and think about it, in the normal course of a product life cycle, or in the course of the business cycle, there are almost as many down periods as up periods. Hence, value fluctuates both up and down.

Keep in mind that an impairment charge is always a one-way street. The author sometimes refers to this as the "Roach Motel: You can check in but you can't check out!" Once an impairment charge is taken, even if the value of the item subsequently returns to its previous level or even higher, you simply *cannot* undo a prior charge by writing back up any amount previously charged to expense.

Many people view this inability to restore previously written-down value as draconian. That is, until you point out that once accountants start measuring assets each year and booking all the changes, up or down, we would be in the dreaded "Fair Value accounting" arena. Very few readers would want to have to determine the FV of all of their firm's assets every year. First, there are not enough appraisers in the world to perform the valuations; and, second, the increases and decreases in FV would totally swamp the results of operations. Only academics and the FASB want to go to full Fair Value accounting, and neither group has made a persuasive case that the world would be a better place with Fair Value accounting.

A number of years ago the FASB issued SFAS 121, updated more recently by SFAS 144. Without going into excruciating accounting detail, we can summarize the impairment testing requirements for amortizable assets very simply. Step one is to identify the group of assets with identifiable or separable cash flow. So if you have a machine tool or a patent that you think has lost its value, you don't simply compute its FV today.

Instead, you have to see if you can identify cash flows associated directly with that asset. You may not be able to match future cash flows from production or product sales to the single milling machine. Rather, you would look at the machine shop or factory where the tool was used. In the case of a specific patent for a manufacturing process, you would look at the cash flows from the products that utilized the patented process.

Now comes the unusual part. SFAS 144 says you add up the future cash flows on an arithmetic basis, that is, *without* discounting. If the sum of the future cash flows exceeds the carrying value of the asset(s), then, by definition, you do not have impairment. In fact, even if you wanted to, you simply are not permitted unilaterally to write down the patent or machine tool irrespective of what the FV of the individual asset may be. Admittedly, this is not totally logical, nor is it in accord with modern finance theory, which says you should always discount future cash flows to today's values.

The absence of discounting does one thing and does it well. It precludes numerous writedowns. Whether this is good accounting or even good public policy we have to leave to others. As of right now, SFAS 144 is part of GAAP and cannot be changed without the vote of the FASB's members. There is virtually no support currently for changing SFAS 144. The practical result is that for assets that are being amortized or depreciated, it is rare to find an impairment charge.

The only time amortizable or depreciable assets end up being written down is when the underlying business is suffering truly long-term decline. Even one or two bad years won't cause an impairment charge because if you assume that things will get better in years three, four, and five, the cash flows in the out years will usually more than offset current losses.

TESTING GOODWILL FOR IMPAIRMENT

This may be the single most difficult topic for appraisers and accountants to explain to businessmen and their advisers. The reason is that goodwill, as discussed earlier in the book, is not a specific asset such as a patent or a trade name. The latter can be identified and valued directly. Goodwill, however, is a *residual* that results from a series of valuation and accounting steps.

The way goodwill is defined by the FASB and enshrined in GAAP, you arrive at a number for goodwill only after developing a series of other values; you then subtract the sum of those values from the purchase price of a business or the FV of the business. This sounds complicated, and it is.

Earlier in the book we discussed the requirements for allocating the purchase price of a newly acquired business, and we refer readers to Chapters 4 and 8. For purposes of testing goodwill now on the books for possible impairment, the FASB asks companies to determine the FV of the business unit *as though it were to be sold*. Of course, the business isn't really going to be sold, but GAAP asks you to *assume* such a theoretical sale, hence the confusion.

We will briefly describe the process that appraisers have to go through, but this section can be skipped without a loss of continuity. The following steps must be undertaken, pretty much in the order shown.

1. The company has to split up its business into discrete *reporting units*.
2. The FV of each reporting unit must be determined as of the testing date.
3. The FV of the reporting unit is compared to the book value of the reporting unit, and one of two situations exists:
    - The FV exceeds the book value.
    - The FV is less than the book value.
4. If the FV of the reporting unit exceeds the book value (the total dollar amount on the reporting unit's balance sheet), you stop because the FASB defined goodwill impairment this way, and by their definition there is no impairment.
5. If the FV of the reporting unit is *less* than the book value, then you have to go to Phase II.
6. Phase II is identical in definition and methodology to an allocation of purchase price, as discussed in Chapter 4. One must determine the FV on an individual basis of *all* assets and liabilities.
7. The sum of the FVs is subtracted from the FV of the reporting unit, as shown in Step 2 above.
8. The difference between the FV of the reporting unit and the sum of the FV of all the assets and liabilities is the new "computed" goodwill.
9. The newly computed goodwill is subtracted from the goodwill currently on the books, and the difference is the dollar amount of the impairment charge.

We could write an entire chapter, if not a brand new book, on the details of how this work is to be performed. Nonetheless, every company that has goodwill on its books must go through this exercise at least once a year and always on the same date (e.g., at the end of the third quarter).

CAN YOU CONTROL IMPAIRMENT CHARGES?

At the beginning of this chapter we alluded to the fact that the market may be forgiving of a single impairment charge but looks unfavorably at a series of such charges. Many financial executives, agreeing with this assessment, attempt to make sure that if things are not going according to plan with a prior acquisition, then all the bad news comes out at once.

We now discuss some of the tools that can be applied to increase or decrease the amount and timing of any impairment charge. We do not want the reader to believe that companies are permitted to do anything they wish, which would be considered manipulation of the financial statements. Rather, what flexibility there is in GAAP for testing goodwill impairment is there for a reason; it is simply up to management to avail themselves of whatever ambiguities exist.

Getting right to the point, the reason for the flexibility comes from one simple fact: The determination of FV almost always depends on one's assessment of the *future* course of events. Valuing a business or a reporting unit (testing for goodwill impairment always deals with reporting units that are similar to the business segments required for financial reporting) involves judgment about future sales and future income.

Values tend to be high if one has an optimistic perspective, and values will be much lower if one takes a conservative or even pessimistic perspective. Valuing a business always starts out with a projection, and the issue is what assumption one makes about the future.

In making an initial acquisition, companies go through a complex and comprehensive Due Diligence process (see Chapter 5). The board of directors will review management's assumptions. Inasmuch as real money is being expended and the cost of making a mistake is high, most business combinations are based pretty closely on economic reality. If management paints an unduly bright picture for a proposed acquisition, then they themselves will have to live with the bad decision. On day one, too conservative an outlook means the deal won't get done; too optimistic an outlook is setting up the company for future criticism from shareholders and analysts. A really bad acquisition may cause an involuntary change in the continuity of employment for those recommending the decision. In short, there are checks and balances on the purchase price paid—what management determines is the true FV of an acquisition.

The situation is totally different in subsequent years, when previously acquired goodwill now has to be tested in order to comply with SFAS 142, the portion of GAAP that deals with this topic. Remember that the first step (only in the first year do you determine the reporting unit, which, once done, stays the same) is to value the reporting unit. For simplicity, we assume that a newly acquired company is, in fact, a separate reporting unit.

For example, what is the FV of a business (reporting unit) that was acquired two or three years ago and has now been partially integrated into the parent company? Remember that the FV must be determined from the perspective that you would (theoretically) be selling the business to a third party or what that third party would pay you for the business.

Assuming a valuation specialist has been hired to perform the goodwill impairment test, at this point management is going to be requested to provide projections for the next three to five years. What will those projections look like? If the business has been performing above expectation, is quite profitable and there are no clouds on the horizon, the projection is easy and not subject to challenge.

The issue, however, is far more serious if the unit has been performing *below* expectations, perhaps even running at a loss. The critical question may be whether management wants to take an impairment charge this year. If the company wants to own up to a prior mistake, then it is pretty simple. One only has to prepare a five-year outlook with little or no improvement. Presumably, the current outlook is well below that assumed when the deal was done. Consequently, the FV of the reporting unit or business will be below the acquisition price.

Following the logical steps listed above, the company immediately goes to Phase II, which is the separate valuation of each asset and liability. In valuing the intangibles now, looking to the prospect of one major write-down instead of a series of smaller charges, again one would take a very conservative perspective. Customer lists would be written down, the value of trade names questioned, patents and unpatented technology questioned, inventories and receivables scrubbed down, and so forth.

The result would be low values for the individual assets, summing up to a new low FV for the reporting unit. When subtracted the amount of permissible goodwill would be substantially written down, if not totally written off. Going forward from then on, unless the unit actually ceased operations, there would *likely be no future impairment charges*, simply because there was little goodwill and low values for intangible assets left on the books.

This scenario is not common, although it does happen, and we often recommend it to clients. Much more common, however, is the situation where the newly acquired business is performing poorly, but, for whatever reason, management does *not* want to take a write-down. In this situation, care must be taken.

Remember, if a recent acquisition is not performing well, the company's auditors will be aware of this. Presumably, if it is a public company, the management comments in the quarterly SEC filings will have discussed the business and its outlook. The SEC may start asking the question, "If the unit is not doing well, why *isn't* there an impairment charge?" So management has to tread carefully. (Of course, the opposite happens, and when an impairment charge is taken, the SEC asks, "Why didn't you take the charge earlier?") But assume that, despite the poor performance, the company simply does not want to accept a write-off.

The answer for the first year and possibly a second year is to prepare an optimistic projection or forecast. Recognition is made that so far things have not turned out as planned, but "the future is *really* going to improve." Who on the outside can quarrel with this assessment? Management controls the business, knows what went wrong, and is in a position to say what will be done to improve things.

Given the methodologies employed by appraisers, an overall optimistic forecast that shows a continuing loss in the current year—but projects substantial improvement in the out years—will have a favorable FV. If management "pounds the table" and says this is what is going to happen, neither an appraiser nor an auditor can call them liars. Nobody knows what the future holds, and it is always possible for management's optimistic projections to come to pass. Even the SEC cannot substitute its judgment for that of management, no matter how much they question the reasonableness and reliability of the projections. This is because the projections themselves (unless they are outright ridiculous) are determinant of the FV.

Any management can postpone, for at least one year, the necessity of taking impairment charges. The crunch will come in year two. Now people can both review the prior projections and look at newly prepared projections made with the benefit of an additional year's operations.

A very persuasive management team can, in year two, admit to undue optimism the previous year, but assert, "Well, this time we have got it right!" The only thing that auditors and appraisers can do is to challenge the assumptions and ask what is the basis for the continued optimism when the business itself continues to go south. Specific changes have to be committed to and then, in effect, monitored. Maybe things will turn out as management asserts, or perhaps they won't.

The crunch comes in year three. If there has been no progress in the prior two years, most auditors and appraisers will then insist on a dose of reality and require management to face up to the real situation. At that point, impairment charges will be required, and as discussed earlier, it is probably best to take the "big bath," getting everything out of the way at once.

In summarizing this section, we cannot stress too much that almost everything depends on the business unit's forecast. If management has a solid "game plan" and then implements it, there will be no need for impairment charges. A "pie in the sky" forecast, however, will probably stall things for one year, but at that point the appraiser and auditor will hold management responsible and require that SFAS 142 be fully implemented.

CHOICE OF REPORTING UNIT

In this example we assumed that a newly acquired business was treated as a separate reporting unit. In fact, this is, in practice, not necessary at all. A new acquisition can be incorporated into an existing reporting unit. The rules for defining reporting units are clear, but the rules rely on management's assertions as to the internal reporting system it uses and how it manages the business. Thus, a company can almost completely control into which existing reporting unit a new acquisition will be placed.

The FASB was fully aware of this anomaly when they developed SFAS 142 and decided to live with the consequences. The consequences, perhaps not immediately obvious, are that a poorly performing acquisition, when placed in an existing profitable reporting unit, may never have to take an impairment charge on goodwill.

The reason is straightforward. Step 1 in the impairment analysis is the determination of the FV of the total reporting unit. If the newly acquired business is no more than, say, 25% of the total reporting unit's results, the FV of the entire unit will be driven by the profits of the good 75%. Even losses in the newly acquired business will probably not cause the total reporting unit to have an FV below book value of the total unit. In short, the good can cover up the bad.

We mentioned before that once the reporting units are identified, they continue from year to year. This is not totally accurate, because if the company actually reorganizes how it is run, then SFAS 142 permits the reporting units to be reconfigured to match the new organization chart. What is not possible is to reconfigure reporting units simply to preclude an impairment charge. We have yet to see a situation where, to avoid an impairment, the company actually changes its management structure. That would be a true case of "the tail wagging the dog."

TRADE-OFF BETWEEN ASSIGNING VALUE TO INTANGIBLES AND TO GOODWILL

In the initial allocation of purchase price, almost without exception, company management wants the maximum portion of the purchase price to go to goodwill. Every dollar not assigned to amortizable intangibles increases nonamortizable goodwill, with a positive impact on EPS. Between appraisers and auditors reviewing the final appraisal, there may not be a lot of flexibility, but without doubt there is some degree of choice.

The issue is usually discussed in the context that if you have more dollars in goodwill, you increase the risk of an impairment charge. The reason relates to the undiscounted cash flow test for amortizable intangibles and fixed assets. As mentioned earlier, it is almost impossible to have an impairment write-down of amortizable intangibles and property, plant, and equipment (PP&E). When you add up future cash flows for 15 or so years, any assumption as to future profitability over that long a period will be hard to challenge.

Thus, putting more dollars into amortizable intangibles and PP&E effectively precludes any amortization charge, at the cost of higher profit-and-loss (P&L) charges each year. Putting fewer dollars of goodwill on the books also minimizes the potential for any future goodwill impairment charge.

These are real-world choices that management has to make at the time of an acquisition. We, in fact, recommend that this analysis be performed as part of the Due Diligence effort prior to the acquisition. The choices are real, but we don't want to overemphasize the degree of flexibility that exists. You cannot put all the dollars into goodwill; neither can you put no dollars in goodwill. The facts and circumstances effectively control the overall allocation, but there is still room for judgment. This judgment call should be made by management, not by appraisers or auditors.

SUMMARY AND CONCLUSION

Anytime a business combination (M&A transaction) is contemplated, thought should be given to the potential for future impairment charges if the deal does not work out as anticipated.

There are three types of impairment tests, one each for amortizable intangibles and PP&E, a second for nonamortizable intangibles, and a third for goodwill. The methodologies, as discussed, differ, but at the end of the day, one assumption will hold true. If values equal or exceed initial expectation, there will never be an impairment. If the business does not do as well as anticipated, one can count on a lot of resources being applied to the impairment testing process.

Finally, if you are facing an impairment, thought should be given to getting as much off the books as possible. The valuation methodologies that appraisers use provide some leeway in accomplishing this objective. While reporting a loss is never good, the market does not seem to penalize a large write-down any more rigorously than a much smaller charge. If you have a loss, take one as big as can be supported.

CHAPTER 10

Customer Relationships

For financial executives and their advisers, the concept of Fair Value (FV) most often arises in the context of a business combination, as the Financial Accounting Standards Board (FASB) calls mergers and acquisitions (M&A). In virtually every transaction, *management's goal is to make future earnings per share accretive* just as soon as possible. Shareholders, by and large, react poorly to a specific M&A transaction if the buyer's stock goes down and stays down. Yet, unless earnings per share (EPS) get back to premerger levels, the stock price is likely to continue to flounder.

As discussed throughout this book, reported earnings, at least in part, are a function of accounting requirements promulgated by the FASB. It is true that actual cash flows are rarely directly affected by accounting choices. Most privately held companies, and many public companies, pay particular attention to cash flows; but the relationship between cash flows and reported EPS is somewhat tenuous in the short run. In the long run, accounting choices make little difference, but as Lord John Maynard Keynes once opined, "But this *long* run is a misleading guide to current affairs. *In the long run* we are all dead!" Consequently, short-term earnings are important to Wall Street and, by extension, to management.

Calculating anticipated EPS requires fairly detailed assumptions about how the overall purchase price will be allocated over each asset category. Amounts charged to land, goodwill, and trade names do not get amortized and in the short run do not impact EPS. All other allocated dollars (other than cash and marketable securities) will hit the profit-and-loss (P&L) statement sooner or later.

Dollars assigned to receivables and inventory will flow to P&L or balance sheet within the first year as receivables from the seller are collected in cash, and the seller's inventories flow quickly into cost of goods sold. Amounts assigned to property, plant, and equipment (PP&E) will be depreciated over the remaining useful life of the respective assets, often from five years (computers) to 39 years (real estate). The remaining dollars of the adjusted purchase price (amounts paid plus assumption of liabilities) must be assigned to identifiable intangible assets, as set forth in Statement of Financial Accounting Standards (SFAS) 141 R and then those amounts must be amortized over their useful lives. As discussed in Chapter 4, the single most troublesome intangible asset identified by the FASB is customer relationship.

WHAT IS A CUSTOMER RELATIONSHIP?

If you stand back and ask just why one company buys another, there are a limited number of reasons. These might include:

- Buyer's CEO wants to run a larger company.
- Buyer wants to reduce or eliminate competition.
- Buyer acquires supplier to reduce operating costs of combined firms.
- Buyer acquires customers to increase sales.
- Buyer thinks he can increase profits in the target company, over and above what present management is accomplishing.
- Private equity buys company to prepare for a new initial public offering (IPO).

In almost every one of these types of acquisition, the buyer is essentially acquiring only a limited number of asset categories. These include:

- Assembled workforce.
- Product/service lines and resources to produce product or service.
- Existing customers.
- Technology, research and development (R&D), know-how, and potential new products/services.

With the exception of the assembled workforce (the FASB explicitly precludes buyers from recognizing this as an asset on the financial statements), each of the remaining categories can, and must, be valued. In this chapter we focus solely on the customer aspect of any M&A transaction.

Other than for a start-up business, a company without customers is an oxymoron. For a company to generate continuing cash flows requires sales to customers, followed by collection of the subsequent accounts receivable. For a company to remain viable, those sales to customers must ultimately be profitable. It is virtually impossible to think of a company without thinking of who its customers are and how those customers behave.

This focus on customers and their profitability is probably the single most significant part of any Due Diligence effort. Other than in a private-equity transaction, the acquiring company usually is familiar with the relevant market, the customers, and the competition.

There is a reason for discussing what may seem intuitively obvious. The FASB in SFAS 141 requires buyers to place an explicit value on the acquired customer relationships. Understanding how this intangible asset is valued, and the subsequent P&L implication of the valuation, is the area with which a valuation firm's clients have the most trouble. There are more discussions among buyers, their accountants, and valuation specialists on the subject of customer relationships than with virtually all other asset categories combined.

DEFINING A CUSTOMER RELATIONSHIP

Every reader undoubtedly has a mental image of customers in relation to a particular type of business. A wholesale wine distributor calls on and sells to wine and liquor stores and some restaurants. A supplier of parts for new automobiles calls on and sells to the major auto manufacturers or their first- and second-tier suppliers. An oil well service firm calls on and sells to drillers. A law firm has a base of customers who look to them for legal advice. The picture is clear. Anyone buying another business has to obtain a feel for who the customers are and how they behave (i.e., are transactions based solely on price, on service, on product availability, or on personal relationships—maybe some combination of these?).

Defining a customer or a customer relationship is not quite as simple as describing it. Just as Justice Potter Stewart of the Supreme Court had trouble defining pornography ("I can't define it, but I know it when I see it"), so do accountants have trouble actually defining customers and customer relationships. For example, an individual buys a Toyota hybrid car at a dealership, and then six months later returns to buy a small pickup truck. Is that individual a customer after buying the car? Obviously, yes, but most retail customers of retail establishments are totally anonymous. So would you identify a car buyer from six months ago as a customer today? When the individual returns and buys the truck—a second transaction—at that point, does it make him a customer?

The problem is that to put a value on something, you have to be able to define it and then measure it in terms that are understandable to all. Does a law firm have a client if somebody stops in to get a new will, but has no other legal business? Is an individual with a broken arm who goes to one of those stand-alone "doc in a box" medical businesses a patient, one who might have ongoing value? A gasoline station ordinarily buys from the Shell distributor, but if Shell has a refinery problem, then the dealer may have to take delivery of a tanker of gasoline from an unbranded distributor. Does that make him a customer of the new distributor?

This discussion is not meant as a "stump the expert," but, hopefully, it highlights the issue. To value a customer relationship for financial reporting, it is critical that we define just who the customers are and then obtain a projection of what the likely sales will be to those customers.

The FASB *initially* defined a customer relationship in terms of a two-part test. The relationship had to be contractual, or it had to be severable, that is, capable of being sold to a third party.

A contractual relationship would be like the remaining eight years on a ten-year lease for office space, or a take-or-pay contract for natural gas between a pipeline and a public utility. In those clear-cut contractual situations one knew who the customers were, and the contractual amounts of future cash flows could be calculated with a high degree of certainty.

The "severable" relationships envisioned by the FASB were actually few and far between. The example always used by the Board was that of bank deposits, where there is a history of specific bank branches being bought and sold. The purchaser expects, based on past history, that a relatively high number of the depositors will continue to keep their accounts at the branch, almost irrespective of what bank's logo is on the building. Frankly, appraisers had great difficulty identifying many other severable relationships. It certainly would not apply to a parts supplier to General Motors. The supplier could not tell the GM purchasing department, "Well, we sold your account to our competitor, and we expect you to continue buying your parts from them from now on."

The severable and contractual tests the FASB originally put into SFAS 141 meant, in practice, that very few dollars were assigned to this specific intangible asset. Very few companies had actual contracts with their customers enabling the seller to go to court to enforce the contract in case of a perceived breach. An unenforceable contract is no contract at all. At that point, appraisers were comfortable with interpreting the FASB's rules, and auditors had very few problems.

The Securities and Exchange Commission (SEC), however, became very unhappy. If dollars in a purchase allocation are *not* assigned to customer relationships, they end up in nonamortizable goodwill, with no subsequent charge to P&L, absent a major impairment. The practical import of the FASB's contractual/severable definition was that a lot of dollars went to goodwill and very few dollars ever were charged to subsequent P&Ls through amortization of the customer relationship intangible.

It may be unfair to assert that the SEC never misses a chance to object to companies making accounting entries that boost reported earnings. Once in a while, as in the case of reserves against future contingencies, the SEC comes out in favor of lower charges, with a boost to current P&L. It almost seems at times that the SEC staff argues reflexively against whatever it is companies want to do, and then makes them do the opposite.

In the case of customer relationships, however, the SEC complaints hit a very responsive chord among auditors. Most auditors are bright, and they understand the economics of an M&A transaction. The buyer always wants (needs) the sellers' customers. Putting zero value against the customer relationships, because of the strict FASB definition, seemed to fly in the face of the decision process used by buyers. So with the SEC unhappy about the financial reporting impact of a narrow FASB decision as to what constituted a relationship, and with auditors seeing accounting entries that did not comport with the actual business decision making, a change in accounting took place.

The Emerging Issues Task Force (EITF) took up this issue of customer relationships. In one of the most strained arguments ever seen, the EITF stated that a single purchase order open as of the transaction date meant that the buyer truly had a contractual relationship with the seller. In other words, a nonenforceable one-time purchase order put the buyer into a long-term contractual relationship with the seller, even if there was zero ability of the seller to "compel" the buyer to perform in the future. As mentioned earlier, a nonenforceable contract appears to be an oxymoron and would be an interesting subject for discussion in a law school class on contracts.

In the last paragraph we referred to the EITF decision as "strained." It gets better. The EITF opinion went ever further, with concurrence from the SEC (perhaps the concurrence came after the SEC told the EITF what to decide, which the SEC has the power to do). The EITF, in its decision 02–17, says that if anyone in the past had *ever* sent the company a purchase order, that in itself defined a contractual relationship. So a past purchase order that had been fulfilled and closed now represented the basis for an ongoing future contractual relationship that had to be recognized as an asset and then subsequently amortized to P&L. Some financial managers, as well as valuations specialists, have had trouble understanding this logic.

Rather than trying to define customer relationships in terms understood by the average business executive, the FASB and the SEC, under the aegis of EITF rule making, totally twisted around the definition of *contractual relationship*. There is no gain from arguing against this tortured definition. It is being enforced by auditors, the SEC, and the Public Company Accounting Oversight Board (PCAOB), so, as the saying goes, "Live with it!"

HOW TO INTERPRET THE EITF DEFINITION OF CUSTOMER RELATIONSHIP

We go into substantially more detail on customer relationships in this chapter than we provide detail in the rest of the book on other aspects of FV. There are two reasons. First, every dollar assigned to customer relationships is going to be written off to P&L quite quickly, adversely affecting future income. Second, the absolute amount assigned to customer relationships is a direct function of how you define the asset.

The first step in developing a supportable value for this new customer relationship asset is to project the sales one anticipates being made to those customers. As we saw, the EITF defined a customer effectively as anyone who had ever bought something from the company since most business-to-business transactions involve a purchase order. Effectively, only retail transactions are made without the contractual element of a purchase order, and the FASB exempts retailers from trying to value these anonymous buyers who pay with cash or by credit card.

Almost every business combination involves Due Diligence, and the key aspect of any such study is a projection of future sales, operating expenses, and profitability. So the starting point for the appraiser in valuing these customers is to look at the overall sales projection. Most companies, if they analyze past sales history, will find that over a period of years large customers often reduce or eliminate their purchases, while other new customers are developed. Put a different way, turnover of customers is inherent in almost every line of business. How does this impact the valuation of customer relationships?

Keep in mind that, by definition, customer relationships relate *only* to past and current customers, and the definition does not apply to *new* customers not yet on the books. The overall sales projections developed during a Due Diligence study cover *total* anticipated sales; the projections virtually never break down the projected amounts between current and new customers. But, for purposes of valuation, we must exclude future sales from future customers, since this is not an asset of the business acquired at the closing. One can hope and reasonably expect the target company to acquire new customers in the future, but one basic premise of accounting is never to anticipate future profits. Customer relationship valuation can be applied only to the current base.

The consequence of this is that most appraisers start with the current year's sales and apply a *decrement* in each subsequent year. Each year, some of today's customers will go out of business, change direction, or start buying from competitors.

The appropriate decrement rate ideally should be derived from the past history of the subject company. In effect, a simple actuarial analysis is performed. Decrement rates can be as low as 5% and as high as 25% or 30%. A constant rate of decrease will never get to zero, so, typically, we will cut off the projection at perhaps nine or ten years. For any established business, the probabilities are pretty high that the sales to customers ten years ago bear relatively little connection to today's sales.

ONE MAJOR CUSTOMER

Occasionally, a business will have just a few very large customers, the loss of any one of whom would significantly affect the company. In those situations, as long as service, price, and delivery are maintained, one might anticipate very low losses of future sales from today's customers. A company whose major customer is Wal-Mart is a good example. It is hard to become a Wal-Mart supplier but, by and large, the retailer tends to stay pretty loyal. They are tough bargainers, but basically fair.

In a situation such as this, it is very difficult to estimate a reasonable decrement rate. In fact, the outlook is basically binary in nature. You either continue selling to Wal-Mart or you lose them altogether. Actuarial analysis of past customer behavior provides little help in this situation.

We have recommended in this case that the computation of the value of the single customer (e.g., Wal-Mart) relationship be developed. But the amount should not be amortized each and every year. Rather, the FV of the Wal-Mart relationship would be tested for impairment each year. As long as sales to the customer continued and were profitable, the intangible customer relationship asset would stay the same.

When Wal-Mart ceased buying from this supplier, then and only then would the total FV be written off because of the impairment. The SEC will not allow a company to say that customer relationships in total have an indefinite life. They do permit this designation for trade names but not for customers, because history does suggest that trade names last a lot longer than specific customers. But, in the case of a single large customer, treating that one customer relationship as having an indefinite life makes sense.

We are often faced with valuing business enterprises where there is a single large customer, sometimes accounting for 70% or more of volume. By and large, we tend to value such businesses much lower than a comparable firm (same sales and profit) that has a diversified customer base. The reason is simple. There is higher risk if you have only one major customer. Higher risk translates into lower present value, as almost all finance textbooks confirm.

SELLING NEW PRODUCTS OR SERVICES

Growth is the mantra for most American businesses. Yet there really are only three ways to grow organically, that is, without buying another business:

1. You can sell *more* of today's product or service to today's customers.
2. You can sell today's product or service to *new* customers.
3. You can start selling *new products* or services to both current and new customers.

In determining the FV of today's customer relationships, should you include anticipated sales of *new products* to existing customers? Opinions differ on this point, and the implications of answering the question one way or another can be significant.

To a certain extent, this is a matter of the facts and circumstances, how close a new product would be to today's product or service. It is hard to draw what many accountants call a "bright line," a clear-cut rule that allows for little judgment. Paraphrasing former President Clinton ("It depends on what the meaning of 'is' is"), it depends on what the meaning is of "new" product or service.

A projected sales increase caused by the addition of new products or services that are effectively a *new line of business* appears to this appraiser to be ineligible for adding to the value of today's customer relationships. The reason is that a company can reasonably expect a high proportion of existing customers to continue buying existing products and services. Absent deterioration in pricing or service most companies continue to buy from existing suppliers. The cost of changing suppliers is high, and long-term relationships with vendors, in and of themselves, have value.

When we look to new products, our experience suggests that a prior relationship really only allows the vendor to make an initial sales pitch. Assume you have been buying office supplies from Staples, and Staples now starts to sell custom software. You may well agree to hear the sales representative pitch the story of the new service, but Staples faces a lot of competitors in a software product or service that you cannot relate to them based on existing experience. Good experience in office supplies does not translate into purchases of totally different products or services.

What we really have is a spectrum. At one end is a supplier that simply repackages existing products, and most observers would add projected sales into the FV calculation. At the opposite end of the spectrum would be a totally different product, as if K-Mart suddenly started selling motorcycles. Would you really think of buying custom software from Staples or motorcycles from K-Mart?

The answer, of course, is "It depends...." The critical point is that if a vendor goes into a new line of business, he is now competing in a new space against new and different (to him) competitors. If all that an existing relationship does is to provide a "foot in the door," then we do not believe that those sales and anticipated profit properly can be included in the FV of today's customer relationship.

For this reason, when we are asked to determine the FV of existing customer relationships, we very often exclude from the projections anticipated new products or services. In short, we limit our view of the value of such relationships to projected sales of today's product line(s) to today's customers.

In practice, this means that while the buyer will have comprehensive sales projections for the target, these almost always include new products. We recommend that companies try to estimate the amount that new products or line of business will be as a percentage of total future sales. So, for example, one could assume that only 5% of next year's total sales will be of new products, while in five years 40% of total sales will be of products not now carried.

The total future sales projection, utilized in the Due Diligence process, can be bifurcated with only sales of existing products being the starting point. Then the decrement rate for loss of customers is applied to the total projected sales of existing products to arrive at a dollar value representing future sales of current products to current customers. This approach appears to meet both the letter and the spirit of valuing customer relationships.

The next step undertaken by the valuation specialist is to determine the anticipated cost of sales and related gross margin. From this gross profit is subtracted selling, general and administrative (SG&A) expenses related to those future sales of current products to current customers. Because these sales will probably not require as much selling expense and marketing effort, some analysts feel it necessary to adjust the overall corporate SG&A to reflect this savings.

At this point, one will have developed a pretax income; and can then apply the projected tax rate, providing an after-tax amount. If depreciation and amortization are low and offset by new capital expenditures, it is often possible to assume that the after-tax income equals projected cash flows; we essentially discount cash flows, not income, so the relationship between income and cash flows must be made explicit.

RETURNS ON OTHER ASSETS

About ten years ago, when valuation of intangible assets became an everyday event for appraisers, a number of analysts came to the conclusion that the net cash flows derived above really overstated the benefit of the existing customer base.

The reason was simple: To generate sales and profits from these customers, the company had to have made investments in working capital, PP&E, and the other intangibles such as a trade name and technology. Simply taking the after-tax cash flows from sales to customers, on a stand-alone basis, gave no recognition to the company's overall investment.

The solution was to provide a nominal return on the company's investment in all these contributory assets. So, for example, one might assume that the company should earn 6% after tax on working capital. One would estimate how much working capital was required to support the current sales to current customers, apply 6% to the total dollar amount of inventory and receivables (less payables), and subtract that required return from the cash flows for the year.

This process would be carried out for each of the future years in the calculation, not only for working capital but for the PP&E and each of the major intangible assets. Interestingly, the FASB permits a company to calculate a required return on the "assembled workforce," even though the dollar value of that asset cannot be put on the books. The FASB argues that one cannot "sever" a workforce from a company, so it cannot be considered an asset. Here, the FASB is walking a very narrow definitional line, whereas in valuing the customer relationships, they have strained to make the definition as broad as possible.

In all events, we are permitted to subtract an allowance for the use of the assembled workforce in valuing customer relationships. The reason this is so important is that the more required return there is for working capital, PP&E, and other intangibles, the lower the value of customer relationships.

Why do companies desire low values for this customer relationship intangible? In buying another company, aren't they really buying the customer base? Shouldn't they want to "brag" about the magnitude of this newly acquired asset? Well, yes, it is nice to have the customers. But the more value placed on customer relationships, the *lower* will be the reported profit over the next few years.

One is simply not permitted to assume that the customer base has an indefinite life. Rather, a specific life must be assigned and the total value of the customer relationship intangible is then written off over that time period. So, the greater the dollar amount of the asset, the larger will be the amortization charge each year, and the smaller will be reported earnings.

As noted much earlier in the book, most companies want an acquisition to be accretive to reported earnings. The greater the future amortization charge for intangible assets, the harder it is to report accretive EPS.

This is the reason why companies sometimes disagree with appraisers. At other times, the company and the appraiser are on the same side of the argument, and it is the auditing firm that objects to the determination of FV for customer relationships.

Most auditors do not want to receive a comment letter from the SEC questioning how the value of any intangible asset was calculated. The thrust of SEC inquiries in this area always is to see if the company is *under*stating the FV of intangible assets that must be amortized, and *over*stating the FV of goodwill, which is not amortized. Thus, auditing firms often put themselves in the position of the SEC in relation to the client and will argue for higher values to be assigned to amortizable intangibles.

This tension among the company, its auditors, and appraisal specialists is very expensive. In effect, two professional firms are involved, each charging the client for time spent. Ordinarily, the client and the appraiser are on one side and the auditor is on the other. The auditor has the trump card, because the company must obtain a clean certificate, and if the auditing firm "digs in its heels," there is very little the company can do—at least in the short run.

There have been situations, however, where the auditing firm is so rigid and, apparently, unreasonable in its position that the company acquiesces this year and changes auditors the next—usually the change in auditors is stated because of 'fees.'

The statement that the old auditing firm's fees were too high is supported by the often inordinate time that had been spent arguing the appropriate level of the FV of specific intangibles. At times, the auditor will win the battle but end up losing the war.

TESTING CUSTOMER RELATIONSHIPS FOR IMPAIRMENT

Once the acquiring company has integrated the new company into its operations, it is almost impossible two or three years later to measure whether the then remaining balance in the customer relationship account is overstated. The reason, of course, is that if the acquisition is to be successful, duplicate costs and overhead are eliminated, sales forces will have been combined, and it is difficult to satisfactorily extract or isolate the cash flows today from the customers acquired years ago. Problems with new product introductions, mergers among customers, and many other factors make it too expensive to try and reconstruct history.

Because customer relationships are being amortized, however, the impairment test is undiscounted future cash flows. So if the company has any kind of positive cash flow from operations, it is highly unlikely that summing up those future cash flows will ever be less than the balance sheet amount.

The situation is different, of course, if the company is now losing money overall. It is going to be hard to argue that the old customers that were acquired in the merger are still profitable, and that the overall losses are due solely to all the other customers. When a company is in more than a temporary loss position, it is likely that many of the intangible assets will have to be written down, as well as the goodwill itself. Applying the "big bath" maxim at that point, the company will probably *want* to write off as much of the customer relationship asset as can be supported. And when the outlook is bleak, then the auditors will also probably be arguing for conservatism; auditors at that point will be encouraging impairment charges pretty much across the board.

The bottom line is that there are many arguments about the dollar amount to be ascribed to customer relationships in the initial allocation of purchase price. There are very few controversies involved in subsequent impairment testing.

CHAPTER 11

Selecting and Working with an Appraisal Specialist

ntuitively, most businessmen and women have a good grasp as to what assets are worth. In practice, most clients have a pretty good idea as to what value appraisers "should" come up with, even before the appraisal process is begun. What is it that differentiates a businessman's opinion from an appraiser's professional determination of value as set forth in an appraisal report? We may even arrive at the same answer, so why should someone pay an appraiser thousands of dollars for a report that may do little more than confirm what was already known?

It would be possible to argue that the benefits are similar to a healthy executive who goes in for his annual physical. No problems, feels good, weight under control. The report comes back from the physician, "Keep it up; whatever you are doing is working." The executive asks himself, "Well, why did I spend a half a day finding out what I already knew, that I was fine?" The answer is that reassurance, from a trusted source, provides peace of mind and is, in and of itself, worthwhile.

For a question of value, however, peace of mind is not that meaningful a concept. An owner of a privately held business says to himself, "Well I think my business is really worth $5 million and I probably could sell it for at least $4.5 million." If an appraiser does a full-scale valuation and comes back with a report that the business is worth between $5 million and $6 million, the report really accomplishes little unless the owner plans to sell or gift some of the stock or borrow money from the bank. In the absence of some sort of transaction, an appraisal really provides relatively little comfort, more like the clean bill of health from the physician.

So while many executives submit to an annual physical exam, virtually no one voluntarily asks an appraiser for an opinion of value. In fact, in 40 years not a single client has asked the author to determine the value of something just to satisfy their intellectual curiosity. Many businessmen would like to know what their business is worth, but only up to the point where they have to spend money obtaining an answer. Spending actual cash to determine a theoretical number, with limited practical results, does not rank very high in the priority list of hardheaded businessmen.

It is a truism in the valuation profession that a client always has some sort of transaction in mind when he requests a formal valuation study. There is nothing wrong with that; it is simply a fact of life.

Recall that at times a valuation report will be misused; for example, an insurance valuation (high values) will be submitted to a lending institution that wants liquidation value (much lower value). The only real protection is for the reader of any valuation report to actually read it, not just turn to the last page and get an answer.

So we assume for this chapter that the reader has an actual need to know the value of some asset, and needs a formal opinion of value that can be obtained from a valuation specialist. Why can't the person simply tell a prospective lender, independent auditor, retired partner, divorcing spouse, or friendly IRS agent, "Well, *in my opinion*, the asset is worth 'X.'

The answer to this question is why thousands of appraisers make a living, generating over \$1 billion in revenue each year. Put the opposite way, people are spending over \$1 billion each year to answer the question, "What is this asset really worth?"

The reason for hiring an appraiser, for relying on his report when decisions have to be made, is that the appraiser brings two related factors to the process. One is *independence*, and the other is *experience*. Any third party who needs information about the value of your business is far more likely to believe an independent party than the owner himself. Why do used car salesmen suffer from a bad reputation? The answer is that they are not independent, and a prospective buyer has to be very cautious that the car's good points are not overstated and any problems remain hidden. So, if a used car salesman tells you, "This car runs like it just came from the factory—in fact, it is even better because it has been broken in," you might be tempted to hold on to your wallet. The car salesman has a financial interest in selling you the car, right then and there.

If a business owner wants to borrow money from a lending institution, the bank will often ask for collateral (e.g., a lien on the tangible personal property.) The bank usually wants assurance that the *value* of the collateral will equal or exceed the amount of the prospective borrowing. Why does a bank often request that the borrower obtain an appraisal of the assets that will serve as the collateral? From the bank's perspective, the borrower is neither independent, in terms of establishing value, nor necessarily experienced about asset values in the used equipment and auction markets.

In these situations, a prospective car buyer will ask a trusted friendly auto mechanic to look at the car, while the bank will suggest an appraiser who specializes in used equipment asset values. Appraisers are almost always independent, and if—in the rare instance—they are not, they must disqualify themselves from performing a valuation. Further, appraisers usually specialize by type of asset and develop expertise in certain areas. You would not ask a jewelry appraiser to value your house, or a business appraiser to value your grandmother's antiques. Experience in a field can be developed in only one way: time.

EVALUATING AN APPRAISER'S EXPERIENCE

The very first question an appraiser is asked by a prospective client invariably is, "Have you recently valued any businesses similar to mine?" It is a truism that an advertising agency cannot have two clients in the same industry; similarly, attorneys cannot represent both parties to a dispute. But it appears to be all right for an auditing firm or an appraisal firm to have two or more clients in the same industry. Why professional accountants and appraisers can be trusted to keep information from two competitors confidential, but advertising executives cannot be so trusted, has never been clear.

Clients are comforted if their chosen valuation specialist has recently valued very similar assets. The ultimate inquiry this author received dealt with a lawsuit regarding fax machines. In all seriousness the attorney trying the case asked, "Have you ever valued spare parts for fax machines?" When told that we had never done this, but it was equally unlikely that any *other* appraiser ever had either, we soon got down to the real issue, which was whether he felt we were qualified for this important legal battle.

Just how important is experience in a particular field? *The basic principles of valuation are the same for every valuation ever performed.* There are three, and only three, approaches to valuing any asset (or liabilities, as considered by the Financial Accounting Standards Board [FASB]). These, as discussed earlier, are the cost approach, the income approach, and the market comparable approach.

A jewelry appraiser, after identifying the stones by size and quality, will determine the value by reference to the existing market for comparable jewelry. In turn, this requires experience and expertise in telling diamonds from zircons and truly identifying exactly the nature of the asset. The same holds true for an antiques expert, the most important aspect of the job being the ability to tell an original from a fake. So, for some types of appraisals, knowledge of prices in the market may actually be less important than being able to tell the real from the artificial.

For a real estate appraiser, knowledge of all three approaches to value is critical because the *cost* of a building, the *income* to be derived from the building, and the *market* for comparable properties all enter into his final determination. Real estate appraisers, however, do not have a problem in identifying a house from a warehouse from an apartment complex—different experience, different skills, same valuation approaches.

Now let us look at the primary topic of this book, which is valuations for Fair Value (FV) of businesses and business assets, both tangible and intangible. Virtually any individual setting himself forth as an appraiser of businesses and business assets will understand the valuation concepts of the cost, income, and market approaches to value. Any competent master of business administration (MBA) or certified public accountant (CPA) can grasp these concepts immediately. In fact, every reader of this book understands these.

What separates skilled appraisers is the *experience* they bring. That experience tends to become more specialized over time. So, for example, many appraisers work in the area of gift and estate taxes. The issues there usually revolve around taxes, with the IRS on the other side, and with final judgments being rendered by the courts. Appraisers in this area are thoroughly familiar with the relevant cases and precedents, and are able to craft a valuation report that will have a high probability of standing up in a court challenge by the IRS. Other appraisers specialize in valuing damage awards in cases of product liability or wrongful death. The issues there tend to revolve around the appropriate methodologies, and what types of income and expense are appropriate to recognize.

For the topic of this book, Fair Value for business situations, an appraiser requires experience in, and understanding of, financial accounting and reporting requirements. In turn, this has to be combined with an ability to quickly grasp business policies and relate to the subject's business model. A good business appraiser can look at a company, its management, and its business model, and swiftly determine what its prospects are. Then, when provided financial forecasts, the basis of FV, he can rapidly evaluate how likely management's outlook is to occur; is management's projection based more on hope and wishes, or is it based on solid economic reality?

This suggests that experienced appraisers can develop supportable indications of value fairly quickly, and this is correct. But any third party planning to rely on the appraiser's professional judgment is highly unlikely to accept only an oral indication of value with an implied "trust me" from the valuation specialist.

We tell our clients over and over again, "We can arrive at the correct answer pretty quickly; what takes our time is writing the report that *supports* our position." As mentioned several times in this book, readers of an appraisal report are entitled to understand the appraiser's thought process, the logic he used in arriving at a final conclusion of value. By the same token, however, when this is provided in the report, but the user goes only to the final answer, the potential misuse of the valuation increases geometrically.

How can a prospective client properly evaluate whether a specific appraisal firm—or appraiser, for that matter—will perform up to expectations? There appear to be three different approaches:

1. Some clients put out a request for proposals (RFP) and evaluate written responses.
2. Some clients ask for the names of previous clients and then may or may not contact them.

3. Some clients truly interview the prospective valuation specialist and then make an individual judgment one way or the other.

Having participated on multiple occasions in each of these situations, here are my personal observations:

- An RFP approach may well be the most efficient way of obtaining a low-cost valuation report. If you have a mandated requirement, say, for an allocation of purchase price in a business combination or to value collateral for a loan, and you don't really care what the answer is as long as the regulator, lender, or auditor is satisfied, then go for the RFP. Individuals and firms tend to "sharpen their pencil" when they know there is competition. In an RFP environment, undoubtedly one firm or another will be motivated to submit a low bid to obtain the assignment. Perhaps they have idle time prospectively on their schedule and any fee appears better than no fee.

  The problem with the RFP approach to hiring an appraiser is that there is unlikely to be close rapport between the parties. It will be viewed by the appraiser as just another assignment, without necessarily becoming involved in the client's real goals and opportunities. From the client's perspective, if this is seen as nothing more than a compliance issue, it may not make too much difference who does the work. When a low fee is the ultimate criterion, the professional is unlikely to do anything more than the bare minimum contracted for. Many times in a valuation assignment, things turn up that require consultation and further decision and action. How likely is an appraiser, under time and cost pressure, to go the extra mile?

- Contacting previous clients sounds like a good idea. How often will the appraiser choose his most satisfied accounts, as compared to the prior assignments that most closely resemble the current requirement? We have stated many times that no two valuation assignments are the same. In fact, this is what helps retain skilled professionals in the field. The tremendous variety of both requirements and industries represents an intellectual challenge that most appraisers find attractive. By the same token, a happy client in a totally different valuation requirement may not provide a relevant answer to the prospective client's real issues.

■ It should be obvious at this point that the writer strongly prefers the third of the three approaches, and that is a meaningful interview, either in person or by phone. The client should be willing to spell out the issues and the expectations. The appraiser should be able to ask intelligent questions and, in most cases, provide the client with an idea as to how the assignment would be undertaken, who would do the work, what information would have to be supplied, a reasonable time frame for the work, and an estimated fee. At that point, the client can either say, "Yes, you're hired," or that he would like to talk to one or two more appraisers before making a decision. Painful as that may be to an appraiser who may have spent an hour or so discussing the issues, in the long run both parties will be more satisfied; a long-term relationship between a company and an appraisal firm has a lot of benefits.

The most successful client assignments come about when the appraiser has a clear understanding of what information is needed by the client and how it will be used. By the same token, the appraiser should not only understand the client's needs, but have at least some empathy toward the requirements. Empathy, however, does not mean giving up independence.

INDEPENDENCE AND ETHICS IN FAIR VALUE

The topic of ethics has become almost commonplace. For example, every self-respecting MBA program teaches at least one ethics course, and it is usually mandatory. CPAs in many states, as part of their continuing education requirements, have to take an ethics refresher every year. There are ethical standards in the appraisal field, primarily relating to the requirement that appraisers have no financial interest in the assets being appraised. Put simply, an appraiser cannot put a value on his own house and submit this to the mortgage company as support for the loan. The ethical issue for appraisers comes when they become advocates for the client.

Lawyers are expected, even required, to argue their client's position to the best of their ability, coming up with whatever approach and argument may be successful. While not permitting perjury or other obviously illegal behavior, lawyers are supposed to use every technique at their disposal. Even if the lawyer knows a client is guilty as charged, the lawyer still fights for acquittal. The rationale, of course, is that it is up to the prosecution to make their own case, and if they do a poor job, then perhaps the accused should go free.

Here is where appraisers have to walk a very fine line. We know what answer our client would like us to come up with and support. We want satisfied clients, both for repeat business and for referrals. Happy clients receive the answer they are looking for. Unhappy clients are the recipients of news that the appraiser "just can't get there."

The pressure on appraisers to meet client expectations is great. While we have never seen a case of an appraiser valuing his own assets for some third party, we have often seen appraisers under severe client pressure. Sometimes, unfortunately, appraisers have been known to give in to the wishes of the client.

The topic of lawsuits was discussed in Chapter 3. Here, it is appropriate to look at what went wrong, and why otherwise respected appraisers produced reports that, in hindsight at least, were badly flawed.

In the case of a newly formed subsidiary that was taking on way too much debt, a "solvency opinion" was prepared for the board of directors that asserted the new company was solvent, that it could meet its debts as they became due. Some two years after the transaction, during which hundreds of millions of high-interest debt ("junk bonds") had been sold, the new company filed for chapter 11, being hopelessly insolvent. What went wrong? How could the valuation firm have so badly missed?

In the course of a protracted lawsuit, the author was retained to review the solvency opinion and the related determinations of value. It all went back to the management of the parent company, who were desperate for cash. The spin-off of the subsidiary, and the incurrence of debt that would be upstreamed as a dividend, was seen as the solution to the company's cash-flow problems. Lawyers, accountants, and investment bankers put in thousands of hours of work and racked up millions of dollars in fees, and all the professional effort was successful. The deal was ready to go—buyers had been found for the bonds. All that was lacking was a piece of paper, prepared by a valuation firm, that the new company was solvent.

The bond buyers relied on the solvency opinion as some assurance that the interest and principal would be paid. The board of directors relied on the solvency opinion to prevent a charge that the deal was not a "fraudulent conveyance."[1]

Yet even a casual scrutiny of the solvency opinion revealed a major flaw. The projections prepared by management showed some totally unbelievable sales and profit projections (in the prior three years, the company had run at a loss, and for the next ten years was projected to be substantially cash-flow positive—without any real indication as to how the turnaround would happen). Worse, the valuation firm, for some reason never clearly explained, simply neglected to put into the cash-flow projections the future interest expense related to the sale of the newly issued junk bonds. Without the interest expense, things were tight, but one could hope that maybe good things would happen and the company would pull through.

Had the interest expense been incorporated into the cash flow projections it would have been impossible for the solvency opinion to show anything other than that the borrower (the spin-off company) was insolvent. Showing that the borrower was insolvent would have killed the deal, wasted millions of dollars of fees and a half-year of effort by lawyers, accountants, and investment bankers, not to mention that the parent company would have been in dire straits financially.

One can only imagine the pressure on the valuation firm to come up with the "right answer," that the spin-off was solvent. The last line of the last page did indeed say something to the effect that "based on everything above, we believe the company is solvent within the legal definition of solvency [which is a three-part test]." It would not be surprising if everyone at the board meeting where the solvency opinion was presented gave a big sigh of relief when they heard the oral report and were handed a copy of the opinion; they must then have gone on to hold a celebration.

Obviously, the participants wanted to hear that the new company passed the solvency tests and were probably in no rush to question the

---

[1]It is outside the scope of this book to go into the details of fraudulent conveyance. Suffice it to say that if money is paid out, as in this case in the form of a dividend, at a time when the payer is insolvent, the deal will not stand up, and there can be substantial legal liabilities for those involved.

valuation firm in depth about their analysis. But a casual reading of the total report might have raised a few eyebrows, and a very careful reading would have sent up major warning signs. The valuation firm in question had crafted a masterpiece of obfuscation, with all sorts of "we have relied on ... " and "we have assumed ... " and "we take no responsibility for.... " They even managed to come up with some words that did not excuse leaving out the future interest expense, but labeled the exhibit in such a way that a careless reader might miss the exact and literal wording, which was very "cute."

The facts, of course, could not be buried for long. The company did go bankrupt because the interest and principal had to be paid, whether or not the appraisers had or had not included this in their projections. A large and expensive lawsuit followed; the case did not bring much credit to the parties involved and ended up with a major payout for damages.

The moral is twofold. Clients must read the full appraisal report, not just accept the single estimate of value from the last page and *assume* that everything else in the report supports the conclusion. Second, when a transaction rises or falls on the word of an appraiser, ask the question, "In your heart, do you *really* believe the conclusion, not based on the assumptions stated in the report, but on the *real* business economics?"

At the end of the day, appraisers and their appraisal reports only provide guidance to someone else who is ultimately responsible for the final decision. Put a different way, appraisers do not make decisions; appraisers only provide their own professional estimate of FV so someone else can make a financial or business decision. Actually, for an appraiser, this is not too bad a position to be in.

AUDITORS: ARE THEY THE FINAL QUALITY CHECK?

Prior to about 2003, appraisal reports prepared by the major independent valuation firms were reviewed by independent auditors, and this was considered by many as part of the "normal audit process." But the level of review more often than not was cursory. As long as the value conclusions seemed to flow logically from the assumptions, and the assumptions themselves appeared reasonable, there was little reason for the auditors to question the value indication in the final report.

A second factor was at work prior to 2003, and that was the fact that, right or wrong, *auditors were often performing valuations for their own audit clients*. That this represented a conflict of interest did not seem to bother either the auditors or their clients. In fact, on more than one occasion, our valuation firm lost business to a client's audit firm when the audit partner told the chief financial officer, "If you let us do the valuation, the audit will go a lot easier." [This actually happened.]

As a consequence of (1) the audit firms having plenty of valuation business, which they essentially obtained "over the transom" without any selling effort; and (2) little real pressure on auditing the accuracy of valuations because the FASB had not yet moved to an FV orientation, the relationship between auditors and independent valuation firms was reasonable. You might say it was perceived as a "live and let live" situation.

Then came Enron, WorldCom, HealthSouth, and so forth, followed by the Sarbanes-Oxley Act (SOX). SOX explicitly forbade audit firms to perform valuation work for their own audit clients. Further, with the Public Company Accounting Oversight Board (PCAOB) now looking over the shoulder of auditors trying to find "audit lapses," auditors have really dug in and started questioning *everything*. Concurrently, there was a sudden decline in valuation work for the audit firms' appraisal staff because of the prohibition against doing valuation work for audit clients. Because the Big Four audit firms had never really developed a marketing operation for their valuation work, they were having idle time. Previously, the argument had been, "Why spend resources on business development when we have all the valuation work we can handle?" This work, of course, had been brought to them on a platter by their audit partners.

Put together a sudden drop in workload of new valuations and a PCAOB requirement that toughened audit standards, and we had a recipe for auditor/appraiser conflict. After about 2004, when the full import of SOX had become apparent, the valuation work of independent appraisers had been subjected to an unprecedented degree of scrutiny. It is somewhat ironic, at least to the author, that the same work he performed five years ago and was deemed fully sufficient for financial reporting, now is so questionable that it has to be reviewed down to the smallest nit.

In at least half of the situations we are familiar with, audit firms are charging audit clients at least as much, if not more, to review independent appraisals as the valuation firm charged initially. This does not count the additional time the appraiser now has to spend answering all the auditor questions, time that ultimately is paid for by the client. Put a different way, *the cost of obtaining FV information has essentially doubled* since the adoption of SOX. This is another example of the law of unintended consequences.

EXPERIENCE IN YOUR INDUSTRY VERSUS OVERALL EXPERIENCE

As mentioned earlier, potential clients invariably ask if we have performed appraisal work for clients in the same industry. There is always the implicit assumption by those saying that if we had just valued a supermarket chain last month, then valuing a supermarket chain for the new client would be a far superior product; or, if we have not recently valued a supermarket chain, how in the world are we ever going to perform the assignment on the subject supermarket in a timely and competent manner?

It is reasonable for a prospective client to inquire about the background and competency of any professional before engaging him or her. Not just any doctor with an MD degree should be engaged for plastic surgery, much less brain surgery. The MD degree by itself tells you little.

The same holds true for appraisers, albeit in a somewhat different manner. The fact is that a competent financial appraiser can value almost any type of business enterprise. A competent real estate appraiser is fully capable of valuing almost any type of real property. Appraisers who specialize in machinery and equipment are able to go into almost any manufacturing or distribution facility and provide reasonable and supportable answers.

The experience that an appraiser should have is *not* related to industry background, contrary to popular belief among attorneys and CFOs. What is required is the appropriate technical background. So, for example if you have a complex gift or estate tax valuation issue, it probably would be better to identify an appraiser with significant experience with the IRS. If the issue relates to the application of FV to financial reporting, then the appraiser should be familiar with FASB and Securities and Exchange Commission (SEC) requirements. If a client has a complex series of financial instruments and derivatives to be valued, an appraiser with quantitative experience should be engaged.

Put a different way, it is the *type of appraisal* that calls for specific experience, not the particular company or industry in which that experience was gained. Clients are asking the wrong question when they question an appraiser, before deciding whether or not to engage him, about prior engagements in the same or similar industries. What *should* be the primary emphasis in a Due Diligence process of engaging a valuation specialist is the purpose(s) for which prior valuations work was performed. For example, the author has had significant experience as an expert witness in various litigations involving questions of value and damages. It is the testimony experience that is relevant, not whether the cases dealt with the paper industry or milk processing.

One point we stress with prospective clients is that even if we have not recently worked in that industry, we know how to go about obtaining the relevant background and industry-specific knowledge. Our skill is in "getting up to speed" very quickly. After all, if you have worked in 50 different industries, when it comes to the 51st, there are bound to be many similarities, and the differences can be overcome quickly.

Consider two appraisers who appear to be equally competent competing for the same assignment; one had worked in that industry last fall, while the other has no specific experience in that industry. But the assignment involves transfer pricing, an issue with significant IRS ramifications. The client should choose the appraiser with transfer pricing experience, even if not in that industry, over the appraiser who knows the industry but has little background in transfer pricing.

REDUCING COSTS—WORKING WITH INDEPENDENT AUDITORS AND THE SEC

We have mentioned that as an unintended result of SOX, the cost of valuation work has essentially doubled. Auditing firms are spending as much time reviewing the work of valuation specialists as the appraiser spent initially. This may provide employment for Big Four accounting firm valuation staff, but the incremental effort is totally non-value-added. However, this book can describe only what is, not what should be. So the real issue is: "Can companies reduce the cost of valuation work?"

The ideal way to minimize costs, for any valuation assignment that will be used for financial reporting, is to hold an initial meeting with the company, the auditor, and the independent valuation specialist. At the meeting, the client can lay out what he feels are the valuation issues. The appraiser will discuss what valuation approaches he will utilize, what assumptions will be necessary, and what will be his sources of information. At that point, the auditor *should* be in a position to say, "Well, if you do exactly what you say, and the information is as we assume, then it looks as if all we will have to do is to review your work. The approach itself makes sense."

Notice that we said this is what the auditor *should* say. All too often, the auditor says, "As a result of Sarbanes-Oxley, I can't discuss what you are going to do because I would lose my independence! You, Mr. Appraiser, do your work first, and then we will decide if we like the approach you took."

It is this latter approach that doubles the cost for the client. Each of the Big Four audit firms has their own proprietary approach to valuations. In practice, they want the independent appraiser to have followed their unique approach. Consequently, all we can do is deliver our valuation report to the best of our ability, and then sit back and wait while the audit firm tries to get us to reconstruct our work in their format.

It is my belief that both the SEC and the PCAOB have expressed the opinion that discussing valuation methodology with a client and the appraiser prior to the commencement of the work does *not* constitute an impairment of the auditor's independence. Nevertheless, this is a common response.

Is there a good solution? At the end of the day, the company, which is a client of both the appraisal firm and the auditor, must step in and take charge. *Separate budgets must be established in advance*, by both the appraiser and the auditor, for performing *and* reviewing the total valuation assignment.

Then, if either the appraiser or the auditor wants to charge more than the agreed-upon budget, he should have to communicate with the company prior to charging more time. At that point, it is reasonable for the company to ask, "Well, what do you have to do now that you did not know about then? Why didn't you anticipate this initially, since everyone had a chance to discuss, in as much detail as needed, an understanding of the assignment, the methodology, the assumptions, and required information?"

The author has used this exact approach several times, and it works. Auditors may be unhappy, but there is no reason for a company to give the audit firm a "blank check" by running up untold hours on unnecessary work. The reason we used the term *unnecessary* is that many of the questions asked by auditors come off a printed checklist developed by the audit firm. Usually, quite junior staff is assigned the task of checking the audit report against the predetermined checklist. There are two possible reasons why the appraisal report does not check out to the auditor's list. The first would be that the appraiser left out a crucial step, made an erroneous calculation, or simply did not explain clearly and concisely what was performed and why it was done. In such situations, questions from the audit firm may be appropriate.

There is a second scenario that is all too common in practice. The appraiser produced a good report, with sound methodology and appropriate assumptions. But the junior auditor or junior valuation specialist at the audit firm simply does not know enough about valuation to realize that a departure from his firm's checklist is actually appropriate. Going even further, had the appraisal firm done what the junior interprets the checklist to mean, the valuation actually might be incorrect.

The author and many of his colleagues, who average at least 15 to 20 years of experience, face this situation time and time again. In effect, we have to educate the audit firm's employees, and it is very hard to charge our client for that time. Many appraisal firms will put into their engagement letter notice that the estimated fee encompasses, say, a half-day of auditor discussion, and any additional time spent on the audit responses will be charged for. Appraisers are reluctant to bill for this time, however, because unless the appraiser is 100% correct and the audit firm 100% wrong (which is seldom the case), we get into a judgment area. If the audit firm legitimately questions the appraiser's judgment, then it is incumbent on the appraiser to defend his judgment. Consequently, when and how much to charge for incremental auditor interchange becomes a gray area.

SEC INTERACTION

It is public knowledge that as the FASB moves toward FV accounting, and more information is presented in financial statements as being at FV, the SEC simultaneously is getting more involved in valuation. Valuation specialists are being added to the SEC staff, and it is assumed that they have the ability to review registrant filings containing FV information. The author has participated in several of these discussions, and in some ways they are more difficult than comparable discussions with auditors.

The reason is the clout the SEC has. Auditors can always threaten not to sign off if they disagree with a particular valuation issue. In practice, and after discussion, any differences are usually resolved in the context of the overall financial statements. The application of materiality also enters into an auditor's final determination as to what can or should be "passed." But when an issue receives the attention of an SEC staffer, the focus is always on that one issue, with no consideration of the big picture.

The SEC often seems to want companies to do exactly the opposite of what the company itself wants. For example, in the interest of conservatism, banks often want to boost their bad debt reserve even before delinquencies are going up. This can be based on past experience with economic ups and downs, and the bank can be pretty certain that future loan losses will occur, and it makes sense to accrue for them now. But the SEC, fearing possible manipulation, precludes additions to bad debt reserves without "hard" information, not informed management judgment.

Alternatively, if a company has to take an impairment charge for goodwill, the SEC will ask, "Why didn't you take this earlier?" In one case the SEC does not want the company to be conservative, and in the other they question why the firm was not more conservative earlier. No wonder many registrants and their auditors have an adversarial position with the SEC, feeling that whatever the company wants to do, the SEC wants just the opposite.

The previous statement may be perceived as both biased and unfair. Nevertheless, the author truly believes it to be true. In fairness, it is very easy for a staff accountant or valuation specialist at the SEC to become cynical about filings. Many companies do try to play games; egregious accounting and/or valuation positions are taken all too often. The problem is that this small minority of registrants truly poisons the pond for everyone. So companies that really are trying to do the right thing will get "dinged" by the SEC if for no other reason than that they did not sufficiently explain their decisions.

We have discussed valuation problems companies have with their auditors and valuation issues with the SEC. Another category of problems, perhaps the most troublesome of all, arises when the audit firm asserts to a company, "You have to do it this way because the SEC insists on it." When this statement is made, it is usually without specific support—just a "feeling" by the auditor that the SEC wants or does not want a specific position taken. In effect, the SEC is brought into the discussion to preclude the audit firm from arguing their own position. It is much easier to say, "This is the way it should be done because the SEC [not us] wants it that way."

Certainly, companies should rely on their audit firm to keep them out of trouble if at all possible. But we have seen many cases where the company feels they are correct and the auditor's position is wrong. In other words, there is a legitimate difference of opinion, and the auditor justifies his position that "this is what the SEC wants." Yet the company believes that following the auditor's advice will actually provide incorrect information to shareholders and creditors.

Is there a solution? In these situations, we have recommended that the company approach the SEC staff directly. Accounting firms do not like registrants going to the SEC without the auditing firm's having a presence at the meeting. It is our belief that in the case of a significant disagreement with an auditor, and the only evidence adduced by the auditor is the shibboleth that "the SEC wants it this way," then the company should go alone. Put your best case in front of the SEC staff, showing that for you to rigidly follow the auditor's requirement will actually be counter-productive. If the auditor is at the meeting, he will try to justify his previous position, which you don't want or need.

We can think of at least two real-life cases where the company ultimately decided *not* to go to the SEC, and instead (unwillingly) adopted the auditor's position on the valuation issue. For some reason, in both cases, the company had a new auditor the following year, perhaps based on "too high fees."

We cannot explain why auditors are getting extremely stubborn in the area of valuation, and we predict there will be more of these disputes. But rather than fight with the auditor, it is our recommendation that you go around the auditor directly to the SEC. Individually, it is our observation that the SEC staff is of very high caliber. They want to do a good job, and when the proper facts are put in front of them, they will ultimately make a pretty sound decision.

It is the "shoot from the hip" *initial* SEC comments that perhaps are taken way too seriously by audit firms, because they somehow view this as an affront to their manhood. For some reason, tax professionals do not mind taking on the IRS. But financial auditors do not seem to have established the same independent relationship with the SEC. Many auditors simply advise their clients, "Well if the SEC wants it this way (based on just the initial review by the Division of Corporate Finance), you had better do it." Auditors do not seem to be ready to take on the SEC the way tax attorneys and accountants won't hesitate for a minute to challenge the IRS or state tax authorities.

If the auditors won't challenge the SEC, and you think the Commission staff is wrong, you have very little to lose by going and discussing this directly in Washington.

A final comment on auditor review of valuations and the impact of the PCAOB on this issue: Audit firms probably are correct to take PCAOB reviews very seriously.

The bad news is that the PCAOB often seems to be more interested in the "process" than in the final results. There is tremendous emphasis by PCAOB on completeness of work papers. So just as audit firms review our valuation reports by ticking off a checklist, so also do the PCAOB inspectors follow a checklist approach. As long as an audit file has a complete set of work papers, things will probably pass. Woe if the checklist finds a gap.

This probably explains the interminable questions that auditors ask of us in the valuation field—they are really preparing for a possible PCAOB inspection. But if they documented an initial discussion as to how the valuation work was going to be done, and exercised professional judgment that the appraiser's approach made sense, then all they would have to do is verify that the appraiser did what he said he would do.

SUMMARY AND CONCLUSIONS

In this, the last chapter, we provide our overall conclusions and recommendations. There is little doubt that Fair Value is going to become an ever more important part of financial reporting. Whether this is going to help companies or their shareholders and creditors is a matter of opinion.

As close as the author is to the valuation field after 40 years, he sees the problems all too clearly, and may not totally understand the benefits of Fair Value financial reporting. Having said that, we still believe that the same asset can have two or more different values at the same time, depending on the use to which the value information will be put and who is the recipient of the information.

Yet the FASB continues to insist that there is "one" value and that they can tell companies, in advance, what the definition of value should be and the appropriate methodology for arriving at that answer.

The FASB has been under pressure to adopt a "principles-based" approach to standards, rather than a "rules-based" approach as they have for the last 35 years. Just look at the accounting rules for leases, derivatives, pensions, or income taxes, and you will see that we are far from principles-based standards. Unfortunately, in writing Statement of Accounting Standard (SFAS) 157, the FASB continued down the previous rules-based path they were on, putting in a requirement that values be determined on an exit price and for the still-unknown "market participant." By turning on its head 115 years of experience with Fair Market Value—the concept with which businessmen, appraisers, the IRS, and the courts were all familiar—the FASB has now created its own rules-based world of valuation.

We hope this book has provided some clarity in the potentially confusing world of Fair Value. We do predict, however, that before all the dust settles, there will be sufficient changes to justify a new and revised edition of this book.

Sample Capital Stock Report

**SUMMARY APPRAISAL
REPORT OF ABC
CORPORATION AS OF
DECEMBER 31, XXXX**

XX-XX-XXXXX

DATE   File Reference: XX-XX-XXXXX

Mr. Sam Jones
President
ABC Corporation
123 Main Street
CITY, STATE ZIP

Dear Mr. Jones:

In accordance with your authorization, we have made an investigation and appraisal of the outstanding shares of the capital stock of ABC Corporation and submit this *Summary Appraisal Report* of our findings. The date of our valuation is December 31, XXXX.

The purpose of this appraisal is to estimate the market value of the capital stock of ABC Corporation, on both a controlling interest basis and a minority interest basis. It is our understanding that this appraisal will be used for corporate planning purposes ; it may be invalid if used for any other purpose.

The applicable standard of value for this appraisal is market value, which is defined as:

> the amount at which property or common stock of a business enterprise would exchange between a willing buyer and a willing seller, each having reasonable knowledge of all pertinent facts, neither being under compulsion to buy or sell, and with equity to both parties. Market value is synonymous with the legal term "fair market value.'[1]

---

[1] American Society of Appraisers – Business Valuation Standards, Definitions

XX-XX-XXXXX

Mr. Sam Jones
DATE
Page 2

Based on the information and analysis contained in our *Summary Appraisal Report*, it is our opinion that the market value of the total common equity, on a controlling interest basis, in the business enterprise known as ABC Corporation, as of December 31, XXXX, was

$XX,XXX,XXX

In addition, based on the information and analysis contained in our *Summary Appraisal Report*, it is our opinion that the market value of the total common equity, on a nonmarketable, minority interest basis, in the business enterprise known as ABC Corporation, as of December 31, XXXX, was

$XX,XXX,XXX

or

$XXX,XXX per share

(Based on XXX total shares outstanding)

The attached appraisal was conducted in accordance with generally accepted appraisal standards, as promulgated by the American Society of Appraisers (ASA) and the Uniform Standards of Professional Appraisal Practice (USPAP).

An appraisal report presenting the perspective of value, scope of the appraisal, data, procedures, conclusions, assumptions and limiting conditions, and certification is attached to this letter of transmittal.

Very truly yours,

MARSHALL & STEVENS INCORPORATED

AN APPRAISAL OF THE

MARKET VALUE OF

TOTAL COMMON EQUITY OF

ABC CORPORATION

VALUATION DATE AS OF DECEMBER 31, XXXX

APPRAISED BY

MARSHALL & STEVENS INCORPORATED
VALUATION AND FINANCIAL CONSULTANTS

PROFESSIONAL RESPONSIBILITY FOR THE APPRAISAL BY

SENIOR APPRAISER

PERFORMING APPRAISER

XX-XX-XXXXX

Table of Contents

Title Page

XX-XX-XXXXX

Table of Contents (Continued)

Exhibit A—Comparative Balance Sheets
Exhibit B—Comparative Income Statements
Exhibit C—Comparative Adjusted Income Statements
Exhibit D—Comparison of Industry Data
Exhibit E—Projected Cash Flows
Exhibit F—Discounted Net Cash Flow
Exhibit G—Publicly Traded Guideline Companies Business Descriptions
Exhibit H—Publicly Traded Guideline Companies Balance Sheet Comparison
Exhibit I—Publicly Traded Guideline Companies Income Statement Comparison
Exhibit J—Guideline Companies Financial Statement Comparisons
Exhibit K—Guideline Companies Ratio Analysis and Growth Rates
Exhibit L—Publicly Traded Guideline Companies Market Multiples
Exhibit M—Market Approach—Guideline Companies Method
Exhibit N—Summary of Restricted Stock Studies
Exhibit O—Summary of Court Cases

Certification
Assumptions and Limiting Conditions
Corporate Professional Qualifications
Appraiser's Qualifications

ABC Corporation

SECTION 1 - PERSPECTIVE OF THE APPRAISAL

Appraisal Background

Marshall & Stevens Incorporated was retained by Mr. Sam Jones, president of ABC Corporation, to prepare an appraisal of the entity known as ABC Corporation (hereinafter also referred to as "ABC" or the "Company"). The purpose of this appraisal is to estimate market value of the total common equity of the Company on both a controlling and minority basis. The premise of value is as a going concern and assumes control and minority transactional circumstances. The function of the appraisal is its use for corporate planning purposes. The date of the appraisal is December 31, XXXX.

The applicable standard of value for this appraisal is market value, which is defined as:

> the amount at which property or common stock of a business enterprise would exchange between a willing buyer and a willing seller, each having reasonable knowledge of all pertinent facts, neither being under compulsion to buy or sell, and with equity to both parties. Market value is synonymous with the legal term 'fair market value."[2]

Scope of the Appraisal

The scope of the appraisal summarizes the extent of data gathering and the analytical process employed in order to reach a credible conclusion.

The Appraisal Background section of this appraisal identified the client, the property appraised, the purpose and function of this appraisal, the applicable standard of value, and the effective date of the analysis.

In the course of this appraisal, certain members of the Company's management group were interviewed. The due diligence consisted of a review and assessment of underlying corporate documents, relevant financial data, and meetings/discussions with representatives of the Company. Specific due diligence included, but was not limited to, the following:

---

[2] American Society of Appraisers – Business Valuation Standards, Definitions

ABC Corporation

- A review of the Company's audited financial statements for the fiscal years ended June 30, YYYY through June 30, XXXX, prepared by _____ ;

- A review of the Company's reviewed financial statements for the six months ended December 31, ZZZZ and December 31, XXXX, prepared by _____;

In addition, we have reviewed publicly available economic information concerning the industries in which the Company is a part of and various other materials provided by the Company and their representatives. Sources of market and industry financial data included, but were not limited to:

- The Capital IQ Database

- The Value Line *Investment Survey*

- The IBISWorld Industry Report

- Business Valuation Resources' *Fourth-Quarter XXXX Economic Outlook*

- *Stocks, Bonds, Bills and Inflation Valuation Edition XXXX Yearbook* published by Ibbotson Associates

- Houlihan Lokey Howard & Zukin's *XXXX Mergerstat Review*

- Risk Management Association's *Annual Statement Studies ZZZZ-XXXX*

There are many factors to consider in determining the market value of the interest in the Company. We employed an appraisal framework typified by the Internal Revenue Service's Revenue Ruling 59-60, which issued these factors as a valuation guideline:

- The nature of the business and the history of the enterprise from its inception;

- The economic outlook in general and the conditions and outlook of the specific industry in particular;

ABC Corporation

- The book value of the stock and the financial condition of the business;

- The earning capacity of the Company;

- The dividend-paying capacity;

- Whether or not the enterprise had goodwill or other intangible value;

- Prior sales of the stock and the size of the block of stock to be valued; and

- The market price of stocks and the sizes of companies engaged in the same or a similar line of business having their stocks actively traded on an exchange or over-the-counter market.

Following a discussion of valuation techniques and procedures, we developed the selected techniques and procedures to derive a final, credible conclusion of value.

ABC Corporation

SECTION 2 – ENVIRONMENT

The environment section of the appraisal presents a description of the Company and an assessment of the macro and microeconomic influences, essentially an analysis of the Company's operating environment.

Business Description

Overview

ABC Corporation was incorporated as a C corporation in the state of Illinois in XXXX. The Company is engaged in the distribution of aluminum and steel, and manufacturing of related products for industrial and architectural metal users. Nearly 85% of ABC's business is in the construction industry (65% steel, 35% aluminum) and 15% in industrial (coils, stainless steel, etc.) applications. ABC acquires its aluminum and steel raw materials directly from the mill and cuts the metal and performs other manufacturing process to meet customer specifications. The Company is currently headquartered in a leased facility located in _____, Illinois.

In April 1973, ABC acquired 100% of the outstanding stock of _____Industries, Inc., a _____ corporation that is primarily engaged in the manufacturing of metal signs. It continues to manufacture and sell commercial signs and other metal products and serves as a southeastern point of distribution for the Company's aluminum and steel products.

Products and Manufacturing Facilities

Currently ABC has full production facilities in _____, ; _____, ; _____, ; and _____,. Each plant services customers within a 200-mile radius.

The Company's products include _____, _____ panels, _____ panels, _____ panels, integral panels, M&R panels, flush panels, soffit panels, framing systems, coping systems, gravel stops, flashing & trim, column covers, and metal fabrications.

The Company maintains extensive roll forming equipment in each of its plants. Each of its roll formers provides panels that have been _____ corrective leveled. Standing seam, flush, wall, and soffit panels are all factory formed in lengths up to 40 feet. _____ panels are tension leveled to provide superior flatness and feature an optional factory-applied sealant bead for improved water

ABC Corporation

resistance. The panels feature a 1-3/4" leg height and a continuous interlock for improved structural performance and wind resistance. _____ is available in prime quality aluminum, 24 and 22 gauge G-90 galvanized steel, and other metals. A strippable vinyl film can also be applied for protection during fabrication and installation, if desired. Vinyl masking is recommended on all applications requiring extra handling. The vinyl is removed immediately after installation.

ABC fabricates a wide range of roofing accessories. Coping, gravel stops, gutters, and downspouts are all formed from 25 standard _____ colors. With an inventory of over 5 million pounds and extensive processing capabilities, the Company is able to offer just-in-time service with a wide selection of colors and accessories.

Competition

ABC's primary competitors in the metal products manufacturing area include _____Manufacturing Co., ____ & Co., _____Co., Ryerson _____, Inc., _____ Building Systems, and _____ Steel & Aluminum. As an aluminum distributor, it also competes with _____ Metals, Inc. and _____ Metals, Inc.

Description of Stock Ownership

The Company's capitalization included one class of capital stock as of the valuation date. A total of 145 shares were outstanding as of the date of our appraisal. Following are the shareholders of the Company and their respective capital stock holdings as of the valuation date.

ABC Corporation

Shareholder	Number of Shares	Percentage Ownership
Sam Jones, Trustee under Agreement dated July 25, xxxx, Trust A	10	6.8966%
Michael Jones, Trustee under Agreement dated July 25, xxxx, Trust B	96	66.2069%
John Brown	8	5.5172%
Michael Jones as Trustee of Ann R. Jones Irrevocable Trust of September 6, XXXX	4	2.7586%
Michael Jones	9	6.2069%
Margaret Jones Brown	5	3.4483%
Kathryn Jones Smith	5	3.4483%
Jonathan S. Smith	4	2.7586%
Michael S. Brown	4	2.7586%
Total	145	100.0000%

ABC Corporation

Economic Review

In the appraisal of a business, the state of the general economy has influence over the future prospects of a company. Value of a company is indirectly related to the state of the general economy by virtue of factors such as inflation, interest rates, and consumer confidence levels.

The Fourth-Quarter XXXX edition of the Business Valuation Resources' *Economic Outlook Update* served as the source document for valuation purposes near the date of value. Specifically, the *Economic Outlook Update* is a review of the state of the U.S. economy that is updated on a quarterly basis. This summary provides an overview of the primary economic factors that prevailed as of the quarter nearest the date of value. Topics addressed and reviewed in the valuation analysis included:

- **General Economic Conditions**
  This section discusses the gross domestic product, consumer spending, government spending, business investments, rebuilding inventories, and the trade deficit. Each of these areas included quarterly and annual data and compares the quarter's performance with previous performance.

- **Consumer Prices And Inflation Rates**
  This section reviews various pricing indexes and the latest trends in inflation including: the producer price index, the consumer price for all urban customers, and the consumer price index for urban wage earners and clerical workers.

- **Interest Rates**
  This section presents the levels and recent changes in the level of the federal funds rate, the discount rate, and the treasury issues of various maturities. This section also reviews recent meetings and decisions by the Federal Reserve Board.

- **Unemployment**
  This section presents a review of monthly, quarterly, and annual changes in the unemployment rate, number of unemployed persons, employment in manufacturing, retail jobs, average hourly and weekly earnings.

- **Consumer Spending and Confidence**
  This section reviews indicators such as consumer spending on durable and nondurable goods, retail sales, the index of consumer confidence and the University of Michigan's Index of Consumer Sentiment.

ABC Corporation

- **The Stock and Bond Markets**
  This section presents a review of the quarterly and yearly development of major stock market indexes such as the Dow Jones Industrial Average, the Standard & Poor's 500 Index, the NASDAQ Composite Index, The Russell 2000 Index, and the Wilshire 5000 Index.

- **Construction**
  This section reviews housing starts, building permits, construction of single-family homes, thirty-year mortgage rates and more relevant economic indicators.

- **Manufacturing**
  This section presents a review of the monthly manufacturing index and the manufacturing capacity utilization, along with orders for goods made in U.S. factories.

In addition to reviewing the economic indicators referenced above, additional analysis was performed on near-term economic projections which may impact the Company's business operations moving forward. The following section was abstracted from the *Economic Outlook Update* and presents the Economic Outlook as of the Fourth-Quarter XXXX

With an improving trade deficit and solid consumer spending, coupled with mild weather conditions and low inflation rates, the economy posted a stronger than expected fourth quarter of XXXX. While most economists in the financial press feel the nation's economy will grow steadily during the next year, growth in the first half of 2007 may be somewhat slower, due to the return of more seasonable winter weather and the ongoing slump in the housing market.

According to Consensus Economics, Inc., publisher of Consensus Forecasts - USA, the real GDP is expected to grow by 2.3% in the first quarter and by 2.6% in the second quarter of 2007 (percentage change from previous quarter, seasonally adjusted annual rates). For 2007 and 2008, the real GDP growth rate is expected to be 2.4% and 3.0%, respectively (average percentage change on previous calendar year). In the long term, the real GDP is expected to grow by 3.1% for 2008-2016 (average percentage change over previous year).

According to the survey, consumer prices will increase 1.8% in 2007 and 2.3% in 2008. In the long term, Consensus Forecasts - USA also predicts consumer prices will grow by 2.3% for 2008-2016 (average percentage change over previous year). Producer prices are expected to increase 0.9% in 2007 and 1.7% in 2008.

ABC Corporation

Interest rates on three-month Treasury bills will decrease, while 10-year Treasury bonds will rise slightly over the next year, according to the forecasters of Consensus Forecasts - USA. According to the survey, three-month Treasury bills will fall from 5.0% at the end of April 2007 to 4.7% by the end of January 2008. The yield on 10-year Treasury bonds is expected to rise from 4.8% at the end of April 2007 to 4.9% by the end of January 2008. According to the survey, the three-month Treasury rate will average 4.6% for the years 2008-2016, while the 10-year Treasury bond yield is expected to average 5.3% over the same time period.

The forecasters polled by The Livingston Survey in December XXXX posted slightly more optimistic expectations about the level of the S&P 500 index in 2007 and 2008 than they did in the June XXXX survey. The Livingston Survey, which reports the median value across the 40 forecasters on the survey's panel, predicts that the S&P 500 index will rise steadily during the next two years. The December XXXX survey estimates that the index will reach 1433.6 by June 29, XXXX, while the June XXXX survey estimated the index would reach 1363.0 over the same time period. The index is projected to rise to 1475.0 by December 31, 2007 and 1563.7 by the end of 2008. The growth rate in after-tax corporate profits is expected to be 5.1% in XXXX followed by 5.7% in 2008.

The semiannual White House economic forecast, which was released on November 21, XXXX, predicted solid economic growth and a strong labor market, as well as a steady inflation rate. The administration's new forecast calls for the economy to grow 2.9% in XXXX, down slightly from 3.1% in XXXX and revised down 0.4 percentage points from the last forecast issued in June XXXX. The forecast predicted CPI inflation to grow at 2.6% in XXXX and XXXX, which were both revised upward from 2.4% in the previous survey. The White House also predicted that the nation would add about 129,000 jobs a month in XXXX and that the unemployment rate would remain at 4.6% through the end of XXXX, before growing to 4.8% in 2008. The same source forecasts that the Federal Reserve will keep short-term interest rates fairly steady over the next few years, but will raise interest rates on 10-year Treasury notes over the same time period.

In the fourth quarter, the FOMC decided not to change the federal funds rate, which remained at 5.25% for the second consecutive quarter. At the end of the fourth quarter, the Committee noted that, "Readings on core inflation have been elevated, and the high level of resource utilization has the potential to sustain inflation pressures. However, inflation pressures seem likely to moderate over time, reflecting reduced impetus from energy prices, contained inflation expectations, and the cumulative effects of monetary policy actions and other factors restraining aggregate demand." The Committee went on to say, "Nonetheless, the Committee judges that some inflation risks remain. The extent

ABC Corporation

and timing of any additional firming that may be needed to address these risks will depend on the evolution of the outlook for both inflation and economic growth, as implied by incoming information."[3]

Finally, the following chart was abstracted from the subject Economic Outlook Update, and provides historical economic data for the last five years, as well as forecasts for the next ten years of the US economy.

EXHIBIT 2: Historical Economic Data 2002-2006 and Forecasts 2007-2016

	HISTORICAL DATA					CONSENSUS FORECASTS**			
	2002	2003	2004	2005	2006	2007	2008	2008-2011	2012-2016
Real GDP*	1.60	2.50	3.90	3.20	3.40	2.40	3.00	3.10	3.00
Industrial Production*	0.00	1.10	2.90	3.90	4.60	2.50	3.20	3.28	3.50
Personal Consumption*	2.70	2.80	3.90	3.50	3.20	2.90	2.70	2.98	2.90
Nonresidential Investment*	-9.20	1.00	5.90	6.80	7.40	6.10	5.20	5.28	4.80
Government Spending*	4.40	2.50	1.90	0.90	2.10	1.90	1.60	NA	NA
CPI*	1.60	2.30	2.70	3.40	3.20	1.80	2.30	2.30	2.30
Unemployment Rate	5.80	6.00	5.50	5.10	4.70	4.80	4.90	NA	NA
Housing Starts *(millions)*	1.71	1.85	1.95	2.07	1.80	1.52	1.58	NA	NA

Source of historical data: www.bea.gov, www.bls.gov, www.census.gov, www.federalreserve.com

Source of consensus forecasts: *Consensus Forecasts-USA,* January 8, 2007, www.consensuseconomics.com

Notes:

*Numbers are based on percent change from preceding period, seasonally adjusted rates.

**Forecast numbers are based on average percent change on previous calender year.

*** Long term forecasts last updated in *Consensus Forecasts - USA,* October 9, 2006.

Personal Consumption includes spending on services, durable, and nondurable goods.

Government Spending includes federal, state, and local government spending.

---

[3] *"All of the contents of the economic outlook section of this valuation report are quoted from the* Economic Outlook Update™ *4Q XXXX published by Business Valuation Resources, LLC, © XXXX, reprinted with permission. The editors and Business Valuation Resources, LLC, while considering the contents to be accurate as of the date of publication of the* Update, *take no responsibility for the information contained therein. Relation of this information to this valuation engagement is the sole responsibility of the author of this valuation report."*

ABC Corporation

Industry Review

The Company's growth prospects will vary according to the conditions of the markets they operate in, as well as their own particular competitive strengths. In the current instance, the March 15, XXXX IBIS World Industry Report for the Ornamental and Architectural Metal Products Manufacturing in the US Industry served as the source document for valuation purposes.

Specifically, the IBIS World Industry Report contains trends, statistics, and analysis on market size, market share of competitors, and growth rates for the subject industry. Furthermore, the comprehensive study addresses the following topics for additional analysis in the valuation:

- *Industry Definitions*: consisting of products and services, similar industries, and demand & supply industries within the specific industry.
- *Key Statistics*: consisting of constant prices, current prices, real growth, and ratio tables for the specific industry.
- *Market Characteristics*: which includes market size, linkages, demand determinants, domestic and international markets, basis of competition and life cycles for the specific industry.
- *Segmentation*: including products and service segmentation, major market segments, industry concentration and geographic spreads for the specific industry.
- *Industry Conditions*: consisting of barriers to entry, taxation, industry assistance, regulation and deregulation, cost structure, capital and labor intensity, technology and systems, industry volatility and globalization for the specific industry.
- *Performance*: including current and historical performance for the specific industry.
- *Key Competitors*: consisting of major players and player performance for the specific industry.
- *Key Factors*: consisting of sensitivities and success factors for the specific industry.

ABC Corporation

In addition to reviewing the industry/economic indicators referenced above, additional analysis was performed on the near-term industry outlook which may impact the Company's business operations moving forward. The following section was abstracted from the subject IBIS World *Industry Report* and presents the current performance and industry outlook over the next five years from the publication date.

CURRENT PERFORMANCE

Industry Performance

In ZZZZ, IBISWorld estimated that sales revenue was 7.4 per cent or $2.928 billion lower at $36.590 billion. Manufacturing revenue per establishment was 4.5% lower (2000: $4.4 million; ZZZZ: $4.2 million). Productivity per employee (revenue and value added per employee) was stable in the five years to December ZZZZ. Lower sales revenue was reflective of the general economic slowdown affecting the US manufacturing sector over the period. The effect of the economic slowdown was further compounded by the events of September 11th, and the subsequent uncertainty in the economy after it. Furthermore, investment expenditure on non-residential fixed investment, particularly expenditures on structures in petroleum refineries; chemical plants; pharmaceutical plants; plastics plants; fertilizer plants; breweries and titanium plants; liquefied natural gas production; and food processing firms influenced the industry over the current period.

Product and market trends in the residential and nonresidential construction industries (demand for metal doors, windows, sheet metal air-conditioning, roofing, drainage etc.) have impacted revenue growth in the past five years. Important product and market trends in the industry (particularly in regards to metal windows and door products) include: (a) product design is becoming an ever more important factor in designing, manufacturing, and distributing hardware products. Customers are being given greater choice regarding shape, color and finish, and this adds value to the product. These features also add higher profit margins; (b) increased technical standardization has made it easier to integrate the different components with one another. This means that, to remain competitive, manufacturers will be forced to specialize and focus on specific product segments; (c) firms in lower-cost countries are increasing their market shares in the lower-price segments of the market.

The industrial nonbuilding structures construction industry it is estimated to have recorded cyclical revenue growth averaging around 3.0 per cent per annum during the five years to December ZZZZ, and roughly matching the pace of US GDP growth. Since the late 1990s, the expansion in industry activity has principally stemmed from the solid average growth in the value of electric power infrastructure construction (3.0 per cent per annum), and to a lesser extent the resurgent growth in gas infrastructure construction (4.8

ABC Corporation

per cent per annum), however demand from most other downstream markets slowed with the onset of general economic recession in 2001, and the corresponding collapse in gross fixed capital investment and industrial production. Over the five years to December ZZZZ, real gross fixed capital investment averaged 2.5 per cent per annum, while US industrial production is estimated to have averaged just 0.5 per cent per annum with declining trends in the downstream heavy materials industries.

A key driver of the Ornamental and Architectural Metal Products Industry (because of their comparatively higher demand for metal doors, windows, sheet metal air-conditioning, roofing, drainage etc.), the commercial and institutional building industry maintained an unprecedented high level of activity from the mid-1990s to 2000, driven by the robust pace of domestic demand, buoyant company profits and solid employment growth. However, from 2001 onwards the demand for new building construction in the commercial building segment (offices, hotels, retail stores, etc.) contracted sharply in response to the recessionary downturn in the US economy, increased volatility on equity markets, and excess stock on commercial property markets (these trends have corresponded to a fall in industry revenue). During the early 2000s, demand for industry services was partially cushioned by the buoyant conditions in the institutional building market, particularly the publicly funded educational building market, and the privately funded health building market.

Impacting on industry profitability over the past 5 years has been the cost of inputs. As a percentage of revenue total costs have risen from 47 per cent to 48 per cent of total industry revenue. Over ZZZZ, the domestic price of steel (as measured using the producer price index for steel mill products) rose strongly, up 34 percent. This follows two years of significantly smaller price increases. A strong recovery in the domestic and world economy led to expansion in many sectors, including construction. As such steel products were in high demand. World demand for steel has been particularly strong from China, causing a shortage in world steel supplies. Prices are expected to ease over the remainder of the XXXX, as domestic and world demand slows. Higher interest rates in the US together with government intervention in China will see steel demand for steel fall in the medium term. The Chinese government has slowed bank lending by forcing banks to keep more money in reserve, and has also banned new investment in certain industries to avoid overheating.

Year-on-Year Analysis
In XXXX, the Ornamental and Architectural Metal Products Manufacturing Industry was estimated to have generated sales of $39,518 million, representing an increase of 5.7 per cent compared to 1XXXX With more internationally manufactured goods available in the domestic market (and lower than expected export revenues), US manufacturers were forced to cut prices and material costs in a bid to remain competitive (value added was 1 per cent lower over the year). In XXXX, demand from the US Construction sector was

buoyed a number of factors including continued strong GDP and further increases in the level of fixed nonresidential investment of 8.7 percent. This surge in activity reflected the strong growth across both the commercial building and institutional building markets in XXXX, with the fastest growing market segments (demanding higher volumes of inputs) including: offices; education buildings; healthcare facilities; and retail stores.

In XXXX, the Ornamental and Architectural Metal Products Manufacturing Industry was estimated to have generated sales of $xx,xxx million, representing a decrease of 5.3 per cent compared to XXXX (besides the price of metal windows and door sash and frames prices increased by less than 1 per cent over XXXX). In the wider Manufacturing sector, weak GDP growth and increased levels of national unemployment, a decline in the lending interest rate, weak growth in income and a severe contraction in the consumer sentiment index combined to restrict spending patterns. In the Construction sector, fixed investment by the residential sector rose by just 0.4 percent. The nonresidential fixed investment sector performed worse, contracting by 4 percent. The decline in the value of work put into place on commercial and institutional building was most pronounced in office construction; hotel construction; and retail store construction. The fortunes of both the residential, but in particular the nonresidential construction sector affected demand.

In yyyy, the Ornamental and Architectural Metal Products Manufacturing Industry was estimated to have generated sales of $33,126 million, representing a decrease of 10.8 per cent compared to 2001. A 3.6 per cent fall in the price of metal windows and door screens, and price growth of less than 1 per cent in most other product segments conspired against the industry in yyyy. At the wider manufacturing level, consolidated revenues decreased by 3.6 percent compared to 2001 - the recessionary environment continued to impact the sector throughout the year. Despite a further decline in the lending interest rate to 4.7 percent and a return to positive growth in GDP of 1.9 percent, the Construction sector performed poorly in yyyy. A poor operating environment over the year lead to a decline in demand for metal window, doors, and sheet metal products from the Construction sector during the year.

In 2003, the Ornamental and Architectural Metal Products Manufacturing Industry was estimated to have generated sales of $xx,xxx million, representing a decrease of 1.9 per cent compared to the previous year. Industry revenue was negatively affected by a 8.9 per cent increase in import competition, and a 2.4 per cent decrease in export sales. A recovery from the economic downfall experienced in 2001 and YYYY was exhibited through growth in GDP of 3.0 percent. Lower lending rates and growth in personal consumption also aided a wider economic recover in the US. Overall demand from the Construction sector throughout the year was aided by a rise in fixed residential investment of 8.8 percent and growth in non-fixed residential investment of 3.3 percent.

In XXXX, the Ornamental and Architectural Metal Products Manufacturing Industry was estimated to have generated sales of $xx,xxx million, representing an increase of 5.5 per cent compared to XXXX. In XXXX, producer prices were stronger across the industry (metal windows and door screens were 7 per cent higher, the price of iron and steel doors increased 9 per cent, as the price of iron and steel residential doors rose by 4.5 per cent). Demand from the Construction sector was supported by the recovering economic environment, and continued growth in enterprise numbers of 1 percent. Industry revenue was estimated to have been underpinned by growth in the total value of construction in the commercial and institutional building markets, and particularly the cyclical upswing in the commercial building market.

In ZZZZ, the Ornamental and Architectural Metal Products Manufacturing Industry was estimated to have generated sales of $xx,xxx billion, 6.7 per cent higher than the previous year. Prices across most product segments were higher (on average 3.0 per cent higher) than the previous year because of higher input costs, particularly ferrous and nonferrous metals. In the first half of ZZZZ economic conditions in several downstream markets favorably impacted the profitability of firms in the industry as did the industry's ability to increase the efficiency of machinery and equipment (capacity utilization and return on equity were higher in ZZZZ as compared with XXXX). End year inventories suggest that industry participants expect a stronger XXXX. IBISWorld estimates that industry revenue will grow by 2.2 per cent to $xx,xxx million in XXXX.

OUTLOOK

Table: Revenue Growth

	Revenue $ Million	Growth%
XXXX	xx,xxx.0	5.6
XXXX	xx,xxx.0	6.7
XXXX	xx,xxx.0	2.4
XXXX	xx,xxx.0	2.4
XXXX	xx,xxx.0	2.3
XXXX	xx,xxx.0	2.2
XXXX	xx,xxx.0	-1.5

US Economic Outlook ZZZZ-XXXX

IBISWorld forecasts annual average real US GDP growth rates of around 3 percent in the ZZZZ- XXXX period. Consumer spending will be positively affected by rising household income, on the back of healthy productivity gains, and the relatively low unemployment rate. However, the growth in spending will be less strong than in the mid-to-late 1990s due to a slowdown in overall job creation, rising interest rates (that increase debt repayments), the waning effects of mortgage refinancing and tax cuts and the possibility of increasing taxes (as the government seeks to reduce the fiscal deficit) and a gradual rebound in household saving. IBISWorld believes that investment will remain robust, especially from corporations keen to exploit productivity gains from new technology.

Outlook for the Ornamental and Architectural Metal Products Manufacturing Industry
In XXXX, sales revenue is expected to be $xx.x billion (annual average growth of 1.5 per cent per annum). A significant key sensitivity of the industry is revenue growth and capital expenditure patterns in the construction. The industry is primarily dependent upon residential and nonresidential construction, which includes single and multifamily housing construction. Demand for this type of construction is sensitive to the changes in the level of interest rates and income growth. Strong revenue growth is likely to continue within the industry between XXXX and XXXX (before a fall in revenue in the final year of the outlook period), caused by a decline in the number of new privately-owned housing unit starts, which will reduce demand for construction materials in the residential construction market. Conditions in the nonresidential construction market will buoy industry conditions in the period ahead.

In terms of demand for sheet metal products demand from the commercial and institutional building industry is expected to return to stable growth conditions over the outlook period to XXXX, with industry revenue forecast by IBISWorld to average growth of 3.0 per cent per annum, matching the projected pace of US GDP growth. All key commercial and institutional building markets are projected to return to a pattern of synchronized cyclical growth over the outlook period, although the pace of expansion is likely to be moderate by comparison with previous cyclical upswings due to the continued oversupply conditions in the several commercial building markets. Factors which support a cyclical recovery in downstream demand include: (i) a relatively low interest rate environment thereby buoying investor confidence; (ii) the gradual absorption of vacancy levels in commercial premises, and (iii) further expansion in several institutional building markets (notably health and public safety).

In the outlook period companies within the industry will increasingly compete on the basis of cost leadership as prices and margins within the industry continue to fall. As import competition grows to around 3.5 per cent of domestic demand and export revenue declines to around 0.5 per cent of industry revenue, industry structure will become more conducive to mergers and acquisitions. In this environment firms will try to obtain low operating costs in all market segments in which they operate (businesses survive on the competitiveness of their products). IBISWorld believes that these cost advantages will arise from economies of scale, technological systems and design, and cheaper access to raw materials. Companies that can achieve cost advantages and command industry-average prices will earn above average profits in the period ahead.

ABC Corporation

IBISWorld forecasts that employment trends among the various machine setters, operators, and tenders within the Ornamental and Architectural Metal Products Manufacturing Industry will diverge over the outlook period. A decline in employment is projected for many machine tool operators, including cutting, punching, and press machine setters, operators, and tenders; and lathe and turning-machine tool workers as a result of a surge in retirements. Going forward job opportunities are expected to be stronger for sheet metal workers, reflecting both rapid employment growth and openings arising each year as experienced sheet metal workers leave the occupation (and retire). The Bureau of Labor Statistics indicate that the prospects are expected to be better for sheet metal workers in the construction industry than for those in manufacturing because construction is expected to grow faster than the manufacturing industries.

ABC Corporation

Financial Review and Analysis

This section of the valuation presents the historical financial performance of the Company. A review and analysis of the financial statements affords an understanding of the earning capabilities and risks associated with the Company.

Financial Position (Exhibit A)

The financial position of a company reflects the capital structure and quantifies long-term solvency and the ability of the Company to deal with financial problems and opportunities. The financial position of the Company for the fiscal years ended June 30, *ZZZZ* and June 30, XXXX, and as of December 31, XXXX is summarized as follows:

Financial Position Summary							
	6/30/ZZZZ		**6/30/XXXX**		**12/31/XXXX**	
Current Assets	$xx,xxx,xxx	89.3%	$xx,xxx,xxx	90.1%	$xx,xxx,xxx	87.4%
Fixed Assets, Net	x,xxx,xxx	6.8%	x,xxx,xxx	5.9%	x,xxx,xxx	3.8%
Other Assets	x,xxx,xxx	3.9%	x,xxx,xxx	4.0%	x,xxx,xxx	8.8%
Total Assets	$xx,xxx,xxx	100.0%	$xx,xxx,xxx	100.0%	$xx,xxx,xxx	100.0%
Current Liabilities	$ x,xxx,xxx	20.1%	$ x,xxx,xxx	18.4%	$ x,xxx,xxx	19.9%
Long Term Liabilities	xxx,xxx	1.3%	xxx,xxx	1.0%	xxx,xxx	0.7%
Stockholders' Equity	xx,xxx,xxx	78.6%	xx,xxx,xxx	80.6%	xx,xxx,xxx	79.4%
Total Liabilities & Equity	$x,xxx,xxx	100.0%	$xx,xxx,xxx	100.0%	$xx,xxx,xxx	100.0%

Activity Ratios

Activity ratios are a general measure of liquidity and how efficiently a company uses its assets. One measure of liquidity and efficiency is an assessment of short-term liquidity ratios and working capital. The trend in the current ratio, quick ratio, and working capital for the period reviewed was as follows:

ABC Corporation

Working Capital Summary						
	6/30/yyyy	6/30/2003	6/30/2004	6/30/ZZZZ	6/30/XXXX	12/31/XXXX
Working Capital	$xx,xxx,xxx	$xx,xxx,xxx	$xx,xxx,xxx	$xx,xxx,xxx	$xx,xxx,xxx	$xx,xx,xxx
Current Ratio	4.2	4.9	3.8	4.4	4.9	4.4
Quick Ratio	2.1	2.0	1.5	1.5	2.0	1.2

Total assets and equity were as follows for the period reviewed:

Total Asset and Equity Trend Summary							
	6/30/yyyy	6/30/2003	6/30/2004	6/30/ZZZZ	6/30/XXXX	12/31/XXXX	CAGR
Total Assets	$xx,xxx,xxx	$xx,xxx,xxx	$xx,xxx,xxx	$xx,xxx,xxx	$xx,xxx,xxx	$xx,xxx,xxx	
Growth (Decline)	*N/A*	*6.6%*	*17.8%*	*8.9%*	*4.9%*	*4.8%*	*9.5%*
Stockholders' Equity	$xx,xxx,xxx	$xx,xxx,xxx	$xx,xxx,xxx	$xx,xxx,xxx	$xx,xxx,xxx	$xx,xxx,xxx	
Growth (Decline)	*N/A*	*10.9%*	*11.8%*	*13.8%*	*7.5%*	*3.2%*	*10.4%*

Review of Operating Results (Exhibit B)

A summary of the Company's unadjusted operating results, for the fiscal years ended June 30, ZZZZ and June 30, XXXX, and for the trailing 12 months ending December 31, XXXX is summarized as follows:

Unadjusted Historical Operating Results Summary						
	FYE 6/30/ZZZZ		FYE 6/30/XXXX		TTM 12/31/XXXX	
Net Sales	$xxx,xx,xxx	100.0%	$xxx,xxx,xxx	100.0%	$xxx,xxx,xxx	100.0%
Cost of Goods Sold	xx,xxx,xxx	77.1%	xx,xxx,xxx	80.5%	xx,xxx,xxx	81.1%
Gross Profit	xx,xxx,xxx	22.9%	xx,xxx,xxx	19.5%	xx,xxx,xxx	18.9%
Operating Expenses	xx,xxx,xxx	15.4%	xx,xxx,xxx	15.4%	xx,xxx,xxx	15.7%
Income From Operations	x,xxx,xxx	7.6%	x,xxx,xxx	4.1%	x,xxx,xxx	3.2%
Other Income (Expense), Net	(x,xxx,xxx)	-1.0%	(xxx,xxx)	-0.6%	(xxx,xxx)	-0.5%
Profit Before Income Taxes	x,xxx,xxx	6.5%	x,xxx,xxx	3.5%	x,xxx,xxx	2.7%
Income Tax Expense	x,xxx,xxx	2.7%	x,xxx,xxx	1.2%	x,xxx,xxx	0.9%
Net Income	$ x,xxx,xxx	3.8%	$ xxx,xxx	2.3%	$ x,xxx,xxx	1.8%

ABC Corporation

The following chart is a comparison of the Company's unadjusted historical operating performance over the period reviewed.

Unadjusted Historical Operating Results Summary							
	6/30/XXXX	6/30/XXXX	6/30/XXXX	6/30/XXXX	6/30/XXXX	12/31/XXXX	CAGR
Net Sales	$x,xxx,xxx	$xx,xxx,xxx	$x,xxx,xxx	$x,xxx,xxx	$x,xxx,xxx	$x,xxx,xxx	
Growth (Decline)	N/A	0.2%	14.6%	23.3%	2.8%	4.1%	9.8%
Gross Margin	22.8%	23.0%	22.6%	22.9%	19.5%	18.9%	
Operating Margin	6.3%	4.3%	5.4%	7.6%	4.1%	3.2%	
Pretax Margin	5.4%	3.5%	4.5%	6.5%	3.5%	2.7%	

Review of Adjusted Operating Results (Exhibit C)

Exhibit C presents the normalization of the Company's financial statements, which adjusts for any nonrecurring or extraordinary expenses incurred in the period under review. A review of the Company's financial statements and discussions with management indicated that no adjustments were necessary to arrive at normalized income from operations.

In addition, Exhibit C presents the development of the Company's EBITDA indication (earnings before interest, taxes, depreciation, and amortization).

Risk Management Association (RMA) Industry Comparison (Exhibit D)

Exhibit D presents a comparison of the Company's historical financial status and unadjusted operating results, as of the latest period to comparable companies in the same industry as defined by the North American Industry Classification System (NAICS #332323), with sales of $25 million and over, as published by Risk Management Association (RMA) in their *Annual Statement Studies ZZZZ-XXXX*.

A highlight of the comparisons between the Company and the RMA data is as follows:

ABC Corporation

- The Company's current assets as a percentage of total assets are greater than the industry median, at 87.4% compared to RMA's industry composite of 57.1%.

- The Company's net fixed assets as a percentage of total assets are less than the industry median, at 3.8% compared to RMA's industry composite of 31.8%.

- The Company's concentration of current liabilities as a percentage of total liabilities is less than the industry median, at 19.9%, compared to RMA's industry composite of 33.2%.

- The Company's long-term debt as a percentage of total assets is less than the industry median, at zero compared to RMA's industry composite of 13.1%.

- The Company's stockholders' equity as a percentage of assets at 79.4% is greater than the industry median at 44.7%.

- The Company's profitability, as indicated by unadjusted pretax margins, is less than the RMA median. The Company has a pretax profit margin of 2.7% compared to an industry median of 5.4%.

- The Company's current ratio of 4.4 is greater than the industry ratio of 1.6.

- The Company's quick ratio of 1.2 is greater than the industry ratio of 0.9.

- The Company's return on stockholders' equity of 5.4% is less than the industry median of 13.4%.

- The Company's return on stockholders' assets of 4.3% is less than the industry median of 4.7%.

Summary – Financial Analysis and Review

In summary, a financial analysis was performed in order to identify and quantify the historical financial condition and performance of the Company. In addition to the above, the financial condition and operating performance of ABC Corporation was compared to industry benchmarks

ABC Corporation

and public companies similar to the subject in business type and operations. This analysis, in addition to discussions with management, served as the basis of selecting the applicable approaches used in developing a value indication for ABC Corporation, as discussed in the subsequent sections of this report.

ABC Corporation

SECTION 3 - VALUATION

Valuation Procedures

There are many factors to consider in any appraisal. An excellent guide is the Internal Revenue Service's Revenue Ruling 59-60, which issued these factors as a valuation guideline:

- The nature of the business and the history of the enterprise from its inception;

- The economic outlook in general and the conditions and outlook of the specific industry in particular;

- The book value of the stock and the financial condition of the business;

- The earning capacity of the Company;

- The dividend-paying capacity;

- Whether or not the enterprise had goodwill or other intangible value;

- Prior sales of the stock and the size of the block of stock to be valued; and

- The market price of stocks and the sizes of companies engaged in the same or a similar line of business having their stocks actively traded on an exchange or over-the-counter market.

Traditionally, the development of an opinion is based on the utilization of three basic approaches to value: the income, market, and cost approaches. Value indications derived through these approaches are reconciled to formulate an opinion in accordance with the perspective of the appraisal.

The income approach is based upon the valuation principals of anticipation and substitution. The foundation of the approach is reflected in the value of anticipated future benefits. These benefits are discounted or capitalized at an appropriate market rate of return to indicate a value.

Two techniques are typically employed in the income approach, a discounted cash flow technique and a capitalized earnings technique. A discounted net cash flow analysis provides an indication of value based upon the present value of anticipated future cash flows, discounted at an appropriate present worth factor reflecting the risk inherent in the investment. The capitalized earnings

XX-XX-XXXXX

ABC Corporation

technique applies a capitalization rate to a single period economic measure to convert that measure to a value indication.

The market approach is based upon the valuation principal of substitution. The approach develops value measures based upon prices for comparable interests. There are two techniques typically employed in the market approach, the guideline publicly traded company method and the guideline merged and acquired company method.

The guideline companies method of the market approach utilizes financial and market information regarding publicly traded securities of companies engaged in business pursuits similar to those of the Company so that prevailing investor attitudes and expectations can be abstracted. Differences in the comparable companies are noted and adjustments are made in order to develop appropriate market multiples which can be applied to the Company's income and cash flow streams to develop value indications. The market approach merged and acquired (transaction) method utilizes market transaction information regarding privately held companies engaged in business pursuits similar to those of the Company. This method involves deriving value indications from prices at which entire companies or percentage ownership interests have been sold. Differences in the transactions are noted and adjustments are made in order to develop appropriate market multiples. These multiples are applied to the Company's income and cash flow streams to develop value indications.

In the cost approach, the underlying assets of the enterprise are considered individually, and the sum of these assets indicates a value. From this value, various adjustments can be applied to generate a value indication reflecting the premise of value.

In this appraisal, the income and market approach guideline companies method were determined to be the most applicable to the perspective of value. The market approach transaction method was not utilized due to a lack of truly comparable transactions in the subject Company's industry. The cost approach was not utilized since an investor would evaluate a company with positive operating margins based upon its earnings and cash-generating potential rather than through an appraisal of its underlying assets.

The income and market approaches were applied on a debt-free basis since a prospective buyer would not necessarily be confined to operating under the same capital structure. Application of the market and income approaches on a debt-free basis results in a value indication representative of the control value of the total invested operating capital of a company.

ABC Corporation

Income Approach

Two techniques are typically employed in the income approach, a discounted cash flow technique and a capitalized earnings technique. A discounted net cash flow analysis provides an indication of value based upon the present value of anticipated future cash flows, discounted at an appropriate present worth factor reflecting the risk inherent in the investment. The capitalized earnings technique applies a capitalization rate to a single period economic measure to convert that measure to a value indication.

The income approach considers a given company's future sales, net cash flow, and growth potential. The Company's debt-free, net cash flow into the future is discounted or capitalized to determine a value indication of the total invested operating capital of the Company.

As a basis for determining the fair value of the invested operating capital of the Company, operating projections were developed in conjunction with management. The overall projections take into consideration historical trends, the outlook for the economy and the industry in which the Company operates, and the specific prospects for ABC Corporation. The financial projections reflect estimates and assumptions that are subject to economic and competitive uncertainties that are beyond the Company's control. However, management believes these projections are based on reasonable assumptions and are attainable, given current industry and economic conditions. To the extent that historical financial performance significantly affects the risk associated with investing in the business, these factors were considered important in developing the discount rates under the income approach to valuation.

Discounted Cash Flow Method

In the discounted cash flow method, we determined a value estimate of the invested operating capital of the Company by projecting revenues and expenses to arrive at debt-free net cash flow. The projections were based on discussions with management, and considered the general economic outlook, industry conditions, and the Company's historical financial results. The future cash flows are estimated for each year of a defined holding period and discounted back to a present value. The last year of this holding period reflects a stabilized cash flow that is capitalized at an appropriate rate and then discounted back to reflect the value impact after the initial holding period.

ABC Corporation

Financial Estimates (Exhibit E)

Again, in applying this valuation method, an estimate of the economic measure is required. The applicable economic measure is the debt-free net cash flow. In this analysis, the projected cash flows are utilized. The assumptions associated with the projections are as follows.

- Net revenue was projected at approximately $62.9 million for the six months ending June 30, 2007. Thereafter, net revenue was projected to grow at a compound annual growth rate of 4.2% throughout the 5-Year forecast period, increasing from approximately $128.3 million in Year 1 to approximately $151.5 million in Year 5. Overall, the Company's revenue projections were based on discussions with management, observations of the Company's historical performance, and reflect demand estimates which are in-line with current industry and economic indications.

- Cost of goods sold was projected at approximately $51.0 million, or 81.0% of revenue, for the six months ending June 30, 2007. Thereafter, cost of goods sold, as a percentage of revenue, was projected to improve from 80.3% of revenue in Year 1 to 80.1% of revenue in Year 5 of the forecast period. The forecasted cost of goods sold indications was developed in conjunction with management, and reflect expense levels necessary to support the projected sales volume.

- Operating expenses were projected at approximately $9.0 million, or 14.3% of revenue, for the six months ending June 30, 2007. Thereafter, operating expenses, as a percentage of revenue, was projected to improve from 15.4% of revenue in Year 1 to 14.6% of revenue in Year 5 of the forecast period. The forecasted operating expense indications were developed in conjunction with management, and reflect expense levels necessary to support the ongoing operational aspects of the business.

- Other income and expense items were projected at approximately -0.7% of revenue throughout the forecast period.

- Income taxes were projected at a combined federal and state corporate income tax rate of 39.0%.

ABC Corporation

- Depreciation expense was based on current depreciation schedules and estimated depreciation on anticipated additions each year throughout the forecast period. Capital expenditures were based on management's capital budget expectations and equal depreciation levels in perpetuity.

- ABC Corporation's debt-free working capital requirement was based on industry and guideline company research, and discussions with management concerning the Company's historical level of required working capital. Sources of industry data included: Value Line *Investment Survey*, Capital IQ Database, *RMA Annual Statement Studies ZZZZ-XXXX*, and the selected guideline company's historic levels of working capital. Based on the information provided in these research databases, we estimated the annual increase in Petersen's debt-free working capital requirement to be 20.0% of the change in yearly sales.

Discount Rate

The magnitude of the discount rate varies with the analyst's degree of optimism or pessimism relative to the financial projections; increasingly optimistic projections will require a higher discount rate, and vice versa. Stated differently, as the degree of certainty with which the projections are believed attainable increases, the discount rate falls correspondingly, and vice versa.

The economic measure of the discounted cash flow method reflects a releveraged, debt-free amount. The economic measure presents the cash flow available to both debt and equity investors. To be consistent, the discount rate applied to the cash flows was based upon a weighted average cost of capital (WACC) that accounts for the return requirements of both debt and equity investors.

Debt Component

The Capital IQ database and the Value Line *Investment Survey* served as sources for determining the capital structure of the industry. This industry capital structure is representative of the market capital structure.

The cost of debt capital was estimated based upon the rate on high-grade corporate bonds, adjusted to account for the specific risk of the Company's size, capital structure and other specific debt characteristics. The cost of debt capital was tax-effected using a 39.0% blended federal and state

ABC Corporation
corporate income tax rate (presented in the rate conclusion chart).

Equity Component

In this instance, the Capital Asset Pricing Model was used to estimate the rate of return on the equity component of the WACC.

The starting point for developing an appropriate equity component of the discount rate is the alternative investment opportunities in risk-free or relatively risk-free investments. An indication of these market rates of return near the valuation date follows:

Market Rates of Interest	
Security	**Yield**
Treasury Securities—5-Year [1]	4.65%
Treasury Securities—10-Year	4.67%
Treasury Securities—20-Year	4.88 %
Corporate Bonds—Aaa	5.43 %
Corporate Bonds—Baa	6.32 %

1. Source: Federal Reserve Statistical Release, December 31, XXXX

All of these investments offer less risk than an investment in the Company. In addition, these securities are readily marketable. The rate of return expected from an investment by an investor relates to perceived risks. General risk factors relevant in our selection of an appropriate equity component of the discount rate for the Company include:

1. Interest rate risk, which measures variability of returns caused by changes in the general level of interest rates.

2. Purchasing power risk, which measures loss of purchasing power over time due to inflation.

3. Market risk, which measures the effects of the general market on the price behavior of securities.

4. Business risk, which measures the uncertainty inherent in projections of future

ABC Corporation

cash flow.

Consideration of risk, burden of management, and other factors affect the rate of return acceptable to a given investor in a specific investment. An adjustment for risk is an increment added to a base or safe rate to compensate for the extent of these risk factors.

The large company stock return and the long-term government bond return, as published by Ibbotson Associates in the *Stocks, Bonds, Bills, and Inflation Valuation Edition XXXX Yearbook*, was used in determining the equity risk premium. The large company stock return was based upon Ibbotson's Large Company Stocks Total Returns from 1926-ZZZZ, arithmetic average, while the long-term government bonds return was based upon Ibbotson's Long-term Government Bonds Income Returns from 1926-ZZZZ, arithmetic average.

The Capital IQ database and the Value Line *Investment Survey* served as sources for determining the median beta of the industry; therefore representative of the market.

The cost of equity capital was adjusted for a size risk premium of 6.36%, which was based on the "XXXX Ibbotson's Long-Term Returns in Excess of CAPM Estimation for Companies in the 10th Decile" study.

Based on the information presented previously, we selected a discount rate of 14.75% as being reasonable, derived as follows:

ABC Corporation

Cost Of Debt Capital	
Rate On Baa Corporate Bonds	6.32%
Debt Premium	0.00%
Cost Of Debt Capital	6.32%
Tax Rate (T)	39.00%
After-Tax Cost Of Debt Capital (CDC)	3.86%
Cost Of Equity Capital	
Rate On 20-Year U.S. Government Bonds (Rf)	4.88%
Beta Coefficient (ß)	1.23
Large Company Stock Return	12.30%
Less: Long Term Government Bond Return	5.20%
Less: Equity Risk Premium Adjustment	1.25%
Equity Risk Premium (ERP)	5.85%
Size Risk Premium (SRP)	6.36%
Cost Of Equity Capital [Rf+ß(ERP)+SRP]	18.45%
Weighted Average Cost Of Capital	
Debt As A Percentage Of Capital (D)	25.00%
Equity As A Percentage Of Capital (E)	75.00%
Weighted Cost Of Debt: (D)(CDC)	0.96%
Weighted Cost Of Equity (E)[Rf+ß(ERP)+SRP+CSRP]	13.84%
Weighted Cost Of Capital	14.80%
Weighted Cost Of Capital (Rounded)	**14.75%**

ABC Corporation

To account for the value of the business enterprise beyond the 5-year forecast period, the fifth-year projected, net debt-free cash flow was forecasted for one additional period into the future at a long-term growth rate of 3.0% and capitalized using a capitalization rate of 11.75%. The capitalization rate, applying the Gordon Growth Model, was derived from the discount rate of 14.75%, less 3.0% for the assumed residual stabilized long term-growth after the fifth year.

The residual value at the end of our 5-year projection was then discounted to the present at a 14.75% discount rate. The residual value was then added to the sum of the present values of the debt-free net cash flows over the forecast period to arrive at a value indication for total invested operating capital. Exhibit F presents these calculations.

<u>Discounted Cash Flow Method Conclusion (Exhibit F)</u>

Based on the analysis discussed above, the estimated value indication of the Company, as of the valuation date, utilizing the discounted cash flow method of the income approach, was $XX,XXX,XXX (rounded).

Present Value Cash Flow—Forecast Period	$ X,XXX,XXX
Present Value Cash Flow—Residual Period	$XX,XXX,XXX
Present Value Cash Flow—Total	$XX,XXX,XXX
Value Indication—Income Approach (rounded)	$XX,XXX,XXX

ABC Corporation

Market Approach

The market approach is predicated on the theory that the market value of a closely held company can be estimated based on the prices investors are paying for the stocks of similar, publicly traded companies and recently transacted companies. This is done through the use of ratios that relate the prices of the public companies and transacted companies to their same economic measures. By analyzing the financial statements of comparable, publicly traded companies and transacted companies and then comparing their performances with those of the Company, price ratios demonstrate value indications.

Guideline Company Method

The guideline company method selects comparable companies to use in the analysis of operating results and future prospects. From these comparable selected guideline companies, appropriate market pricing multiples are abstracted. These multiples incorporate performance, future prospects and risk elements of the guideline companies. A comparison and analysis of the data forms the foundation for the application of the method.

Identification of Guideline Companies (Exhibits G-K)

The first step was to identify public companies similar to the subject in business type and operations. To accomplish this, we used the Capital IQ database. Guideline companies are analyzed relative to industry, lines of business, operating results, risks, and future prospects. The following publicly traded companies were determined to be comparable to the Company.

These publicly traded guideline companies, along with their ticker symbols, are listed below.

Guideline Company	Ticker
AM Castle & Co.	CAS
International Aluminum Corp.	IAL
NCI Building Systems Inc.	NCS
Novamerican Steel Inc.	TONS
Olympic Steel Inc.	ZEUS
Quanex Corp.	NX
Reliance Steel & Aluminum Co.	RS
Steel Technologies Inc.	STTX
Worthington Industries, Inc.	WOR

XX-XX-XXXXX

ABC Corporation

A description of the guideline companies is presented in Exhibit G in the Addenda to this *Summary Appraisal Report*. Balance sheet, income statement, financial statement ratio and growth rate comparisons between the Company and the comparable companies are found in Exhibits H - K.

Analysis of Guideline Companies

An investor is usually concerned with the cash flow generating capacity of a business. In this instance, we selected the invested capital-to-latest fiscal year and trailing 12 month EBITDA (earnings before interest, taxes, depreciation and amortization) as the most appropriate measure for valuing the invested operating capital of the Company. An invested capital-to-EBITDA basis was selected because the EBITDA cash flow measure eliminates the effect of different capital and income tax structures from the market multiples. EBITDA is synonymous with the term "operating cash flow."

The total invested capital of a firm is the control-level market value of the firm's total equity, plus the market value of all other forms of capital financing, including interest-bearing debt and preferred stock among others (hereafter, "Invested Capital"). In the present instance, the Invested Capital of each guideline company was computed by calculating the marketable, minority value of the firm's total equity, applying a control premium to reflect a control level of value, and then adding the market value of the firm's additional financing. That control premium is defined as an amount or percentage by which the pro rata value of a controlling interest exceeds the pro rata value of a non-controlling interest in a business enterprise, to reflect the power of control (hereafter, "Control Premium").

Thus, the first step involves identifying non-synergistic control premiums being paid in the public markets for similar interests. To do so, we relied on Mergerstat/Shannon Pratt's *Control Premium Study*. The *Control Premium Study* tracks acquisition premiums for completed transactions involving publicly traded target companies where a controlling interest was acquired. Analysis compares acquisition prices to the trading prices one day, one week, one month and two months prior to the announcement date of the transaction. In addition, an event study is performed for each transaction to ascertain the target company's common stock price per share unaffected by the acquisition announcement.

ABC Corporation

In determining the control premium applicable to the Company, we searched the *Ornamental and Architectural Metal Work Manufacturing* industry for control acquisitions occurring from January 2, 1998 to December 31, XXXX. The control premiums resulting from the acquisitions were weighted according to occurrence, and concluded to a control premium of 30.0%, as presented in the following table:

Year	Median Premium (Note 1)	Weight Factors	Weighted Product
1998	48.0%	1	48.0%
1999	21.0%	2	42.0%
2000	47.0%	3	141.0%
2001	43.0%	4	172.0%
yyyy	21.0%	5	105.0%
2003	26.0%	6	156.0%
2004	30.0%	7	210.0%
TOTALS		28	874.0 %
WEIGHTED AVERAGE:			31.2%
CONTROL PREMIUM (ROUNDED)			**30.0%**

NOTES:

1. Premiums are based on the Mergerstat/Shannon Pratt's Control Premium Study for target transactions in the *Ornamental and Architectural Metal Work Manufacturing* industry.

Market Multiples (Exhibit L)

In reviewing the profitability, capital structures, and operations of the guideline companies, we concluded that the median multiple provided the most reasonable indication of value in relation to the Company's referenced indication. The following table presents the market multiple selected for application to the Company's EBITDA indication.

ABC Corporation

Total Invested Capital To:	Selected Market Multiples
Latest Fiscal Year EBITDA	7.5
Trailing 12 Month EBITDA	7.5

In comparing the Company to the publicly traded companies, we took into consideration that: (a) many of these companies operate in multiple business segments; (b) they may not share business segments precisely; (c) they are vertically integrated; and (d) they collectively represent only a guide for determining the value of privately held companies such as the Company. The selected publicly traded companies provide the most comparability regarding the type of operations relating to the Company, based on available data.

Before applying the above market multiples to the Company's EBITDA, we considered factors that require adjusting the multiples. *Mergerstat Review* notes that publicly traded companies tend to be larger, more sophisticated businesses with solid market shares, strong public identities, and greater access to various capital resources. These factors allow an investor in the publicly traded guideline companies to place greater reliability on expected future benefits and to minimize risk.

The following table presents data summarized from the *XXXX Mergerstat Review*. The discounts referenced are derived from comparing price-to-earnings multiples paid in change of control transactions for large and small companies. The data reveals that investors require either a greater return, or a discount, as offsetting compensation for an investment in a smaller, less diversified company.

ABC Corporation

SMALL VS. LARGE COMPANIES
MEDIAN P/E PAID

Year	$100 Mil Transactions Or More	$25 Mil Transactions or Less	Size Discount
1996	21.3	16.2	23.9%
1997	25.2	15.9	36.9%
1998	24.2	12.6	47.9%
1999	21.9	14.9	32.0%
2000	19.1	16.1	15.7%
2001	17.7	14.4	18.6%
2002	18.9	14.3	24.3%
2003	21.0	15.1	28.1%
2004	22.1	14.3	35.3%
2005	23.5	13.3	43.4%

Source: Houlihan Lokey Howard & Zukin's *XXXX Mergerstat Review.*

As shown in the preceding table, size discounts have ranged from approximately 15.7% to 47.9% over the last 10 years.

Risk Factor Adjustment

At the valuation date, the selected guideline companies were publicly traded companies with Invested Capital values ranging from approximately $273.0 million to $5.0 billion. These selected guideline companies enjoy significant advantages to the Company as a result of their publicly traded status including lower cost of capital, shareholder liquidity, the ability to use their stock as currency in acquisitions, and higher public profiles. Conversely, the Company is a privately held/thinly traded company, which places it at a disadvantaged position relative to the selected guideline companies in the areas of cost of capital, shareholder liquidity, and acquisition strategy.

Specific factors considered in developing the Company discount included:

- The guideline companies generally exhibited greater financial size, product line diversification, earnings power, financial growth, and more sophisticated operations, in comparison to the Company.

ABC Corporation

- The guideline companies served more diverse geographic area bases relative to the Company, thus creating significant regional concentration risk.

- The guideline companies had less customer concentration, relative to the Company, thus creating significant customer concentration risk.

These factors reduce the value of the Company, relative to the selected guideline companies. Based upon the above discussion and the data summarized from Houlihan Lokey Howard & Zukin's *XXXX Mergerstat Review*, a 25% reduction of the selected EBITDA market multiples has been taken to reflect the above differences between the selected guideline companies and the ABC Corporation.

Guideline Company Method Conclusions (Exhibit M)

The resulting indicated value of the total invested operating capital of ABC Corporation, on a controlling interest basis, as of December 31, XXXX, utilizing the market approach guideline companies method was $XX,XXX,XXX (rounded).

ABC Corporation

SECTION 4 - RECONCILIATION OF VALUATION OF APPROACHES

The reconciliation of valuation approaches is the correlation of results generated from the valuation process in which the appraiser considers and selects from alternate value indications to arrive at a final value estimate. The appraiser weighs the relative significance, applicability, and defensibility of each value indication and relies on that which is most appropriate. Although the reconciliation involves personal judgment, the appraiser's conclusion results from a careful, logical analysis of the procedures leading to each indication of value. The analysis is based on several criteria that enable an appraiser to form a meaningful, defensible conclusion about the final value estimate. These criteria are appropriateness, accuracy, and quantity of evidence.

The market values of the total invested operating capital, on a controlling interest basis, indicated by the two approaches used in this report are shown as follows:

	Value Indication
Income Approach (Exhibit F)	$XX,XXX,XXX
Market Approach Guideline Companies Method (Exhibit M)	$XX,XXX,XXX

The income approach bears significance because it considers the future income potential of the Company, which reflects market participant behaviors. The accuracy of the approach has foundation in the dependability of the economic measure and appropriateness of the selected discount rate.

The market approach is appropriate because it reflects market behavior and the attitudes and actions of market participants. The accuracy of the approach is allied with the dependability of the economic measure and adjustments to the data in the valuation process.

ABC Corporation

After analyzing the approaches to value, and assessing the appropriateness, accuracy and evidence of each approach, we weighted the approaches as demonstrated in the following chart. Based upon the analysis, it is our opinion that the total invested operating capital of the Company is $XX,XXX,XXX, on a controlling interest basis, as of December 31, XXXX, summarized as follows:

Value Indication–Total Invested Operating Capital	Value Indication	Weighting	Indication (rounded)
Income Approach (Exhibit F)	$XX,XXX,XXX	x 50.0%	$XX,XXX,XXX
Market Approach Guideline Companies Method (Exhibit M)	$XX,XXX,XXX	x 50.0%	$XX,XXX,XXX
Control Value of Total Invested Operating Capital (Rounded)			$XX,XXX,XXX

Excess Assets and Asset Deficiencies

To arrive at the control value of the total invested capital, it is necessary to adjust for excess assets and asset deficiencies. Excess assets and asset deficiencies exist when the Company has significantly greater or lesser amounts of certain assets (typically cash and marketable securities) in comparison to industry and guideline company financial positions.

The Company recorded excess working capital in the amount of $8,869,000 (rounded) as of the date of value. We estimated the amount of the Company's excess working capital by comparing the Company's debt-free working capital at the valuation date of $31,668,000 (rounded) to an industry, debt-free, working capital level of $22,799,000 (rounded), based on a working capital-to-sales ratio of 20.0% of the Company's TTM XXXX sales. The Company's debt-free working capital requirement was based on industry and company research and discussions with management concerning the Company's historical level of required working capital. Sources of industry data included: Value Line *Investment Survey*, Capital IQ Database, *RMA Annual Statement Studies ZZZZ-XXXX*, and the selected guideline company's historical levels of working capital.

This amount was added to the unadjusted business enterprise value of the Company, in determining the control value ABC Corporation's total invested capital.

ABC Corporation

Nonoperating Assets & Interest-Bearing Debt

The final step in arriving at the control value of the total common equity is to adjust for nonoperating assets (assets unrelated to business operations that can be liquidated without impairing the subject company's operations) and total interest-bearing debt outstanding at the valuation date.

The computation of the control value of the Company's total common equity, on a controlling interest basis, is summarized as follows.

Control Value of Total Invested Operating Capital	$XX,XXX,XXX
Add: Excess Working Capital	X,XXX,XXX
Control Value of Total Invested Capital	$XX,XXX,XXX
Add: Nonoperating Assets – Cash Value of Life Insurance	X,XXX,XXX
Less: Total Interest-Bearing Debt	0
Control Value of Total Common Equity (rounded)	$XX,XXX,XXX

Applicable Discounts

Lack of Control Discount

In the present instance, we are concerned with a valuation of a minority interest in ABC Corporation. Since minority interest positions are generally void of control factors, it stands to reason that the value of a minority interest is less than the pro-rata portion of controlling interest value. The value of control depends on the ability to exercise any or all of a variety of rights typically associated with control. The owner of a controlling interest in a business possesses valuable rights and benefits that an owner of a minority interest in the same business does not. The most significant prerogatives of control include the ability of a controlling shareholder to:

- Elect directors and appoint management.
- Determine management compensation and perquisites.
- Set policy and change the course of the business.
- Acquire or liquidate assets.
- Select people with whom to do business and award contracts.
- Make acquisitions or divestitures.

ABC Corporation

- Liquidate, dissolve, sell out, or re-capitalize the company.
- Register the company's stock for a public offering.
- Declare and pay dividends.
- Change the articles of incorporation and/or bylaws to establish or enhance barriers to gaining/losing control, such as staggered elections, voting v. nonvoting share classes, supermajority voting provisions, "poison pill" provisions, and so on.

From the above list, it is apparent that the owner of a controlling interest in an enterprise enjoys some valuable rights unavailable to a minority interest stockholder. As a result of a controlling shareholder's ability to control significant aspects of the firm that are expected to generate cash inflows, the per share price at which a controlling interest in a business will be purchased (e.g., an interest greater than 50.0 percent) will almost always be more than the per share price at which a minority interest in the same business will be purchased. This price differential is appropriately termed the "control premium." Conversely, the lack of these valuable rights implies a lower value than, and hence the application of a discount for lack of control to, the control interest valuation. Mathematically, the relationship of the control premium and the discount for lack of control is as follows: Discount for Lack of Control = Control Premium / (1 + Control Premium).

Based on the preceding data contained in this *Summary Appraisal Report*, we determined that an equity control premium of 30% would be appropriate for the subject Company. To determine the mathematical equivalent of a minority discount from a determined premium for control, the following formula was used.

$$\frac{0.30}{(1 + 0.30)} = .231 \text{ or } 23.1\%$$

It is our conclusion that a minority interest discount of 23.1% (based upon the assumed control premium of 30.0%) from control value is applicable for the subject minority interest in ABC Corporation subject to this valuation.

ABC Corporation

Lack of Marketability Discount

We also considered a discount for lack of marketability. The absence of a readily available market for a minority holding of shares in a closely held company also detracts from their value. The selected guideline companies are firms whose stocks are traded freely and actively in the public market. The minority shareholder of the Company, however, has no readily available market in which to sell his/her interest. Hence, the sale of the subject minority interest would involve locating a willing buyer, which would involve a loss of time and money for the minority shareholder of the Company.

The impact of marketability on the market value of common stock has been analyzed and commented upon by a number of sources.

In 1977, the IRS issued Revenue Ruling 77-287 entitled "Valuation of Securities Restricted From Immediate Resale." This ruling and its conclusions were based on the SEC study and recognized that a marketability discount was indeed associated with shares that are restricted from resale pursuant to Federal security laws and thus lack immediate access to an active, public market. Generally, Revenue Ruling 77-287 indicated that no automatic formula could be used to determine marketability discounts: discounts were related to the sales and earnings of the issuing corporation, were a function of the trading market for the equivalent actively traded stock, or were a function for the resale constraints placed on the issue.

In 1983, Standard Research Consultants reported the results of an update of the SEC study in their publication *SRC Quarterly Reports*, Spring 1983, Volume 10, No. 1. This empirical study, involving 28 private placements of restricted common stock from October 1978 through June 1982, showed that discounts ranged broadly—from 7% to 91%--with a median discount of 45% for the group. The revenue size of the issuing companies also appeared to influence the discount level. Those companies within the group's highest quartile, where revenue ranges from $29.7 million to $275 million, had a slightly lower median discount of 36%.

ABC Corporation

In addition, two more recent studies involving marketability discounts indicated substantial discounts for lack of marketability. In a paper titled "Value of Marketability as Illustrated in Initial Public Offerings of Common Stock," written by John Emory, ASA, first vice president, Appraisal Services, Robert W. Baird & Co., and published in the December 1986 issue of Business Valuation News, 130 initial public offerings (IPOs) were analyzed to determine the relationship between prices at which common stocks were initially offered to the public and the prices at which private sales were transacted within five months prior to the public offering. This study was updated several times by Mr. Emory using IPOs from 1980 through 1997. This time, the median and average discounts were 43% and 44%[4], respectively, as reported in the September 1997 edition of Business Valuation Review. In his article, Mr. Emory concluded that:

> The final question to be answered is that if these kinds of discounts are appropriate for promising situations where marketability is probable, but not a certainty, how much greater should discounts be for the more typical company's stock that has no marketability, little if any chance of ever becoming marketable, and is in a neutral to unpromising situation? ... In summary, size of discount for lack of marketability depends on the individual situation. While there is no one discount for lack of marketability applicable at all times and to all situations, it is apparent that the lack of marketability is one of the most important components of value, and the public marketplace emphasizes this point.

Various restricted stock studies and court cases indicate that marketability discounts for closely held shares or restricted securities can be significant—about 25% to 45% on average. In Exhibits N and O in the Addenda, we have listed some of the studies and recent court decisions on marketability discounts that we reviewed. Based upon the above, we concluded that a discount for lack of marketability of 35% would be appropriate.

---

[4] Of the 310 transactions in the eight studies from 1980 through 1997, 67 were sale transactions and 239 were option transactions. On average, sale transactions had higher discounts than option transactions. The eight studies' median discount for the 67 sales transactions was 51%, the mean was 50%.

XX-XX-XXXXX

ABC Corporation

Conclusion

The computation of the market value per share of the outstanding common stock, on a nonmarketable, minority interest basis, in the business enterprise known as ABC Corporation, is summarized as follows:

Control Value of Total Common Equity	$XX,XXX,XX
Less: Lack of Control (Minority) Discount (23.1% - rounded)	(X,XXX,XXX)
Marketable, Minority Interest Value of Total Common Equity	$XX,XXX,XXX
Less: Lack of Marketability Discount (35.0% - rounded)	(X,XXX,XXX)
Marketable, Minority Interest Value of Total Common Equity	$XX,XXX,XXX
Divided By: Total Shares Outstanding	XXX
Nonmarketable, Minority Value per Share (rounded)	$ XXX,XXX

Based on the information and analysis contained in our *Summary Appraisal Report*, it is our opinion that the market value of the total common equity, on a controlling interest basis, in the business enterprise known as ABC Corporation, as of December 31, XXXX, was

$XX,XXX,XXX

In addition, based on the information and analysis contained in our *Summary Appraisal Report*, it is our opinion that the market value of the total common equity, on a nonmarketable, minority interest basis, in the business enterprise known as ABC Corporation, as of December 31, XXXX, was

$XX,XXX,XXX

or

$XXX,XXX per share

(Based on XXX total shares outstanding)

SECTION 6 – EXHIBITS

CERTIFICATION

The undersigned appraiser certifies that:

- Jones's corporate office was visited in the course of this appraisal assignment, and conversations were held with management regarding financial results, operations, and the outlook for the business. The Company has been accurately described based on factual information received from sources considered to be both responsible and knowledgeable.

- The appraiser has no present or contemplated future interest in the subject Company of this *Summary Appraisal Report*. In addition, he has no personal interest or bias with respect to the parties involved.

- Data was obtained from sources believed to be reliable, all facts known to the appraiser, which have bearing on the values of the property, have been considered, and no facts of importance have been omitted intentionally herein.

- The appraiser's compensation for this *Summary Appraisal Report* was in no way contingent upon the value estimates contained in this *Summary Appraisal Report*, nor was it contingent upon anything other than the delivery of this *Summary Appraisal Report*.

- To the best of the appraiser's knowledge and belief, the reported analyses, opinions, and conclusions were developed and this *Summary Appraisal Report* has been prepared in conformity with the Uniform Standards of Professional Appraisal Practice and the Code of Professional Ethics.

- The statements of fact contained in this *Summary Appraisal Report*, upon which the analyses, opinions, and conclusions expressed herein are based, are true and accurate.

- In addition to the undersigned, XXXXX, an Associate Member of the American Society of Appraisers, assisted in the preparation of the *Summary Appraisal Report*.

XXXXXX
Project Manager

ASSUMPTIONS AND LIMITING CONDITIONS

Title

No investigation of legal title was made, and we render no opinion as to ownership of the Company or its underlying assets.

Date of Value

The date of value to which the conclusions and opinions expressed in this *Summary Appraisal Report* apply is December 31, XXXX. The dollar amount of any value reported is based on the purchasing power of the U.S. dollar as of that date. The appraiser assumes no responsibility for economic or physical factors occurring subsequent to the date of value that may affect the opinions reported.

Visitation

ABC Corporation's corporate office was visited in the course of this appraisal assignment, and conversations were held with management regarding financial results, operations, and the outlook for the business.

Non-appraisal Expertise

No opinion is intended to be expressed for matters that require legal or specialized expertise, investigation, or knowledge beyond that customarily employed by appraisers.

Fee

The fee paid to Marshall & Stevens Incorporated in connection with the rendering of this *Summary Appraisal Report* has not been contingent upon the conclusions reached or the substance presented.

Financial Interest

Marshall & Stevens Incorporated have no financial interest in ABC Corporation or any of its affiliates.

Information and Data

Information supplied by others that was considered in this valuation is from sources believed to be reliable, and no further responsibility is assumed for its accuracy. We reserve the right to make such adjustments to the valuation herein reported as may be required by consideration of additional or more reliable data that may become available.

ASSUMPTIONS AND LIMITING CONDITIONS

Confidentiality/Advertising

This *Summary Appraisal Report* and supporting notes are confidential. Neither all nor any part of the contents of this appraisal shall be copied or disclosed to any party or conveyed to the public orally or in writing through advertising, public relations, news, sales, or in any other manner without the prior written consent and approval of both Marshall & Stevens Incorporated and ABC Corporation.

Litigation Support

Depositions, expert testimony, attendance in court, and all preparations/support for same, arising from this appraisal shall not be required unless arrangements for such services have previously been made.

Management

Our conclusions assume the continuation of prudent management policies over whatever period of time is reasonable and necessary to maintain the character and integrity of the Company.

Purpose

All opinions of retrospective market value are presented as Marshall & Stevens Incorporated's considered opinion based on the facts and data appearing in the *Summary Appraisal Report*. *This Summary Appraisal Report has been prepared for the sole purpose stated herein and shall not be used for any other purpose.*

Unexpected Conditions

We assume there are no hidden or unexpected conditions of the Company or the underlying assets that might adversely affect value. Further, we assume no responsibility for changes in market condition, which may require an adjustment in the appraisal.

Hazardous Substances

Hazardous substances, if present within a business, can introduce an actual or potential liability that may adversely affect the marketability and value of the Company or the underlying assets. In this appraisal, no consideration has been given to such liability or its impact on value.

ASSUMPTIONS AND LIMITING CONDITIONS

Limited Assignment

At the client's request, the scope of this appraisal was limited to a *Summary Appraisal Report* format of presentation. The written discussion in this *Summary Appraisal Report* relative to the business overview, economic outlook and industry outlook, and financial review is summary in nature or has been omitted. It is important to note, however, that the magnitude of the supporting valuation analyses and the due diligence conducted is otherwise full and complete.

Future Events/Projections

The reader is advised that this valuation is heavily dependent upon future events with respect to industry performance, economic conditions, and the ability of the Company to meet certain operating projections. In this appraisal, operating projections were developed from information supplied by management, historical trends and the outlook for the economy and the industry in which the Companies operate. The financial projections incorporate various assumptions, including, but not limited to, net sales growth, profit margins, income taxes, depreciation, capital expenditures, working capital levels, and discount rates, all of which are critical to the valuation. The financial projections were deemed reasonable and valid at the date of this appraisal; however, there is no assurance or implied guarantee that the assumed facts and circumstances will actually occur. We reserve the right to make adjustments to the valuation herein reported as may be required by any modifications in the prospective outlook for the economy, the industry, and/or the operations of the Company.

Index